A to Z of Creative Writing Methods

Research in Creative Writing

Series Editors:

Janelle Adsit (Humboldt State University, USA)
Conchitina Cruz (University of the Philippines)
James Ryan (University of Wisconsin-Madison, USA)

Showcasing the most innovative research and field-defining scholarship surrounding Creative Writing Studies, *Research in Creative Writing* strives to discuss and demonstrate the best practices for creative writing pedagogy both inside and out of the academy. Scholarship published in the series wrestles with the core issues at the heart of the field including critical issues surrounding the practice of creative writing; multilingualism and diverse approaches to creative production; representation and the politics of aesthetics; intersectionality and addressing interlocking oppressions in and through creative writing; and the impact of teaching established lore. Responsive to emerging exigencies in the field and open to interdisciplinary and diverse contexts for creative writing, this series is designed to advance the field and push the boundaries of Creative Writing Studies. This series benefits from the guidance of and collaboration with the Creative Writing Studies Organization (https://creativewritingstudies.com/).

Editorial board members:

Ching-In Chen (University of Washington Bothell, USA)
Farid Matuk (University of Arizona, USA)

Titles

The Place and the Writer, Ed. Marshall Moore and Sam Meekings
Craft Consciousness and Artistic Practice in Creative Writing, Benjamin Ristow

Forthcoming titles

Teaching Cultural Dexterity in Creative Writing, Micah McCrary
Digital Voices: Podcasting in the Creative Writing Classroom, Ed. Saul Lemerond and Leigh Camacho Rourks

Related titles

Beyond Craft, Steve Westbrook and James Ryan
Imaginative Teaching, Ed. Amy Ash, Michael Dean Clark and Chris Drew

A to Z of Creative Writing Methods

Edited by (from Z to A)
Deborah Wardle
Julienne van Loon
Stayci Taylor
Francesca Rendle-Short
Peta Murray
David Carlin

BLOOMSBURY ACADEMIC
LONDON • NEW YORK • OXFORD • NEW DELHI • SYDNEY

BLOOMSBURY ACADEMIC
Bloomsbury Publishing Plc
50 Bedford Square, London, WC1B 3DP, UK
1385 Broadway, New York, NY 10018, USA
29 Earlsfort Terrace, Dublin 2, Ireland

BLOOMSBURY, BLOOMSBURY ACADEMIC and the Diana logo
are trademarks of Bloomsbury Publishing Plc

First published in Great Britain 2023
Reprinted 2023

Copyright © Deborah Wardle, Julienne van Loon, Stayci Taylor, Francesca Rendle-Short,
Peta Murray, David Carlin and contributors, 2023

Deborah Wardle, Julienne van Loon, Stayci Taylor, Francesca Rendle-Short, Peta Murray,
David Carlin and contributors have asserted their right under the Copyright,
Designs and Patents Act, 1988, to be identified as Authors of this work.

For legal purposes the Acknowledgements on pp. xvi–xvii constitute an
extension of this copyright page.

Cover design: Eleanor Rose and Rebecca Heselton
Cover image @ potas / Shutterstock

All rights reserved. No part of this publication may be reproduced or transmitted
in any form or by any means, electronic or mechanical, including photocopying,
recording, or any information storage or retrieval system, without prior permission
in writing from the publishers.

Bloomsbury Publishing Plc does not have any control over, or responsibility for,
any third-party websites referred to or in this book. All internet addresses given
in this book were correct at the time of going to press. The author and publisher
regret any inconvenience caused if addresses have changed or sites have ceased
to exist, but can accept no responsibility for any such changes.

A catalogue record for this book is available from the British Library.

A catalog record for this book is available from the Library of Congress.

ISBN:	HB:	978-1-3501-8420-6
	PB:	978-1-3501-8421-3
	ePDF:	978-1-3501-8422-0
	eBook:	978-1-3501-8423-7

Series: Research in Creative Writing

Typeset by Integra Software Services Pvt. Ltd.
Printed and bound in Great Britain

To find out more about our authors and books visit www.bloomsbury.com
and sign up for our newsletters.

Contents

List of contributors	viii
Acknowledgement of country	xvi
Acknowledgements	xvii
Introduction *Deborah Wardle, Julienne van Loon, Stayci Taylor, Francesca Rendle-Short, Peta Murray, David Carlin*	1
Archival-poetics *Natalie Harkin*	7
Aswang Allan N. Derain	10
Atmospherics *Kathleen Stewart*	13
Braiding *Catherine McKinnon*	16
Bricolage *Dominique Hecq*	20
Bung wantaim Steven Winduo	23
Camping *Soile Veijola*	27
Character *Lina Maria Ferreira Cabeza-Vanegas*	30
Chorality *Martina Copley*	33
Code *Benjamin Laird*	37
Collaboration *Quinn Eades*	40
Collecting *Ander Monson*	43
Communitas Francesca Rendle-Short	46
Dialogue *Cath Moore*	49
Drawing *Sarah Leavitt*	52
Ekphrasis *Sarah Holland-Batt*	54
Ensemble *Shuchi Kothari*	57
Erasure *Nhã Thuyên*	60
Experience *Kári Gíslason*	63

Experimentation *Collier Nogues*	66
Facilitator *Ali Cobby Eckermann*	69
Fade out *Stayci Taylor*	71
Feelings *Erik Knudsen*	74
Flow *Mary Cappello*	77
Ghost Weaving *Paola Balla*	80
Hybrid *Marion May Campbell*	83
Imagination *Paula Morris*	86
Iterative thinking *Ames Hawkins*	89
Juxtaposition *Wendy S. Walters*	92
Keepsake *Fiona Murphy*	95
Listening *Marjorie Evasco*	98
Listing *David Carlin*	101
Memory work *Maria Tumarkin*	104
Metaphor me *Selina Tusitala Marsh*	107
Nonhuman imaginaries *Deborah Wardle*	111
Not-knowing *Julienne van Loon*	114
Notebooking *Safdar Ahmed*	117
Observation *Stephen Carleton*	120
Paragraphing *Delia Falconer*	123
Permission *Tina Makereti*	126
Phototextuality *Karen L. Carr*	129
Play *Nicole Walker*	132
Preposition *Martin Villanueva*	134
Procrastination *Aritha van Herk*	138
Queering *Marion May Campbell, Lawrence Lacambra Ypil, Francesca Rendle-Short, Deborah Wardle, Ames Hawkins, Quinn Eades, Stayci Taylor, Peta Murray, Natalie Harkin, Antonia Pont and Anonymous*	141
Radical effrontery *Jeanine Leane*	144
Reading *Belinda Castles*	147
Resistance *James Byrne*	150

Rites *Manola-Gayatri Kumarswamy*   153

Sensing *CM Burroughs*   157

Speculation *Robin Hemley*   160

Taxonomy *Lavanya Shanbhogue Arvind*   163

Translation *Rúnar Helgi Vignisson*   166

Uncertainty *Lawrence Lacambra Ypil*   169

Vocabulary *Peta Murray*   172

Writing-foreign-language *Fan Dai*   176

Xenos *Nike Sulway*   179

Yoga *Antonia Pont*   182

Zim *Alvin Pang*   185

Index   188

Contributors

Safdar Ahmed is an artist, writer and educator who lives on Guringai country. He is a founding member of the community art organization Refugee Art Project and author of *Still Alive: Notes from Australia's Immigration Detention System*. He is also a member of eleven, a collective of contemporary Muslim Australian artists, curators and writers, and plays guitar with the anti-racist death metal band Hazeen.

Paola Balla, PhD, is a Wemba-Wemba and Gunditjmara woman and Senior Lecturer, Moondani Balluk Indigenous Academic Centre, at Victoria University. Artist, curator and writer, her research and publications focus on Blak women's sovereign love, resistance, contributions and disruptions of racism and colonization, including 'Work to Be Done' (*Freize*, 2018) and 'Dark Mofo doesn't deserve our blood' (*The Conversation*, 2021). She was co-editor of Blak Brow–Blak Women's Edition (*The Lifted Brow*, 2018).

CM Burroughs is Associate Professor of Creative Writing at Columbia College Chicago and author of *The Vital System* (2012) and *Master Suffering* (2021), which was long-listed for the 2021 National Book Award and a finalist for the 2022 LA Times Book Prize. Burroughs' poetry has appeared in journals and anthologies including *Poetry*, *Ploughshares*, Cave Canem's *Gathering Ground* and *Best American Experimental Writing*.

James Byrne is a Reader in Contemporary Literature at Edge Hill University, UK. His research interest collections include translation and global poetics. His most recent book is *Places You Leave* (2021).

Marion May Campbell was Associate Professor in Writing and Literature at Deakin University. Her most recent works include the hybrid memoir *The Man on the Mantelpiece* (2018), the poetry collection *third body* (2018), the monograph *Poetic Revolutionaries: Intertextuality and Subversion* (2014) and the experimental novella *konkretion* (2013). A new poetry collection *languish* appeared in 2022. She lives in Gunaikurnai Country.

Mary Cappello is Professor of English and Creative Writing at the University of Rhode Island. A Guggenheim and Berlin Prize Fellow, she has authored seven books of literary non-fiction, most recently *Lecture* (2020). Cappello likes to take on unfathomables and to find, or invent, a form for them. Her current work addresses dormancy and its cognates, incubation, hibernation, late-bloomerism, promise and life *in potentia*.

Stephen Carleton is an award-winning Australian playwright based in Brisbane, where he teaches drama and playwriting at the University of Queensland. Stephen's work is frequently anchored in northern landscape, imagery and politics, and examines the cultural intersections between the Australian north and South-east Asia. He is co-artistic director of Knock-em-Down Theatre with Mary Anne Butler and Gail Evans.

David Carlin is Professor in Media and Communication at RMIT University. Co-founder of WrICE and non/fictionLab, his research interests include essaying and hybrid, collaborative and ecocritical forms and methods. Recent books include *The After-Normal: Brief, Alphabetical Essays on a Changing Planet* (2019) and *100 Atmospheres: Studies in Scale and Wonder* (2019).

Karen L. Carr is Senior Lecturer in the Literary Arts and Studies Department at The Rhode Island School of Design. Her writing encompasses fiction, creative non-fiction and hybrid forms, such as the phototext. She is interested in the politics and poetics of visuality, and is currently working on a memoir that explores adoption through ideas of space and place.

Belinda Castles is Lecturer in Creative Writing at the University of Sydney. She is the author of four novels: *Bluebottle* (2018), *Hannah and Emil* (2012), *The River Baptists* (2007) and *Falling Woman* (2000), and the editor of the essay collection, *Reading like an Australian Writer* (2021). Her research interests include walking, place and writing and writerly reading.

Ali Cobby Eckermann is employed as an Arts and Cultural Facilitator for local government on Ngadjuri country in South Australia where she was raised as an adopted child. A proud Yankunytjatjara woman and internationally published author, Ali is a poet who was inspired by the cultural teachings of her Elders in the central deserts of Australia, where she searched for her birth family for many years. Ali is Adjunct Professor at RMIT University.

Martina Copley is an artist, curator, educator and writer working in the annotative space. Recent publications and readings include *I'm Nearly There and Then I'll Stop*, Liquid Architecture, Melbourne, 2022; *The Movement of the Aside*, University of Melbourne, 2019; Doubting Writing/Writing Doubt, Australian Centre for Contemporary Art + RMIT non/fictionLab, 2019; *No Notes (This is writing)*, with Francesca Rendle-Short, 2017. www.martinacopley.com

Fan Dai is Professor of English at Sun Yat-sen University, China. Her research interests include creative writing in English as a foreign language and as (self) translation, as well as discourse analysis. She has published on these fields. Her most recent papers are 'Workshopping to Better Writing and Understanding' (2021), 'Creative Writing in English as a Foreign Language – From the Classroom to the World' (2021) and 'Self-translation and English-language Creative Writing in China' (2019).

Allan N. Derain is Assistant Professor at Ateneo de Manila University in the Department of Filipino. Their research interests focus on Philippine literature and folklore and they are the author of two novels, *Ang Banal na Aklat ng mga Kumag* (2013) and *Aswanglaut* (2021), and editor of the *aswang* anthology, *May Tiktik sa Bubong, May Sigbin sa Silong* (2017).

Quinn Eades is Senior Lecturer in Gender, Sexuality and Diversity Studies at La Trobe University, Melbourne. A writer, researcher, editor and award-winning poet, Quinn is the author of *all the beginnings: a queer autobiography of the body* (2015), and *Rallying* (2017). He is currently working on two volumes: an essay collection titled *Collaboration as Love*, and *is the body home*, a trans autobiography.

Marjorie Evasco is Professor Emeritus of Literature at De La Salle University, Manila, Philippines. She writes poems and essays in Boholano-Binisaya, her mother tongue, and English. She has published four poetry collections: *Dreamweavers* (1998), *Ochre Tones* (1999), *Skin of Water* (2009) and *Fishes of Light* (2013, with co-author Alex Fleites). Her research focuses on Cebuano Literature and Ecofeminist Literature in the Philippines.

Delia Falconer is a Senior Lecturer in Creative Writing at the University of Technology Sydney. She has published two novels (*The Service of Clouds* and *The Lost Thoughts of Soldiers*) and two works of nonfiction (*Sydney* and, most recently, *Signs and Wonders: Dispatches From a Time of Beauty and Loss*). In 2018, she was awarded the Walkley-Pascall Award for Arts Criticism.

Lina María Ferreira Cabeza-Vanegas works as Assistant Professor at the University of Chicago and has MFAs in creative nonfiction and literary translation from the University of Iowa. She is the author of *Drown Sever Sing* (2015) and *Don't Come Back* (2017), and has published widely, from the *LA Review of Books* to *Poets & Writers*. She has two forthcoming books.

Kári Gíslason is Associate Professor of Creative Writing and Literary Studies at Queensland University of Technology. He is the author of the memoir *The Promise of Iceland* (2011), the novel *The Ash Burner* (2015), and co-author with Richard Fidler of the travel book *Saga Land: The Island of Stories at the Edge of the World* (2017). His fourth book, the historical novel *The Sorrow Stone*, was published in 2022.

Natalie Harkin is a Narungga woman and poet from South Australia. She is Senior Research Fellow at Flinders University with an interest in decolonizing state archives, currently engaging archival-poetic methods to research and document Aboriginal women's domestic service and labour histories in South Australia. Her books include *Dirty Words* (2001) and *Archival-Poetics* (2019).

Ames Hawkins is Professor at Columbia College Chicago in the English and Creative Writing Department and author of the award-winning transgenre work of literary nonfiction, *These are Love(d) Letters* (2019). As a creative-critical scholar, Ames explores the interstices of text, audio and image. They have published widely in scholarly and literary publications – both print and online.

Dominique Hecq was until recently Associate Professor and Research Leader at Swinburne University of Technology, Australia. Hecq has long written across genres and disciplines, including literature, critical theory, pedagogy and psychoanalysis. *Towards a Poetics of*

Creative Writing (2017) deploys this mix of interests. Often experimental, her creative works include a novel, five collections of stories and twelve volumes of poetry. *Kaosmos* (2020), *Speculate* (with Eugen Bacon, 2021), *Smacked* (2022) and *After Cage* (2022) are her latest offerings.

Robin Hemley is Director of the George Polk School of Communications at Long Island University in Brooklyn, New York, as well as founder of NonfictionNOW and co-editor (with Leila Philip) of *Speculative Nonfiction*. His most recent books include *Borderline Citizen: Dispatches from the Outskirts of Nationhood* (2020), *The Art and Craft of Asian Stories* (with Xu Xi; 2021) and the Autofiction, *Oblivion: An After-Autobiography* (2022).

Sarah Holland-Batt is Professor of Creative Writing and Literary Studies at the Queensland University of Technology, and a Prime Minister's Literary Award-winning poet and critic. Her most recent books are a collection of essays on contemporary Australian poetry, *Fishing for Lightning: The Spark of Poetry* (2021), and a new book of poems, *The Jaguar* (2022).

Erik Knudsen is a filmmaker and Professor of Media Practice at the University of Central Lancashire, UK, where he is also the Director of Research for the Faculty of Culture and Creative Industries. His research focuses on film practice, in particular ideation, story and transcendent narrative strategies. His latest feature film is *True Calling* (2021), and his latest book is *Finding the Personal Voice in Filmmaking* (2018).

Shuchi Kothari is Associate Professor in Media and Screen at the University of Auckland. As a New Zealand-Indian filmmaker, she has written and produced several award-winning films (*Firaaq, Apron Strings, Shit One Carries, Coffee and Allah, Fleeting Beauty*) that have screened at over 100 international film festivals. She is the co-founder of the Pan Asian Screen Collective and currently is co-producing a portmanteau feature film *Kāinga*, that brings together immigrant stories by eleven Pan-Asian women writer/directors.

Manola-Gayatri Kumarswamy is Research Associate at the Wits School of Arts, Witwatersrand University, South Africa. They bring Participatory Action Research (PaR) and queer embodied methodologies to ocean research and are interested in reimagining post-decoloniality through artistic thinking. They have published on PAR and decoloniality (2018), gendered citizenship (2017), PaR as Foresting Loss (upcoming) and are co-editing *CTR*'s Special Isssue What's Queer About Queer Performance Now (2022).

Benjamin Laird is a PhD candidate in the School of Media and Communication at RMIT University. His PhD investigates biographical poetry in print and programmable media, which includes the creation of digital and print poems concerning William Denton, a nineteenth-century spiritualist, scientific lecturer and radical. His electronic poems about Denton include the digital chapbook *The Durham Poems* (2016) and 'Psychometric Researches' (2019).

Jeanine Leane is a Wiradjuri writer, poet and academic from southwest New South Wales. Her poetry, short stories and essays have been published in *Hecate: An Interdisciplinary Journal of Women's Liberation, The Journal for the Association European Studies of*

Australia, *Australian Poetry Journal*, *Antipodes*, *Overland* and the *Australian Book Review*. She teaches creative writing at the University of Melbourne.

Sarah Leavitt is Assistant Professor of Graphic Forms in the School of Creative Writing at the University of British Columbia. Her particular areas of interest include autobiographical comics, formal experimentation in comics and comics pedagogy. She is the author of two award-winning comics: *Tangles: A Story About Alzheimer's*, *My Mother and Me* (2010) and *Agnes, Murderess* (2019). Sarah is currently working on a collection of comics about her partner's medically assisted death. More at instagram.com/sarah_leav/

Tina Makereti is Senior Lecturer in Creative Writing at the International Institute of Modern Letters, Te Herenga Waka, Victoria University of Wellington, New Zealand. Her research interests focus on fiction and creative non-fiction, Māori, Pasifika and Indigenous literatures and kaupapa Māori literary approaches and methodologies. Her publications include *Once Upon a Time in Aotearoa* (2010), *Where the Rēkohu Bone Sings* (2014), *Black Marks on the White Page* (2017), and *The Imaginary Lives of James Pōneke* (2018). She is of Te Ātiawa, Ngāti Tūwharetoa, Ngāti Rangatahi and Pākehā descent.

Selina Tusitala Marsh (ONZM, New Zealand Poet Laureate 2017–19) is Associate Professor in English at the University of Auckland, New Zealand. Her research interests focus on Pacific literature, postcolonial theory and creative writing. She has published three award-winning collections of poetry and recently, two award-winning graphic memoirs, *Mophead: How Your Difference Makes a Difference* (2019) and *Mophead TU: The Queen's Poem* (2020).

Catherine McKinnon is Discipline Leader of English and Creative Writing at the University of Wollongong, Australia. Her research interests focus on climate warming, feminism, war and other forms of violence. She is a writer of novels and plays. Her most recent book is *Storyland* (2017). A play adaption of *Storyland* has been commissioned for 2023 by Merrigong Theatre.

Ander Monson is Professor of English at the University of Arizona. His most recent books are *The Gnome Stories* (2019), *I Will Take the Answer* (2019) and *Predator: A Memoir* (2022).

Cath Moore is a teaching associate at The University of Melbourne in Creative Writing. She also teaches at the Victorian College of Arts in the Department of Film and Television. Her research interests focus on script development practices, screenwriting as a creative labour and cultural export. She has published on Danish collaborative script development and story preferences. Her debut novel *Metal Fish Falling Snow* won the 2021 Victorian and Queensland Premier's award for Young Adult literature.

Paula Morris is Associate Professor at the University of Auckland, New Zealand, where she directs the Masters programme in Creative Writing. Her iwi affiliations are Ngāti Wai, Ngāti

Manuhiri and Ngāti Whātua. She is an award-winning novelist, short story writer and essayist. In 2021 she co-edited, with Alison Wong, the landmark anthology *A Clear Dawn: New Asian Writing from Aotearoa New Zealand*.

Fiona Murphy is a Deaf poet and essayist. Her memoir *The Shape of Sound* (2021) explores secrets, stigma and sign language.

Peta Murray is Lecturer in Creative Writing at RMIT University, Melbourne. Her research focus is the role of language and arts-based practices as modes of enquiry and forms of cultural activism. Publications include plays such as *Salt* (2001), fiction including *Indigestion* (2010), collaborative, queer and multi-modal works of live art such as *vigil/wake* (2019) and adventures in the essayesque, *Glossalalalararium Pandemiconium* (2020).

Collier Nogues is Assistant Professor of Creative Writing at the Chinese University of Hong Kong. She writes at the intersection of digital and documentary poetics, with an emphasis on making connections across decolonization and demilitarization movements in the United States and in the Pacific. Her poetry collections include the hybrid print/interactive volume *The Ground I Stand on Is Not My Ground* (2015), and *On the Other Side, Blue* (2011).

Alvin Pang, PhD, is Adjunct Professor in the School of Media and Communication at RMIT University. His research interests include the possibilities of literary practice conducted across multiple languages, genres, careers and communities. A poet and editor from Singapore, his writing has been translated into more than twenty languages worldwide. His recent books include *What Happened: Poems 1997–2017* (2017) and *Uninterrupted Time* (2019).

Antonia Pont is Associate Professor in Writing, Literature and Culture at Deakin University, Australia. Poet, yogi and essayist, she also researches time, creativity, stability, futurity and plainness. Selected works include *A Philosophy of Practising with Deleuze's* Difference and Repetition (2021), the co-authored *Practising with Deleuze* (2017), *You Will Not Know in Advance What You'll Feel* (2019) and 'Private Practice: Toward a Philosophy of Just Sitting' (*Literary Hub*, 2020).

Francesca Rendle-Short is Professor of Creative Writing in the School of Media and Communication at RMIT University. She is interested in a research practice that seeks to subvert normative practices, one focused on ethical enquiry. She is co-founder of non/fictionLab and WrICE (Writers Immersion and Cultural Exchange). Her five books include *The Near and the Far* (Vol I and II; 2016, 2019) and *Bite Your Tongue* (2011).

Lavanya Shanbhogue Arvind teaches at the Tata Institute of Social Sciences, Mumbai. Her research interests focus on feminist theory, gender and social exclusion, critical feminist ethnographies, and gender and sustainability. She is the winner of the Commonwealth Short Story Special Prize (2011). Her most recent book is the novel *The Heavens We Chase* (2016).

Kathleen Stewart is Professor of Anthropology at the University of Texas, Austin. She writes ethnographic experiments to approach the worldings in everyday atmospheres, matters, voicings, rhythms and refrains. Her books include *A Space on the Side of the Road: Cultural Poetics in an 'Other' America* (1996), *Ordinary Affects* (2007), *The Hundreds* co-authored with Lauren Berlant (2019) and *Worlding* (in preparation).

Nike Sulway is Senior Lecturer in Creative and Critical Writing at University of Southern Queensland. Her research focuses on diversity and inclusivity in creative writing practice and research, particularly the writing and writing practices of women and queers. Recent publications include the award-winning children's novel *Dying in the First Person* (2016), *Winter's Tale* (2020) and a chapter on Australian fairy tale history in *The Routledge Companion to Australian Literature* (2020).

Stayci Taylor is Senior Lecturer in the School of Media and Communication at RMIT University. Her research interests include screenwriting, script development, non-fiction and creative practice. She has published in all of these areas, in both scholarly and creative outlets, and often through the lenses of gender and comedy. She is lead editor of *The Palgrave Handbook of Script Development* (2021).

Nhã Thuyên works as a writer in Hanoi. Her most recent books in English are *un\\martyred: [self-]vanishing presences in Vietnamese poetry* (2019), *moon fevers* (2019) and *words breathe, creatures of elsewhere (từ thở, những người lạ)* (2016). Her main practices are writing between languages, experimenting with translations and poetic exchanges. She's been working on a multilingual project that aims to open a discussion of "up\ \rooted beings" in Vietnamese poetry. Her book of poetry *vị nước (taste of waters)* has been waiting to see the moon.

Maria Tumarkin is an Associate Professor in the School of Culture and Communication at the University of Melbourne. She has published books and essays on physical sites of trauma and more-than-representational forms of cultural memory. Her most recent book is *Axiomatic* (2018).

Aritha van Herk is Professor in the Department of English at the University of Calgary in Canada. She is a novelist, essayist and ficto-critical writer. Her creative process focuses on geographical and historical temperament as tonal accompaniment to landscape, especially in relation to women and work. Her recent prose-poem, *Stampede and the Westness of West* (2016) cross-examines notions of *carnivale* and its performance in western mythologies.

Julienne van Loon is Associate Professor of Creative Writing at RMIT University, Melbourne, and Honorary Fellow in Writing at the University of Iowa. Her research interests include feminist literary practice, contemporary narrative fiction and literary value. Publications include *Road Story* (2005), *Beneath the Bloodwood Tree* (2008), *Harmless* (2014) and *The Thinking Woman* (2019). She is managing editor at *TEXT: Journal of Writing and Writing Courses*, see https://textjournal.scholasticahq.com/

Soile Veijola is Professor of Cultural Studies of Tourism at University of Lapland, Finland. Her research has dealt with feminist analyses of disembodied tourism theories, the Hostessing Society, silence in Finnish and responsible tourism planning. Her pieces of experimental co-writing include the articles 'The Body in Tourism' (1994), 'The Disoriented Tourist' (1997) and the book *Disruptive Tourism and Its Untidy Guests* (2014).

Rúnar Helgi Vignisson is Professor in Creative Writing at the University of Iceland. He is the author of eight books of fiction and has translated fiction by numerous well-known authors, such as William Faulkner, Amy Tan, J. M. Coetzee and Jhumpa Lahiri. His most recent project is an anthology of short stories from around the world which he co-edited (2016–20). His short stories have been translated into several languages.

Martin Villanueva is an Assistant Professor in the School of Humanities at Ateneo de Manila University in the Philippines. He is the Associate Editor for the Literary Section of *Kritika Kultura*. He is the author of the essay collection the poetry collection *Account* (2017) and *A Pig Was Once Killed in Our Garage* (2019).

Nicole Walker is the author of several books, most recently *The After-Normal: Brief Alphabetical Essays on a Changing Planet* (2019) and *Processed Meats: Essays on Food, Flesh and Navigating Disaster* (2021). She edits the Crux series at University of Georgia Press, is non-fiction editor at *Diagram* and teaches creative writing at Northern Arizona University.

Wendy S. Walters is Concentration Head in Nonfiction and Associate Professor in the Writing Program of the School of the Arts at Columbia University, New York, USA. She is the author of three books, including *Multiply/Divide: On the American Real and Surreal* (2015). She is completing her next book, an argument against the use of white paint.

Deborah Wardle teaches Creative Writing at RMIT and University of Melbourne, specialising in Ecofiction and Environmental Literature. Her research explores how climate fictions give voice to nonhuman entities, particularly ways to give expression to groundwater. She has publications in Australian and international journals, most recently in, *Scorchers: A Climate Fiction Anthology* (2021). Her book with Routledge, *Subterranean Imaginaries: Groundwater Narratives* is due in 2023.

Steven Winduo lives and writes in Port Moresby, Papua New Guinea. He taught in the Literature Program at the University of Papua New Guinea for many years. He writes poetry, fiction, non-fiction and journalistic pieces. His latest book *Imagination Is Everything* (2021) is a memoir on personal development and success principles.

Lawrence Lacambra Ypil is Senior Lecturer at Yale-NUS College. His work explores the intersection of text and image and the role of material culture in the construction of cultural identity. In 2020, he was a finalist for the Lambda Literary Awards and on the longlist for The Believer Book Awards for *The Experiment of the Tropics* (2019). He has received MFAs from Washington University in St. Louis and the University of Iowa.

Acknowledgement of Country

The editors acknowledge the people of the Boon wurrung, Dja Dja Wurrung, Wadawurrung and Woi wurrung language groups of the Kulin Nation on whose lands this book has been conceived and compiled. We respectfully acknowledge the Traditional Custodians and Owners of Country across the continent known as Australia and recognize their continuing connection to and custodianship of lands, waters, community and culture. We pay respects to their Ancestors and Elders, both past and present. In acknowledging country, we acknowledge that sovereignty has never been ceded, and treaties are yet to be agreed.

Acknowledgements

A previous version of 'Flow' was published in *Bending Genre* (bendinggenre.com), 29 April 2013. Available online https://bendinggenre.com/2013/04/29/flow-mary-cappello/ (accessed 25 November 2021).

'Dear Incubator' appears in the collection *The Vital System*, published by Tupelo Press. Copyright © CM Burroughs 2012. Reprinted by permission of Tupelo Press.

Students work quoted in 'Writing-foreign-language' printed with permission.

Introduction

DEBORAH WARDLE, JULIENNE VAN LOON, STAYCI TAYLOR, FRANCESCA RENDLE-SHORT, PETA MURRAY, DAVID CARLIN

The *A to Z of Creative Writing Methods* is an alphabetical collection of essays to prompt consideration of methods within creative writing research and practice. The volume draws together in one useful glossary many current developments in the creative writing methods and methodologies field. It confirms the specialist lexicon of research practice in creative writing, proposing a vocabulary inherent to creative writing processes, but also recognizing the generative nature of emergent methods.

Glossary, from *glossarium*, its root in the Greek word *glossa* meaning tongue, is a list of words, obsolete, foreign or otherwise difficult. A typical glossary offers an alphabetical list of words relating to a specific subject, text or dialect, with definitions. Our approach, under the guise of an abecedary, is an atypical glossary, more a repository of ideas, a go-to, a testing ground. We invite you to try things out.

In curating and compiling this collection, the editors draw on the experiences and thinking emerging out of non/fictionLab, a research group located within the School of Media and Communication at RMIT University in Melbourne, Australia. Established in 2011, non/fictionLab members experiment with contemporary realities through story, dialogue, poetics and partnerships. The idea for this book came out of a playful dialogue among members of the group and is informed by our looking back on (at the time of writing) ten years of collegial thinking with and alongside one another as writers, practitioners and scholars. The editors, as members of non/fictionLab, work with a multiplicity of practices that are collaborative and non-hierarchical, and we recognize the value of focusing on how we work at writing – both within our membership and also with and alongside visitors and guests of the non/fictionLab. This book, in part, is our way of synthesizing and sharing concepts of methodology and method in terms of how they relate to our own writing practice (and supervisory practices with doctoral candidates) and the reflexive way, as practitioners, we have manifested our creative writing methods into research relationships.

In many disciplines, writing is simply one of many methods that form a part of research practice: it is distinctly not a methodology. At times writing is not overtly recognized as a method in its own right. It is simply what is done. Here we explore writing as more than method. We include how it is understood as methodology. It is not just our methods that evolve, but the ways in which we think about what creative writing *is* and *does*.

In terms of scholarly research practice, it is generally agreed that a method is a tool or a *way of doing*, whereas a methodology is the justification for using a particular tool, or *the thinking behind* employing that tool in the first place. Methodology, as we know, emerges from a domain and the domain we are interested in here is creative writing and while it is a domain largely comprised of creative writers, it is often located with and alongside the domains of literary and cultural studies, sociology, ethnography, media, screen studies, journalism, performance studies, communication design, the visual artists and the broader humanities. *The thinking behind* creative writing is very much influenced by (and in turn influences) the thinking of neighbouring domains. In the creative writing discipline, however, writing can be both a justification and a tool. In creative writing, as is the case with many other creative arts-based research disciplines, we *do*, we *make*, we *think*, in short, we *research* through practice. We discover through practice. The writing practice therefore is not just a tool for thinking but can become a form of thinking in its own right. This book explores how writers and scholars might understand creative writing as *the thinking behind* the writing we do.

Questions of methods and methodologies in any discipline are intricately enmeshed with questions of power and difference. Numerous writers of colour have highlighted the racialized, normative restrictions they have experienced in the learning and teaching of creative writing methods. Viet Thanh Nguyen writes in the *New York Times* of his experience of creative writing classes at the University of California (Berkeley): 'As a young aspiring writer, I was troubled by how these workshops, aside from the "art" of writing, did not have anything to say about the matters that concerned me: politics, history, theory, philosophy, ideology' (qtd in Malla 2017). Namrata Poddar, in her essay 'Is "Show Don't Tell" a Universal Truth or a Colonial Relic' (2016), challenges the edict to 'show, don't tell', which she found ubiquitous in the 'predominantly white American creative writing workshop culture', for its privileging of visuality over orality, and its universalizing and privileging of white Western cultural traditions. Toni Morrison (1984) also articulates how her creative writing methods are grounded in an imperative to resist the effects of Western, white supremacist and colonizing projects on how literature as a field has been constituted:

> [If] my work is to confront a reality unlike that received reality of the West, it must centralize and animate information discredited by the West – discredited not because it is not true or useful or even of some racial value, but because it is information held by discredited people, information dismissed as 'lore' or 'gossip' or 'magic' or 'sentiment' (Morrison 1984: 388).

This book seeks to contribute to the project of decolonizing creative writing through its breadth of perspectives, including Indigenous knowledge systems and cosmologies, as well as methods and methodologies arising in Global South contexts. It embraces practices of resistance and social engagement. For example, Jeanine Leane's 'Radical Effrontery' asks difficult questions about who has the authority to tell someone else's story; she challenges 'Eurocentric-constructed universalisms' such as 'freedom of the imagination'. Natalie Harkin's 'resistance-poetics' is a vision of refusal to be silent or silenced. Steven Winduo outlines the *bung wantaim* method with the view that the production of social knowledge through this 'extended multilogue' promotes a better understanding of the self within the 'culturescape' of the Pacific. Eric Knudsen in 'Feelings-as-method' encourages readers not to become a mascot for other people's political agendas and other people's feelings of social guilt: find stories 'that belong to us all, but that only you can tell here and now'. We acknowledge that writing is inextricably linked with political engagement. This book casts a critical and self-critical eye on the politics as much as the poetics of creative writing methods. It aims to bring into dialogue a multiplicity of different voices, speaking across, alongside and towards each other, and in so doing to push against normative hierarchies of centre and margin.

Creative writing is a field that privileges the imagination. It privileges other things, too: ambiguity, doubt, mess, process as much as product, poetics, the irreconcilable, the question, the sketch, the unconscious and very often, the concept of the active reader. What we do may be left incomplete, or rather, its meaning may be designed to be finished or contributed to by someone other than us, someone we don't know, someone who is yet to come. Sometimes our discipline also privileges non-knowledge, or the unthought known, or the idea that what we are doing is deliberately moving away from knowledge into unknowing. Accordingly, this book examines innovative and generative writing methods that may deliver new texts capacious yet porous enough to speak to difference, to contain multiplicity, to express paradox, to birth concepts and to deliver what is conceived, to point to what remains unformed, or intuited, or in a state of coming into being.

As creative writers, attentiveness to language, to both its complexities and its limitations, is crucial both to what we do with writing and *the thinking behind* what we write. Ours is primarily an imaginative engagement with language. As Maurice Blanchot puts it, 'To write is to let fascination rule language' and thereby open language up to a potentially endless play (Blanchot and Smock 1989: 33). As writers, language is our medium. We are thinking with words. We are caught up in and by language games, and by both the limitations and the (as yet unforeseen) possibilities of the language(s) we and our (potential) readers inhabit. In this sense, the practice of writing can never be decoupled from other language practices, especially reading and speaking. In this volume, A to Z becomes an organizing principle. We acknowledge that categorizing concepts may have limits, despite the inescapable usefulness of the process. Like Glăveanu (2016), who proposes that in research processes we may dissolve categories and add new perspectives, we alphabetize the entries, to invite readers to enter the book according to their own organizing principles and reading desires.

This *A to Z* arrives at a time when creative writing has developed into a well-established discipline in the academy, one with its own critical vocabulary. The list of methods canvassed in this collection are testament to the discipline's maturity, demonstrating terms and approaches that are practice-oriented and that distinguish creative writing from allied disciplines. Our book is a snapshot of a moment in time, capturing some of the multiple practices, voices, purposes and perspectives of those who write and teach, mostly but not exclusively from within the academy.

But creative writing is, as ever, an outward-facing discipline, and our contributors are aware of, and attentive to, readerships beyond the walls of the university. In many ways, the specificities of working with words, and what we may do with them to conceal or reveal, has never been more crucial. We grapple daily with the means to sustain our confidence in 'the known world' (Gibson 2010). As writer Sarah Sentilles has said, there is an urgency to our creative and artistic practices, because they are 'how we exercise our capacity to reinvent the world' (2020). This collection gestures towards how to write and speak to the nuances and subtleties, and to find words and structures equal to the carriage of ideas and experiences well beyond the academic life.

Introduction 3

As editors, we invited our contributors to propose, defend, explain or demonstrate a creative writing method in essayistic form, highlighting the relationship between genre and subject matter, and embodying the idea of *essai*, or 'to try'. We particularly encouraged idiosyncratic, playful, innovative approaches, often personalized (to demonstrate practice in action) and peculiar to the topic/method at hand. The resultant collection of fifty-nine essays from fifty-eight contributors often demonstrates method in action, enacting possibilities, hypothesizing, testing and working to generate further enquiry by others. By enacting the spirit of some of the methods they describe, these essays serve not only as a guide but often as a set of examples or case studies. Some of the essays end with questions or exercises for further consideration as well as suggestions for further reading, including creative works. Our contributors were encouraged to ponder what the relevant key term, approach or practice might mean for creative writing, and how its application in this discipline might differ to its application elsewhere.

In soliciting contributions, we began with a list of more than fifty possible methods and invited academics working in the field to either select from our list or propose a new topic. As curators, we were attentive to including writers from a range of writing traditions and practices across multiple forms and genre, from poetry and nonfiction to fiction writing and writing for performance, from graphic novelists and illustrators to those engaged in multi-media writing and forms of writing-related arts activism. As editors based in Australia, we were particularly enthusiastic about extending invitations to writers and academics based in the Asia–Pacific region. When we reached the limits of academic and writerly networks, we sought suggestions from writers who had already agreed to contribute. 'Who would you suggest?' we asked, and 'who do you know who is doing interesting work on method?' – resulting in rolling rounds of commissions beyond the networks of the non/fictionLab and introducing us to a global cohort of inspiring writers whose work we might not have already encountered. In this way, our list of contributors and their attendant topics, multiplied and diversified to include topics on camping and chorality, procrastination, resistance and uncertainty. The collection gives voice to a lively and innovative interpolation of collaboration-as-love, generative 'mistakes of translation', iterative thinking as the catalyst for alchemical writing, the gift of listening and the paradoxical safe place of permission. In one essay – 'Queering' – all of the current contributors were invited into a shared online document, or 'space of queersomeness', to contribute to a polyphonic, non-binary, irreverent conglomeration that enacts queering as writing method through the doing. Entries of 100 words were encouraged by queer-identifying authors. The contributors to 'Queering' are listed in the order they arrived, and from opening paragraph to the reference list, the remote collaboration pushed against the boundaries of scholarly format.

We worked, as editors, in a collaborative fashion, sharing all the key roles, and reading together, often at the same time and place. Eschewing perhaps more 'efficient' ways of working where the collection was divided into sections and assigned to an editor, each of us read every essay and had input into the editorial and curatorial processes. The editors are listed Z-A – both as a playful gesture and as an act of resistance against entrenched scholarly conventions and hierarchies around 'first author'. While a linear list cannot be avoided, it is hoped our approach to editor-order reflects the editorial process that was inclusive and rigorous, where editors both played to their strengths while also developing new skills, and where decisions were made collectively, following robust discussion and equal input.

This book is a resource for expanding the field of methods with which to encourage and stimulate writing practices. It is designed to work as a handbook for creative writers who are keen to push the boundaries of their current practice and offers a range of approaches with which to expand a creative writing practice. The methods outlined in the essays also comprise a resource for creative writing researchers – from PhD candidates to established scholars – providing ways to understand and extend their own creative writing and research practices. Our contributors bring to this volume their distinct literary and cultural contexts and, in most cases, illustrate the method they describe, giving the writer a sense of what's possible should they try the method themselves. By demonstrating the method in action, these entries enact possibilities for experimentation and innovation in writing practice. In this way, our contributors share methods beyond simplistic 'write and reflect' models to inspire the full spectrum of writers – published writers with an established practice, people who know they want to write but don't know where to start, and everyone in between. Our confidence with this assertion is because our contributors have inspired us already.

All of our authors model how social, cultural and historical forces explicitly and implicitly affect their practice. This allows for a conversation between ideas, concepts and approaches that we hope will open up rather than close down possibilities.

From 'Archival-poetics' and 'Atmospherics' to 'Yoga' and 'Zim', we offer an abecedary of methods that may, at first glance, seem weird, wild or wanton. We have invited wordplay in curating our topic list. This approach is deliberately meandering, subversive and contra-dictory, and we hope to exhort our readership to push back, push around, push through the conventions of creative writing to uncover and expose what may be possible. For these reasons we invite writers to broach this book haphazardly and slant, entering via any aper-ture to follow any pathway that appeals. For those who prefer a little guidance, each entry is followed by a short list of suggestions of essays from within the volume to which a writer may springboard. These 'see also' suggestions are sometimes offered as possible compan-ion essays with obvious coherence, and sometimes because the proposed next reading may collide with the ideas from the first. They offer an extra nonlinear weave to the volume.

It is hoped that the ideas within the pages ahead will give writers of all genres and styles the courage and the impetus to explore new methods. The entries may also embolden some writers to flex new muscles and try out unfamiliar forms, styles or approaches. While we hope this book contributes to debates around methods within creative writing research and practices, this is, in the end, a book about *doing*. By focusing on methods, the collection enables the writer to hypothesize, to test ideas, to generate further enquiry. Ultimately, the *A to Z* is an invitation. It is offered in the spirit of sharing how we write with a playfulness of language, a lightness of touch, attention to the politics and aesthetics of our practice, and our commitment to pushing forms. Most of all, this book encourages writers to write – delve in.

References

Blanchot, M. and A. Smock (1989), *The Space of Literature*, Lincoln: University of Nebraska Press.

Gibson, R. (2010), 'The Known World', in D. L. Brien, S. Burr and J. Webb (eds), *TEXT Special Issue 8: Creative and Practice-Led Research*. Available online: https://www. textjournal.com.au/speciss/issue8/Gibson.pdf (accessed 17 November 2021). https://doi. org/10.52086/001c.31508

Glăveanu, V. P., L. Tanggaard, and C. Wegener (2016), *Creativity, a New Vocabulary*, Basingstoke: Palgrave Macmillan.

Malla, P. (2017), 'What Julio Cortazar Might Teach Us about Teaching Writing', *The New Yorker*, 23 October. Available online: https://www.newyorker.com/books/page-turner/what-julio-cortazar-might-teach-us-about-teaching-writing (accessed 29 November 2021).

Morrison, T. (1984), 'Memory, Creation and Writing', *Thought*, 59 (235), December. Available online: https://blogs.umass.edu/brusert/files/2013/03/Morrison_Memory-Creation.pdf (accessed 29 November 2021).

Poddar, N. (2016), 'Is "Show Don't Tell" a Universal Truth or a Colonial Relic?', *Literary Hub*, 20 September. Available online: https://lithub.com/is-show-dont-tell-a-universal-truth-or-a-colonial-relic/ (accessed 17 November 2021).

Sentilles, S. (2020), 'How Can You Write while the Earth Is Burning? Sarah Sentilles on Why Making Art Matters', *The Writer's Room with Charlotte Wood*. Available online: https://www.charlottewood.com.au/podcast.html (accessed 25 March 2020).

Archival-poetics

NATALIE HARKIN

Archival-poetics emerged as a slow, situated unfolding, an embodied reckoning with Australia's state colonial archive and those traumatic, contested and buried episodes of history that inevitably return to haunt. It developed as a means to rupture and re-imagine contemporary legacies of colonialism, including the inconceivable volume of Indigenous records, objects, artefacts and human remains held in state collections all over the world; material, cultural and intellectual property that was stolen, recorded, categorized and contained in the name of empire and conquest. These archives hold histories of preservation painstakingly maintained, a fixed consignment process of hierarchy and order where provenance, objectivity and security are assured. As institutions of future memory, they also signify sites and histories of immense loss for all that was discarded and deemed irrelevant for the record.

My own family research manifested as feverish gathering and hoarding of primary source materials from state-based collections, tracing file-note paper trails and memory fragments from multiple sources. I unwittingly replicated the very thing I was attempting to disrupt, *the Archive Box*; locked-in and vacuum-sealed with my Ancestors, navigating a violent entanglement of myth and truths, buoyed and sustained by imperial fantasies to shape official realities. The only way for me to reckon with it all was to examine the origins of the archive itself, consider new offerings for the future record, write poetry and weave my way out (Harkin 2019).

A selection of hand-written letters by my Nanna and great-grandmother revealed critical minor histories where the gendered and racialized conditions of empire play out in the mundane intimacies of the everyday (Stoler 2006). They were replete with references to home, to family and a domestic-trained life controlled by the state and provided insight to stories and legacies otherwise smoothed over, hidden or forgotten. As a labour of love, weaving became central to my poetic-praxis culminating in the physical and metaphorical transformation of their letters into a Ngarrindjeri basket (Harkin 2020), a new archival-poetic site of resistance, a shared-history location, and a means to honour a very different story to what was officially recorded about them.

Through ekphrastic markers of relationality and respect, I was drawn to particular Indigenous poets, writers and artists who also engage archive and memory through decolonial praxis. Their work captured me in unexpected-uncanny moments and at potent places, and they told me something new and profoundly nostalgic about my own story. In these moments of embodied recognition, invisible spaces opened up to write and create into. Such literary-ekphrasis can trigger critical interventions beyond the self, towards resounding and collective reckoning, an archival-poetic response where the potency of place, colonial-histories and blood memory collide.

As a signature literary trope (Allen 2002; Momaday 1968), *blood memory* became central to archival-poetics as a reclamation response to personal and collective loss, an active remembering and redefining relationships to knowledge to strengthen a sense of self, identity and place: 'blood trails that we follow back toward a sense of where we come from and who we are' (Owens 1998: 150).

As a narrative tactic, blood memory is a means to write back to the state's colonial discourses and fixed imaginings on blood, constructions of race and identity, and the construction of personal story (Allen 2002). It is also a means to re-imagine history and contribute to communal memory through the intergenerational transmission of knowledge pumping through individual and collective bodies and societies. It is vital and unending, and it does not always flow easily.

As a literary tool, blood memory explored through an epistemology of haunting makes sense to me; a means to understand and theorize that which is silent, hidden or absent, but is nevertheless acutely present and felt. Reckoning with history's ghosts through a framework of *recognition, transformation* and *action* (Gordon 2008; Van Wagenen 2004) enables profound honouring, a form of restorative justice for local stories to rupture and inform larger narratives of history. Theorizing haunting from our local Indigenous standpoints can also challenge and counter problematic representations of the Indigenous *ghost* in literature, interrogate how spectres of colonialism still haunt our Indigenous subjectivities today and dismantle colonial systems, processes and fixed imaginings via reckoning with spectres of, and in, the colonial archive. Offering up new narratives of history and storytelling has the potential to shift local and national consciousness towards some kind of justice, through either a reckoning with ghosts, an aesthetics of action or a politics of vision (Cameron 2008; Cariou 2006). Such a proactive poetics of haunting can expose what Tony Birch calls Australia's 'national secrecy about colonialism' (Birch 2006), unveil what Kim Scott calls 'Australia's continuing neurosis' (Scott 2001) and keep the wounds open, as Alexis Wright states, to reverse the prescribed forgetting with a 'steadfast telling of the truth' (Wright 2002: 19). This can also be described as a *work of mourning* where the possibility of just futures lies in the ability to live in remembrance and in the wake of history's injustices (DeShazer 1994; Galeano 1983; Sharpe 2016).

This method is also framed by Black, queer, postcolonial and Indigenous feminisms that inform decolonial critical-creative praxis, ways to better understand intersecting dynamics of power and oppression, and alternative systems of accountability for race, class and gender-based violence, and grounded in a resistance-poetics vision of refusal to be silent or silenced.

There are multiple ways to bear witness to the violence of colonialism and collectively move through it all to lighten the load. Archival-poetics is one way to repatriate stories, agency and love to our Ancestors for the future record. We trust our intuition. We follow paper trails, heartbeats and signs. We trace our Ancestors' gaze towards future generations where their dignity shines, and this is their lasting impression.

References

Allen, C. (2002), *Blood Narrative: Indigenous Identity in American Indian and Māori Literary and Activist Texts*, Durham: Duke University Press.

Birch, T. (2006), 'Promise Not to Tell: Interrogating Colonialism's Worst (or Best) Kept Secrets', *First Person: International Digital Storytelling Conference*, ACMI, 4 February. Available online: www.acmi.net.au/global/media/first_person_birch.pdf (accessed 20 March 2015).

Cameron, E. (2008), 'Indigenous Spectrality and the Politics of Postcolonial Ghost Stories', *Cultural Geographies*, 15 (3): 383–93.

Cariou, W. (2006), 'Haunted Prairie: Aboriginal "Ghosts" and the Spectres of Settlement', *University of Toronto Quarterly*, 75 (2): 727–34.

DeShazer, M. (1994), *A Poetics of Resistance: Women Writing in El Salvador, South Africa, and the United States*, Michigan: University of Michigan Press.

Enwezor, O. (2008), *Archive Fever: Uses of the Document in Contemporary Art*, New York: International Centre of Photography.

Galeano, E. (1983), 'In Defense of the Word', trans. B. Ortiz, in *Days and Nights of Love and War*, 169–78, London: Pluto Press.

Gordon, A. (2008), *Ghostly Matters: Haunting and Sociological Imagination*, 2nd edn, Minneapolis: University of Minnesota Press.

Harkin, N. (2020), 'Weaving the Colonial Archive: A Basket to Lighten the Load', *Journal of Australian Studies*, 44 (2): 154–66.

Harkin, N. (2019), *Archival-Poetics*, Melbourne: Vagabond Press.

Momaday, S. (1968), *House Made of Dawn*, New York: Harper and Row.

Moreton-Robinson, A. (2000), *Talkin' Up to the White Woman*, St Lucia, Queensland: University of Queensland Press.

Owens, L. (1998), *Mixedblood Messages, Literature, Film, Family, Place*, Oklahoma: University of Oklahoma Press.

Scott, K. (2001), 'Australia's Continuing Neurosis: Identity, Race and History', *The Alfred Deakin Lectures*, 14 May. Available online: https://archive.is/CzH2t (accessed 15 October 2015).

Sharpe, C. (2016), *In the Wake: On Blackness and Being*, Durham: Duke University Press.

Stoler, A. (2006), 'Tense and Tender Ties: The Politics of Comparison in North American History and (Post) Colonial Studies', in A. Stoler (ed.), *Haunted by Empire: Geographies of Intimacy in North American History*, 23–67, Durham: Duke University Press.

Van Wagenen, A. (2004), 'An Epistemology of Haunting: A Review Essay', *Critical Sociology*, 30 (2): 287–98.

Wright, A. (2002), 'Politics of Writing', *Southerly*, 62 (2): 19–20.

SEE ALSO

Ghost Weaving
Memory work
Radical effrontery

Aswang

ALLAN N. DERAIN

The *aswang* is a creature of Philippine folklore, of flesh and blood with a witch's shape-shifting ability and a viscera-sucker's feeding behaviour. Its covert attack is called *pangangaswang*, most notoriously shown by how it absorbs the unborn from the womb of an unwary mother, where from its nightly flights it lands on a rooftop and sends its threadlike tongue to the sleeping target's stomach to suck the life that is inside. The *aswang* would take its time as the operation might need several more visits before it could consume the entire foetus. The procedure is so subtle that the ensuing maternal loss would be taken in the end as a natural case of miscarriage. In its more everyday usage *pangangaswang* means tricking, exploiting and stealing from the unwary.

The first *aswang* was in fact a trickster thief, who stole the primordial fire from *Gugurang*, the guardian deity of Mayon Volcano. This attack against a more formidable being, in the end, has brought fire to mankind, tipping the balance of power between gods and humans nearer to the side of humans. Seen this way, the myth configures the creative and subversive potentials of such a motif. This motif, in turn deployed as poetics, could help describe a disruptive writing act achieved by an alien other where the writer as *aswang* covers the very ground it is most unwelcome. Plato's Republic and Augustine's Celestial City were the classic examples of such hostile grounds. The former a philosophical site, the latter theological, both expelled poets from their respective domains as enemies of the state. For the poets are said to teach heresy and extol human desires, and thereby corrupt the youth who are the future foundation of the city.

As animosity against creative wild imaginings is still alive in various manifestations, it is easy to imagine the walled city in the shape of a fascist regime. This is where the *aswang* writer operates, sometimes in danger of being marked or red-tagged by the agents of political witch-hunt. *Pangangaswang* in this case becomes relevant when the information needed to write with justice is strictly guarded inside the enemy's camp. Coming to a dead end, the *aswang* writer would press on by devising more unconventional ways of doing research.

On the other hand, the walled city can also be the regions inhabited by the writer's cultural other. In this case, the aim of writing is appropriation, which would entail certain ethical issues, especially if the writer belongs to a more dominant segment of the society. Here, the *aswang* arrives in silence and commences to work from the inside. Its modus is achieved by self-effacement through a dispersal of its own spectrality. It can turn invisible or shapeshift itself into a dog, a bird, a pig and in some stories, it was even seen as a flying black umbrella. Its concealment, a play between perceived absence and visual abundance, presents the *aswang* as a disruption of the humanist obsession for essence and totality. It presents the writer the alternative possibilities of multiplicity and liminality, of not only relating with the other, but more significantly, identifying with the other – the stranger, the foreigner, the adversary – and schizophrenically assuming and absorbing these countless others into his/her own positionality. The *aswang* writer both lies within and without, an outsider and an insider.

The contested ground can also be the academic turf where people from the creative departments are never really expected to contribute meaningfully no matter how trans-disciplinary these fields are thought to be. When it comes to articulating the complexities of our present global affairs, creative writing either dies out of parochialism and irrelevance or evolves by understanding the limits of its own metaphors. It sees what its own genre can't say but where literature of other fields has fluently said much, and why. From here, the *aswang* writer flexibly takes and adopts different modes of discourse – even those more familiarly identified with the disciplines of others – but without ceasing to be imaginative and playful. *Pangangaswang* is bricolage with a vengeance.

The *aswang* is always on to something and nobody knows what it is. It works in silence, in the same manner most creative projects are done in silence, with the artist's time invested in confined deliberations, deceptively static and non-productive. The creative process is disclosed only through hindsight, and mostly belated recognitions. Among the ruses the *aswang* is known for is when it conjures upon a banana tree trunk the image of the corpse it wants to snatch from a funeral wake. The only distinction between the real and the copy would be the latter not having fingerprints. With speed and guile, the *aswang* manages to steal away the actual corpse and replace it with the dummy of its own making (hence the warning to always keep awake during funeral vigils). The validity of this simulation lies not in its verisimilitude but in its performativity. The dummy shall substitute for the real in its entombment and the real corpse, now in the hands of the *aswang*, is magically turned into a swine to be fattened for the next town fiesta, which is how it can be said that the original (which is also a trace of what was once living) was cast into a different form of existence. The *aswang* as creator commits to both death and creation as it exchanges one with the other. The work in progress and the *aswang* both undergo transformation.

'The master's tools will never dismantle the master's house', says American poet, Audre Lorde (1984, 111). This is perhaps why the *aswang* does not only grab and use those tools, but pervert them and pervert them even further, changing something that has been declared dead to something new and nourishing, anticipating festive celebration, and transforming its flavour and palatability. In the same vein, the writer may take the truth of others and transform it to create his/her own truth. This truth, which others in turn can also take and use.

Reference

Lorde, A. (1984), 'The Master's Tools Will Never Dismantle the Master's House', in *Sister Outsider: Essays and Speeches*, 110–14, Berkeley: Crossing Press.

Further reading

Lynch, F. (2004), 'An mga Aswang: A Bicol Belief', in A. Yengoyan and P. Makil (eds), *Philippine Society and the Individual: Selected Essays of Francis Lynch*, Quezon City: Ateneo de Manila University Press.

Ramos, M. (1990), *The Aswang Complex in Philippine Folklore*, Manila: Phoenix Publication.

SEE ALSO

Imagination
Xenos
Speculation

Atmospherics

KATHLEEN STEWART

The atmospheric for a subject and a writer is something you're *in* or *of* because you just walked into a cloud of smells or you live in a toxic place. Fog and barometric pressure are atmospheric, so is a mood, an October mountain of maples, an opening in a situation, an aesthetic presenting in paint, clouds, a swagger. A subject subject to an atmospheric takes place on the edge of what's almost there and already surrounding. We lean into the suggestion of a coherence in the air. We write what's already writing itself around us. Raymond Williams wrote the sense of an era through the tilt of his father's hat – where that tilt came from, what heads it rested on, how it was deployed as a character actor in its own lifeworld (1975). LeFebvre attuned to the city as sheer rhythms (2013). Fred Moten writes thought as a sounding (2018).

At the ski area this morning, dozens of snow-making machines on the trails and a hard wind made a wild snow globe of tiny flakes propelled. It was twelve degrees and only early November, the advent of a winter coming. In the parking lot the snow hit sideways into cheeks. Workers raced around on snow mobiles in full winter gear and helmets. The immanence of the first ski of the season had arrived in bodies. Forty ski patrols were getting recertified in CPR and learning to check Covid symptoms in open-sided tents in the parking lot. They walked with loose hips and a little low to the ground, their voices carrying in an excited trill.

An atmosphere swells with imperatives. The subject, the writer, is called to an attention that is also an impassivity. We wait in the company of others for what's still cutting together and apart. Once in a place and a time, a car passing on a street without its lights on could call up a chorus of 'lights, lights, lights'. 'All down the block … voices winking on like fireflies' (Dybek 1996: 31–2). Parents at a soccer game train on the singularities of breaking threats and possibilities for their kids. Ta-Nehisi Coates remembers the fear that permeated the streets 'in the music that pumped from boom boxes full of grand boast and bluster [...] in the girls, their loud laughter [...] how they squared off like boxers, Vaselined up, earrings off, Reeboks on' (2015: 15).

We live and write as plastic subjects, 'improvising with already-felts' (Manning 2009: 30) in the thickness of a duration. A bouncer in a strip club watches for 'pockets':

> those dark human spaces in the room where something has just changed: above the music a man lets out an appreciative yell when before he was quiet; one of the dancers out on the floor laughs a little too hard or steps back too fast; a chair leg scrapes the carpet – something Lonnie can't hear, just feels, a shift of objects in the space there, this change in the air, a pocket of possible trouble (Dubus 2008: 38).

A field opens in a note struck. Something tentative, incidental and powerful hangs suspended (Choy and Zee 2015); an invisible toxicity shows up in a rainbow sheen on water flooding up next to a sidewalk. At Fort Hood in Killeen, TX deployment hangs in the air; it's in PTSD, infidelity, divorce, abuse, drugs. It sutures to the mile-long row of strip malls, fast food chains and auto parts stores on the main street … It's in death by speeding on the widows' highway the day after returning from war … the dull sense of propriety on the base … in ten miles of tanks and then nothing – the open prairie of tornado country (MacLeish 2015).

A milieu forms an elemental, self-sensing surround, like thought taking on water. Things half-seen out of the corner of the eye take on the feeling of a question. Material passes into compounds of sensation, forces are borne, characters are called up, objects become registers. A public intimacy echoes in what's leaning into a mobilization.

I was a townie north of Boston. Townieness was ambient, atmospheric; it seeped into colours, a taste for pecan sandies, a flipped finger at the shitheads of the world. We kept windows uncurtained and open a crack on winter nights; sheets had to be hung out on the line to dry in the fresh air and, in the winter, brought in frozen stiff to finish drying in the basement. Eye contact pinged around the Dunkin' Donuts. When a townie died, a thousand walked to the wake not because community was something stamped on us but to witness *en masse* the weight of the world.

One morning, on my return to the Boston area a year after my father's death, I woke to a precise composition of air, light and sound. Men working on trees in the street, in that crisp October, called out in a joking intimacy. It was my father's townie voice – its tone and timing, the phrasing, the barely suppressed giggle, the way it travelled across the street.

Atmospheric writing suspends in the sharp singularity of oblique events and background noises. Writing folds into matter, words and their objects are exposed to one another in a gathering, a thickening that surrounds (Martin 2011). This critical amplification of an expressivity unfolding is theorized, variously, as Deleuze and Guattari's plane of immanence (1987), Whitehead's speculative realism (1997), Barthes's incidentals (1992), Lingis's imperative (1998), and Nancy's world at its edges (1997).

One night in college I was driving my old Dodge Dart through a snowstorm, half-stalking an escalating love. I came to a town centre. My headlights etched the white clapboards of 300-year-old houses, then sliced the corner of a porch and flood-lit a closed country store. It was pitch black at five o'clock in a kind of place that was news to me. At the crossroads my car went into a 360-degree spin on an endless expanse of black ice; snowbanks careened around me; wind whisked snowflakes sideways and off into the dark. I lived a long minute when there was nothing I could *do* but I was *in* it. The elemental expressivity of a winter's skid threw weight into a turn and hung the scene.

References

Barthes, R. (1992), *Incidents*, Berkeley: University of California Press.
Choy, T. and J. Zee (2015), 'Condition – Suspension', *Cultural Anthropology*, 30 (2): 210–23.
Coates, T. (2015), *Between the World and Me*, New York: One World.
Deleuze, G. and F. Guattari (1987), *A Thousand Plateaus*, Minneapolis: University of Minnesota Press.
Dubus, A. (2008), *The Garden of Last Days*, New York: W. W. Norton.

Dybek, S. (1996), 'Lights', in J. Kitchen and M. Paumier Jones (eds), *In Short*, 31–2, New York: W. W. Norton.

LeFebvre, H. (2013), *Rythmanalysis*, London: Bloomsbury.

Lingis, A. (1998), *The Imperative*, Bloomington: Indiana University Press.

MacLeish, K. (2015), *Making War at Fort Hood*, Princeton: Princeton University Press.

Manning, E. (2009), *Relationscapes: Movement, Art, Philosophy*, Cambridge: MIT Press.

Martin, C. (2011), 'Some Speculative Approaches to Writing through Fog', in M. Fusco (ed.), *Who Is This Who Is Coming? Inscription as Contemporary Art Writing*, 57–74, Birmingham: Article Press.

Moten, F. (2018), *Stolen Life*, Durham: Duke University Press.

Nancy, J. L. (1997), *The Sense of the World*, Minneapolis: University of Minnesota Press.

Whitehead, A. N. (1997), *Science and the Modern World*, New York: Free Press.

Williams, R. (1975), *The Country and the City*, Oxford: Oxford University Press.

SEE ALSO

Nonhuman imaginaries

Preposition

Observation

Braiding

CATHERINE MCKINNON

1

A braided novel is weaved delicately, adventurously, consciously, in order to pay attention to the unconscious: to pay attention to the unknown, the secret and the hidden. Trust is involved, also risk. It's like walking through a forest at night with only the moon as guide; many paths are possible, not all are visible.

2

It's summer, 2020. Where I live – in New South Wales, Australia – forests are burning and smoke drifts through the trees that front my house. I check the Fires Near Me app every hour. In-between, (and with a packed bag by the door ready to leave if the fires come too close), I braid stories for a new novel. There are two different locations for the novel – New Mexico and Papua New Guinea – and five interconnected narratives focused on five characters. The story takes place from November 1944 to August 1945. I'm choosing where and how to jump from one tale to the next. Each crossing offers different meanings. I make decisions quickly trusting a deeper knowledge of story learnt from a life lived entangled with narratives.

3

What is a braided novel? For some (Bancroft 2018), the braid is made up of different tales that belong to one storyworld. For others, the separate braids might belong to the same story and have a shared conclusion – although this type of braid might be confused with subplots. For me, it's about narrative weight. A braided novel interweaves distinct stories that each has their own main characters and narrative drive, whether the story climax is shared or independent.

4

The braided novel form encourages readers to contemplate the gaps between stories. The individual tales create a context for what is unknown. Like the lyric essay, braided nonfiction and poetry, the braided novel is 'full of new spaces in which meaning can germinate' (Miller 2012: 235). Readers are encouraged to 'think across and between gaps' (Krauth 2019: 2).

5

When I wrote my last braided novel, *Storyland* (McKinnon 2017), I wanted the gaps to raise questions about changes to the land and weather. The wartime novel I'm currently writing braids distinct tales connected to the first atomic explosions – cited by some as marking the beginning of the Anthropocene (Zalasiewicz 2019) – but what questions am I attempting to raise?

6

By autumn, the fire season has passed but Covid-19 has arrived. We are in lockdown. I sit by a window that overlooks burnt trees. On brown paper I write out my five story plots. Using coloured pens, I draw lines between plot points, tracing threads of connection and disconnection – a method of sorts. A writer braids with intention, looking for patterns, shapes and motifs that have sometimes formed unintentionally. I use a red pen to trace 'violence', orange to chart racism. Then I'm stumped. How to bind the stories?

7

The binding of a braided novel operates like a bridge across a river or a ravine. When I wrote *Storyland* I set each tale on land adjacent to the same watercourse. Certain places reappear in different stories: a rock with a fish carving, a tree cave, mountain caves, a home. Other things bind the tales: an Aboriginal axe, a small-leaved fig (*Ficus obliqua*), birds. In a crossing from the 1900 story, a white-bellied eagle 'hovers looking for prey' and enters the first sentence of the 1998 story and is seen by a new protagonist diving into 'reeds in the lake' (McKinnon 2017: 118). Jennifer Sinor says that a 'purely lyric form relies on images' (2014: 189) to bind the narrative, likewise for the braided novel.

8

Juxtaposition is key to the braided form. The juxtaposition of stories offers readers a new vision of the world and our place in it (Dicinoski 2017: 2). The whole is more than the part, yet each part is needed to comprehend the whole. A braided narrative can extend the time scale of fictional storyworlds, making leaps from one era to another, one place or character to another – useful when dealing with complex subject matter.

9

In winter, I buy a red notebook. In it, I list the new novel's characters, putting names at the top of the page, qualities in a column below, charting difference and similarity. Does each character have a strong story function? How best to introduce a large cast?

10

A braided narrative offers multiple voices, multiple perspectives. It challenges the idea that there is one 'true' tale to tell about a particular set of events and instead suggests there are many differing ones. Characters, eras and places are entangled; ethics and moralities are varied. Braiding disparate stories and their distinct characters together creates a narrative that confirms individuals as individuals within a more complex system (Bancroft 2018).

11

Nicole Walker says the braided essay 'expands the conversation, presses upon the hard lines of ideology' (2017: 7). The braided novel does this too, illuminating new ways of imagining how we are together. 'Braided narratives do not advocate a particular ethical stance, but rather invite a way of reading and relating that strives to be open to different experiences, aware of the tensions between them, and accountable to these sometimes-conflicting claims' (Bancroft 2018: 264). However, after reading Linda Aronson's thoughts on 'consecutive stories', I understood that a braided narrative often needs one climatic scene to operate as the narrative's moral heart (2010).

12

By spring, 2020, my local area's first lockdown is over but social distancing is still in place. Sheets of paper covered with squiggly lines, dots, circles and loops stretch out beyond my writing room and take over the house. Staring at the story maps, I notice the 'moral heart' scene is missing. Instead, I have a scene that speaks to the loss of a moral code. Perhaps this is okay? Writers write from their own historical moment. Like a virus, it infects the work. You can't force meaning onto the braid; meaning emerges from it. By spring, I still haven't found the image system that will jump readers from one story to another, but I trust it will find me.

References

Aronson, L. (2010), *The 21st Century Screenplay*, Crows Nest, New South Wales: Allen and Unwin.

Bancroft, C. (2018), 'The Braided Narrative', *Narrative*, 26 (3): 262–82.

Dicinoski, M. (2017), 'Wild Associations: Rebecca Solnit, Maggie Nelson and the Lyric Essay', *Text*, 21 (1), in R. Robertson and K. Cardell (eds), *Special Issue Series, The Essay* (39): 1–12.

Krauth, N. (2019), 'Fragmented Narratives: Minding the Textual Gap', *Text*, 23 (2): 1–21.

McKinnon, C. (2017), *Storyland*, Sydney: Fourth Estate, HarperCollins.

Miller, B. (2012), 'A Braided Heart: Shaping the Lyric Essay', in B. Miller and S. Paola (eds), *Telling It Slant: Creating, Refining, and Publishing Creative Nonfiction*, 234–44, New York: McGraw Hill.

Sinor, J. (2014), 'Deserting the Narrative Line: Teaching the Braided Form', *Teaching English in the Two-Year College: Urbana*, 42 (2): 188–96.

Walker, N. (2017), 'The Braided Essay as Social Justice Action: Between the Lines', *Adaption*, 64: 1–8. Available online: https://www.creativenonfiction.org/online-reading/braided-essay-social-justice-action (accessed 5 November 2020).

Zalasiewicz, J. (2019), 'Results of Binding Vote by AWG Released 21 May 2019', *Subcommission on Quaternary Stratigraphy Working Group on the Anthropocene*. Available online: http://quaternary.stratigraphy.org/working-groups/anthropocene/ (accessed 5 November 2020).

SEE ALSO

Juxtaposition
Paragraphing
Dialogue

Bricolage

DOMINIQUE HECQ

Bricolage is a French noun, which refers to the process of tinkering or improvising a solution to a particular problem with tools and materials that are at hand. It can also signify the end product of this process, that is, the handiwork. The French anthropologist Claude Lévi-Strauss coined the term in *La pensée sauva*ge (1962) to describe the activities of so-called primitive people who rummaged around the natural world, experimenting, classifying, combining and re-combining odds and ends to create cultural artefacts, all the while applying their free-associative thinking patterns, or 'wild thought', to construct knowledge.

Lévi-Strauss uses the iconic figure of the *bricoleur* whom he contrasts to that of the engineer as a way to articulate mythopoetic thought, that is, how myths, rituals and social systems come into being:

> The 'bricoleur' is adept at performing a large number of diverse tasks; but, unlike the engineer, he does not subordinate each of them to the availability of raw materials and tools conceived and procured for the purpose of the project. His universe of instruments is closed and the rules of his game are always to make do with 'whatever is at hand', that is to say with a set of tools and materials which is always finite and is also heterogeneous because what it contains bears no relation to the current project [...] but is the contingent result of all the occasions there have been to renew or enrich the stock or to maintain it with the remains of previous constructions or destructions (1966: 20).

For Lévi-Strauss, the key difference between the bricoleur and the engineer is that the bricoleur is constrained by the tools at his disposal whereas the engineer creates tools that are appropriate to the project. In other words, where the bricoleur cannot escape from the system of signs that constitute his language and culture, the engineer stands outside the symbolic system.

In a re-reading of Lévi-Strauss's thesis, Jacques Derrida argues that in using language we cannot avoid being a bricoleur: as speaking beings, we are subjected to language and therefore cannot create our own lexicon and syntax. Derrida therefore declares the engineer to be a myth created by a bricoleur. He adds: 'A subject who supposedly would be the absolute origin of his own discourse and supposedly would construct it "out of nothing", "out of whole cloth", would be the creator of the verb, the verb itself' (1978: 285). For Derrida, the symbolic system of which all texts partake has no origin. Julia Kristeva and Roland Barthes concur. According to Kristeva, every text is an 'intertext' (1969). Expanding on this notion of intertextuality, Barthes famously blurred the distinction between author and reader, writing and reading, and proclaimed readers as creators in their own right (1977).

In the twenty-first century, bricolage is a way of thinking about methods in general. It is intertextual, interdisciplinary and multivocal. Three decades ago, Jean-François Lyotard announced the postmodern in terms of the ruination of modernity, a project founded upon stable systems of knowledge and grand narratives (1984). In a rapidly changing world grounded in nothing but uncertainty, we move from one ad hoc project to another, grabbing tools that may 'come in handy' (Lévi-Strauss 1966: 20). Unsurprisingly, the term 'bricolage' has infiltrated multi-disciplinary discourses – from the social sciences to literature and literary theory, to science and entrepreneurship. Further, the demise of grand narratives generated a proliferation of minor discourses using alterity, or difference, to undermine the hegemony of seemingly stable systems, including that of Western philosophy, theory and language itself. The discursive fluidity that ensued highlighted contradictions and instabilities at the heart of knowledge formation that called for multivocality.

If Derrida's conception of bricolage pertains to any discourse, which means to the system of language in general, then applying it to creative writing methods can only enhance it, transforming Lévi-Straus's engineer and proto-creator into a bricoleur. As users of ready-made tools that are not our own, we cannot escape from the mechanics of bricolage. This bricolage of language need not be formulaic, though. On the contrary: bricolage fosters experimentation with the fabric of language as well as lived realities through critical and creative practice. A superb example of this is Mark Z. Danielewski's *House of Leaves* (2000), an experimental novel in fragments that roams with genre-bending abandon through the landscapes of literature, aesthetics, semiotics and philosophy to re-invent the shape and meaning of narrative.

So, how does one 'do' bricolage? There is no formula, because bricolage works by free association from a particular problem towards a solution that might remain elusive. One would have to embark on the path to creative writing by trying to think the unthinkable, using a combination of tools at hand, that is, language(s), methods, methodologies and knowledge frameworks.

At a micro level one would begin by selecting our tools from a variety of disciplines to address a central question. How could I, for example, disrupt and subvert language in fresh ways? I could conflate writing and speech in an act of semiotic vandalism that would have formal and philosophical implications as is the case in *House of Leaves* where subversion is then applied to other aspects of language. But to do this, I could also forage in the field of neuroscience. Weary of the distinction between *creative* and *research*, I could also devise a research model whereby the research component of my project is integrated in my creative product, fostering a hybrid form of research that explores and directs the theory and analysis of creative writing's processual activities.

At a macro level, bricolage would promote collaborative projects requiring different skills and levels of expertise in partnership with fellow writers, artists and researchers, but also institutions, communities and industries. Multi-disciplinary projects that marry the arts and sciences abound today, often using ethnography as a common methodological tool.

In the atelier of language, with its contexts, intertexts, dynamics and devices, and its sounds, images, metaphors and silences, what we do in practice and theory remains close to what Lévi-Strauss describes as bricolage. In selecting our methods and methodologies, experimenting with theories and realities, not only do we work with 'a set of tools which is always finite', but also reflect on the inadequacy of these tools in order to 'enrich the

Bricolage   21

stock' of knowledge and push at or through the borders of practice, which entails 'previous constructions or destructions'. In the twenty-first century, creative writing methods bear upon modalities of bricolage that are experiential, psychodynamic, existential and conceptual, stylistic, ideological and ethical. Indeed, bricolage opens up our set of tools and equips us for accomplishing ad hoc projects by constantly asking ourselves: What can we do with what is at hand – how do I know what I know, what needs to be done, how do I go about my practice, what is it that I have created or de-created, why and for whom?

References

Barthes, R. (1977), 'From Work to Text', in S. Heath (trans.), *Image – Music – Text*, 155–64, New York: Hill and Wang.

Danielewski, M. Z. (2000), *House of Leaves*, New York: Pantheon.

Derrida, J. (1978), 'Structure, Sign, and Play in the Discourse of the Human Sciences', in A. Bass (trans.), *Writing and Difference*, 278–93, Chicago: The University of Chicago Press.

Kristeva, J. (1969), *Recherches Pour une Sémanalyse*, Paris: Seuil.

Lévi-Strauss, C. (1966), *The Savage Mind*, Chicago: The University of Chicago Press.

Lyotard, J. F. (1984), *The Postmodern Condition: A Report on Knowledge*, trans. G. Bennington and B. Massumi, Minneapolis: University of Minnesota Press.

SEE ALSO

Hybrid
Collecting
Ensemble

Bung wantaim

STEVEN WINDUO

In my work as a poet, short story writer, researcher and scholar at the University of Papua New Guinea, I have engaged regularly in *bung wantaim* sessions (dialogue sessions, conversations, sometimes multilogues) with teachers, students, prisoners, villagers and government officials on various writing projects. *Bung wantaim*, meaning working together or coming together, is the Papua New Guinean equivalent of *talanoa*, a Fijian expression. In *talonoa* sessions, participants move between 'worlds' through visiting and the sharing of perspectives (Nabobo-Baba et al. 2012: xi). The work of Nabobo-Baba and others using *talanoa* as model inspires us to think about *bung wantaim* in a similar vein. *Bung wantaim* brings together voices heard and unheard of to speak out and speak the truth. *Bung wantaim* summons everyone to come together to speak, to learn, to share stories and write their stories.

One of the first books I co-authored using *bung wantaim* as method arose out of a three-day book making workshop facilitated by the Kokoda Track Foundation and SEAM Fund at the National Museum and Art Gallery in Port Moresby, Papua New Guinea. It brought together writers such as Drusilla Modjeska, Russell Soaba, John Kasaipwalova and Andrew Moutu, university lecturers such as Sakarepe Kamene, Aundo Aitau and Eugenie Duque, teachers such as Rachel Fari, and university and primary school students. Out of this extended multilogue, this moving between 'worlds' through visiting and the sharing of perspectives, came two books: *Images at the National Museum* (2016), which I co-authored with seven other participants, and *Singsing Bilas* (2016), also published by Kokoda Track Foundation and SEAM Fund. *Singsing Bilas* was written and illustrated by the grade eight students of Gerehu Primary School with their class teacher Rachel Fari.

Another *bung wantaim* I engaged with was held inside a prison in Papua New Guinea, leading to the publication, *A Turning Point: Buimo Prison Writers* (2015). This collection features the writing of prisoners, prison officers and pastors, making possible a rare sharing of worlds between those with very different experiences of the prison system. Partner organizations included The Bible Society of Papua New Guinea, the Correction Services of Papua New Guinea and the University of Papua New Guinea and these again may seem like 'unlikely' partners for a collection of creative writing. Reflecting on the *bung wantaim* sessions at Buimo Prison closer to the time, I wrote: 'The Buimo Prison writers' workshop began with storytelling. We guided the participants to write these stories down on paper [...] Our view was that using the techniques used in formal university classrooms was intimidating to learners at the village level or in prisons. Our approach was simple, flexible, and allowed a lot of verbal interactions' (Winduo 2015: 2).

Many of us in the Pacific use *bung wantaim* sessions as method. It is the consistent view that the production of social knowledge through *bung wantaim* is promoting a better understanding of the self within the 'culturescape' of the Pacific. Through *bung wantaim* sessions various disjunctures are made visible and their role in the formation of selfhoods in the multiple landscapes and culturescapes of Oceania can be more easily acknowledged. In the words of anthropologist and globalization studies theorist, Arjun Appudarai, this makes possible 'a deeper change, itself driven by the disjunctures between all the land-scapes […] and constituted by their continuously fluid and uncertain interplay' (1990: 306). *Bung wantaim* reveals the emergence of independent ideas from multiple selfhoods and environments.

As a poet, I am particularly conscious of the importance of having a dialogic engagement – a kind of *bung wantaim* session – with others. There is always more we must discover about ourselves. A dialogic unfolding can enable transformational ideas as well as trans-formative understandings that can help us shape our shared future (Holquist 1990). *Bung wantaim* as method was important to me a poet, living and writing in another environment, when I developed this poem:

A Dialogue
>Ten years in silence
>nothing completed,
>everything started,
>about anything
>lives imagined,
>lives told,
>lives fashioned
>I have come to bear
>the burden of living
>with or without it
>I was born to hear voices
>Use the make magic.
>Borges and Beckett's voices
>now covered in snow
>I was here before,
>they were here all along,
>the failure of my art
>never quite right anyway.
>I hear in the silence
>Borges singing down by the river
>Heraclitus spoke about
>Beckett across the river
>building a bridge between us (Winduo 2009: 108).

Foregrounding *bung wantaim* as method allows us to see that individual voices are always in dialogue with others. The dialogic self opens more fully to Indigenous worldviews and epistemologies. Fijian scholar Unaisi Nabobo-Baba describes this, in the context of *Talanoa*, as 'seeing with the eyes, heart, and soul […] to give meaning and interpretation to the realities of the people' (2006: 37). Using these points of reference, for example, a

24 A to Z of Creative Writing Methods

discussion of the Fijian cosmos expands and clarifies as it incorporates Pacific mediations, beliefs, spaces and ways of knowing the world.

In the poem, 'Bark Cloth', written by Iphigenia Soaba in a *bung wantaim* session held at the Papua New Guinea National Museum and Art Gallery, we can see the possibilities for learning material culture opened by *bung wantaim* method:

Bark Cloth
>   Extracted from a mulberry tree
>   Bark cloth is worn by many.
>   Beauty undefined meets
>   the eye
>   With patterns aglow in many
>   Designs
>
>   In celebrations women sing
>   And children play with laughter
>   While dancers prepare to show off
>   Their beautiful tapa
>
>   Coloured using nature's own dyes
>   Thrown over their backs,
>   The dancers
>   Transform into butterflies (Soaba 2016).

Both the production of new writing and the act of reading or sharing literary and material cultures involve 'a certain mode of social cooperation' (Williams 1977: 91). *Bung wantaim* is an exciting method because it can produce new possibilities for knowledge(s) reflected in a shared worldview. As method, *bung wantaim* deliberately creates an environment for different voices and ideas to co-exist and come together to form a new set of understandings, towards a new shared future. It is as Christine Garlough has said of our movement through multiple languages, worlds and histories: 'edges blur when cultural forms, grounded in distinct traditions, interact' (2008: 63). Foregrounding *bung wantaim* as method, it is possible to see *bung wantaim* writing workshops held in different environments, places and landscapes as a powerful means for promoting creativity and transformational stories.

References

Appudarai, A. (1990), 'Disjuncture and Difference in the Global Cultural Economy', *Public Culture*, 2: 1–24.

Fari, R. (2016), *Singsing Bilas*, Port Moresby: Kokoda Track Foundation and Sustain Education Art Melanesia.

Garlough, C. (2008), 'Playing with Boundaries: Self and Dialogue in an Indian-American Fatana Performance', *Folklore*, 39 (1): 63–95.

Holquist, M. (1990), *Dialogism: Bakhtin and His World*, New York and London: Routledge.

Nabobo-Baba, U. (2006), *Knowing and Learning: An Indigenous Fijian Approach*, Suva: Institute of Pacific Studies.

Nabobo-Baba, U., S. Bogitini, T. L. Baba, and G. Lingam (2012), *Rural and Remote Schools in Udu, Fiji: Vanua, Indigenous Knowledge, Development and Professional Support for Teachers and Education*, Suva: The University of the South Pacific and Native Academy Publishers.

Soaba, I. (2016), 'Bark Cloth', in *Images at the National Museum*, Port Moresby: Kokoda Track Foundation and Sustain Education Art Melanesia.

Williams, R. (1977), *Marxism and Literature*, Oxford and New York: Oxford University Press.

Winduo, S. E. (2009), 'A Dialogue', in *A Rower's Song*, Port Moresby: Manui Publishers, 108.

Winduo, S. E., ed. (2015), *A Turning Point: Buimo Prison Writers*, Port Moresby: University of Papua New Guinea Press, Manui Publishers and The Bible Society of Papua New Guinea.

Winduo, S. E., C. Soaba, B. Dinghan, I. Soaba, C. Winduo, E. Kambao, S. Steven, E. Dugue, S. Kamene, and A. Kolomba (2016), *Images at the National Museum*, Port Moresby: Kokoda Track Foundation and Sustain Education Art Melanesia.

SEE ALSO

Dialogue
Facilitator
Communitas

Camping

SOILE VEIJOLA

I propose camping as a method for writing oneself into a community of strangers. Camping allows timing one's writing as well as untiming it, flowing with both fast and slow tides that break into one another. Writing as camping creates good emptiness between many. It starts by – stopping, and having a clueless moment, a moment that lacks any kind of waiting, hastiness or predesigned direction, a pause which, without noticing, may turn into a shore-less time of writing. You may write, but you do not have to. A license at its fullest.

Does camping call for an invitation? It might arise with one. However, even upon an invitation, camping transcends the host and guest relationship. No one opens their door and seats the guests. No one is forced to spend time in the kitchen while others abandon themselves to play. Instead, everyone welcomes everyone. Everything is welcomed as it is.

Camping as a method of writing is dwelling in a potential, playful space, attaching and detaching the strings between one's own venture and those of other campers (Winnicott 2005). All these probing paths into the woods, criss-crossing. Lighter steps and entangled stories afterwards (Veijola et al. 2019).

When writing *as a camper* on, say, travelling and tourism, one could use the possibility to speculate on their current and future ontologies. How do we understand the Tourist and the Traveller, and Host, at the current moment when the realities and baselines (Pauly 1995) of knowing and touring the world are dramatically shifting?

Metaphors have often been useful for making sense of cultural and social phenomena. The classic social figures of the Stranger, Adventurer and Flañeur, the first two cast by Simmel (1971 [1908]) and the third by Baudelaire (1964 [1863]) and later Benjamin (1982 [1927–1940]), tell of a modern subject relating to his immediate social environment. Later, the metaphor of the Tourist has been offered instead – being, likewise, based on a mascu-linist morphology (Jokinen and Veijola 1997).

Alas, the Au Pair and Babysitter have been marched onto the scene to demonstrate how a modern subject could also be analysed with the help of an explicitly, not implicitly, sexed metaphor for a travelling agency. Home and away, how indeed do these two destina-tions, the familiar and the unknown one, each yearned for and escaped from, construct one another in society marked by gender arrangements (Jokinen and Veijola 1997)?

Next, the Untidy Guest and even the Untidy Host perplex the Reader in tourism theory, disrupting a managerial approach to organizing knowledge into segments, edges (cutting ones) and countable deliverables. Messy metaphors, and vital images of 'disruption' and 'untidiness', make both *a clearing* and a *chora*, 'the emptiness through which *being* becomes possible' (Germann Molz 2014: 25); wayward guests are able to give an unexpected twist to everyday situations and the hosts a chance to live their life instead of staging it.

Concepts are active and creative, says Deleuze. They stimulate discussion instead of ending it; they renew existing arrangements of social relations (see Veijola et al. 2014: 7–8).

Let us take the Camper, for instance. Was it just another individualist *antitourist* (Urry 1988), searching for the untouched land or the unfound idea, nothing would have changed by way of politics of authorship and ownership in knowledge production? The world would still yield in front of 'him', symbolically and in real life, or in front of 'his' rivalling contestant, 'her'.

When in plural, however, the Campers might be able to come up with more imaginative solutions for writing worlds, existing and potential ones (Veijola and Jokinen 2018: 545). They could help turning, for instance, *conferencing* from a vast, competitive science fair into camping experiments of post-biopolitical living (Veijola et al. 2014) and companionate writing (Carlin et al. 2014). The regular keynoters' and conference-goers' regular *papers*, those that had travelled so far away from home to be *given* in a conference that does not camp slowly nor build a relation with a place, did not really travel at all. They were mere call cards, passports, CV entries.

What good could come out of camping as a method of writing, as opposed to (for the sake of argument), ambitiously targeted, incessant writing that takes place on so many laptops of knowledge workers and creatives – students, project employees, busy professors, artists – during office hours, late nights, long-haul flights?

Camping as a method of writing leans on an ethical epistemology that is open about its inevitable narrativity and constructed nature.

When *camping as writing* happens, writings become *letters* forming 'a collateral correspondence marked by alongsideness' (Veijola et al. 2019: 26), or tourist ethnographies that touch a place only lightly. 'To camp in clearing, and to clear space and time for camping, is to flirt with inspiration and surprise' (Germann Molz 2014: 24).

Then again, even when thinking of the opposite arrangements, say, a factory or an office, '"fast", "accurate" or "efficient" are not self-evident attributes; they are relative and arguable judgements' (Veijola and Jokinen 2018: 543).

In practice, writings as campings can rather fruitfully be arranged into trialogues between-three which brings social *interaction* into an intimate relationship *in-two* (Pyyhtinen 2009). Writing becomes a kaleidoscope, a kinaesthetic perception of multiple, simultaneous views on a subject or an event (Husserl 1973). 'We-ness' is not led by 'I', 'You', nor 'Them' (Benveniste 1971: 202–3).

It is precisely there where your author name is not – this is the beginning of writing (Barthes 1990: 100). Multiplying, reuniting and perhaps also post-humanizing author names into the Campers cannot, unfortunately, promise a real exit out of this world.

Where you are camping, you speak your plural (Barthes 1990:225).

References

Barthes, R. (1990 [1977]), *A Lover's Discourse*: *Fragments*, trans. R. Howard, London: Penguin.
Baudelaire, C. (1964 [1863]), *The Painter of Modern Life*, New York: Da Capo Press.
Benjamin, W. (1982 [1927–40]), *Das Passagen-Werk*, Frankfurt am Main: Suhrkamp Verlag.

Benveniste, E. (1971), *Problems in General Linguistics*, Florida: University of Miami Press.

Carlin, D., A. Light, and S. Veijola (2014), 'Companion Pieces #1: Walking to the Market', in S. Pink, Y. Akama and Symposium Participants (eds), *Un/certainty*, 43–5, Melbourne: RMIT University.

Germann Molz, J. (2014), 'Camping in Clearing', in S. Veijola, J. Germann Molz, O. Pyyhtinen, E. Höckert and A. Grit (eds), *Disruptive Tourism and Its Untidy Guests*, 19–41, London: Palgrave.

Husserl E. (1973), *Ding und Raum: Vorlesungen 1907*, The Hague: Martinus Nijhoff.

Jokinen, E. and S. Veijola (1997), 'The Disoriented Tourist: The Figuration of the Tourist in Contemporary Cultural Critique', in C. Rojek and J. Urry (eds), *Touring Cultures. Transformations of Travel and Theory*, 23–51, London: Routledge.

Pauly, D. (1995), 'Anecdotes and Shifting Baseline Syndrome of Fisheries', *Trends in Ecology and Evolution*, 10 (10): 430.

Pyyhtinen, O. (2009), 'Being-with: Georg Simmel's Sociology of Association', *Theory, Culture and Society*, 26 (5): 108–28.

Simmel, G. (1971 [1908]), 'The Stranger' (Der Fremde), in D. Levine (ed.), *Georg Simmel: On Individuality and Social Forms*, 143–50, Chicago: University of Chicago Press.

Urry, J. (1988), 'Cultural Change and the Contemporary Holiday Making', *Theory, Culture and Society*, 5 (1): 35–55.

Veijola S. and E. Jokinen (2018), 'Coding Gender in Academic Capitalism', *Ephemera, Theory and Politics in Organization*, 18 (3). Available online: http://www.ephemerajournal.org/contribution/coding-gender-academic-capitalism (accessed 31 May 2021).

Veijola, S., J. Germann Molz, O. Pyyhtinen, E. Höckert and A. Grit, eds (2014), *Disruptive Tourism and Its Untidy Guests*, London: Palgrave.

Veijola, S., E. Höckert, D. Carlin, A. Light and J. Säynäjäkangas (2019), 'The Conference Reimagined: Postcards, Letters, and Camping Together in Undressed Places', *Digithum*, 24. Available online: https://digithum.uoc.edu/articles/abstract/3168/ (accessed 31 May 2021).

Winnicott, D. W. (2005), *Playing and Reality*, London: Routledge.

SEE ALSO

Collaboration

Play

Rites

Character

LINA MARIA FERREIRA CABEZA-VANEGAS

'Lack of character is a sin'. – *My father*

A woman walks into a room, she hurries from room to room, closing blinds, locking doors. She shuts windows and turns on the light. From room to room to room. Shuffling, rushing. The bedroom, the kitchen, the bathroom, the pantry, the flashlights under the sink. Every room, every scrap of light she can gather. Fluorescent daylight shining down on a woman clutching an expired road flare and mumbling to herself. 'Oh God, oh God, oh God'. Spears of light from flashlights scattered across the floor. She checks the locks again. Oh God.

The woman, of course, already knows what's coming. And in many ways, so do we. At least, you suspect it, don't you? It doesn't matter how many flashlights, how much light. She is not likely to see daylight again.

The scene tells us so, and only a few – if any – will mourn her. If something is interesting on the page, it is interesting because of what is about to happen, not because it is happening to her. It is no surprise that narratives with underdeveloped character require more and more things to happen to them, from page to page, paragraph to paragraph, word to word, whilst developed characters can sustain tension even in the quietest scenes. It doesn't make one narrative superior over the other, but it is vital to understand that the narrative arc moves not only forward but inward as well, and a shallow character has no inward into which to-ward. We barely know these characters; we cannot be expected to meet and mourn in the same breath. It is possible, even likely, that some of us are cheering for the inevitability of the ticking of the bomb, the whirring of the chainsaw or the unreliability of battery-operated flashlights. So, we read, we watch. We notice the way this woman in this room turns her head as if she didn't also know what we know. She may die tonight; the scene demands action. And some of us will even want her to stand up and walk over to the door. To undo the locks as if pulling on black lace ribbons, one by one by one by one. Until the door is stripped and bare, and there is nothing left to do but to let the thing on the other side burst in.

Open the door! Go into the basement! Cut the rope, pull the trigger!

But what would happen if we did know her? If we understood what would be lost if she were to be lost, to the night, to the bomb, to herself, to whatever is or is not behind the door she locks.

What would happen if we dared to ask, why hasn't she opened the door yet? Why won't she? Maybe she is a coward, maybe she is weak. Maybe she is one of those iron ladies, or those virgin martyrs. Maybe she isn't locking it out, maybe she is locking herself in. We don't know, of course we don't. Because if we did, we would care, and then what? What would we do if we knew her name was Mary, or Clémence, or Astrid, or Sofia? What if we knew she was eight when she saw her uncle drunkenly stumble towards the ditch in their backyard? What if we knew she watched and said nothing? Or, that she screamed when she saw him fall. 'Took him a few hours to bleed out', she remembers eavesdropping on the officers. That she hid her small face in her small hands and whispered to herself, *wake-up-wake-up-wake-up*, like she always did when she found herself in a nightmare full of creaking darkness and a twisted howling, like that time her uncle kicked a dog that nipped at him: 'Until it stopped howling, stopped everything'. What if we knew the dog wasn't a dog, but a man with a limp who begged on a street corner near their home? What if we knew the thing behind the door wailed like a dying dog and whispered like an uncle when he holds you close and says, 'He tripped didn't he? That's what you saw, isn't that right?'

Do you care? Does it make a difference? To know the man fell into that ditch and the little girl said nothing? To know that maybe he deserved it, or that she thought he deserved it? That in the end that didn't make a difference to her because sometimes she still sees him in the unlit corners of her lonely bedroom. The obtuse angle of a broken neck, the tightness of skin over shattered bones. Does it make any difference that tonight she's sure she saw him sitting in the back of the bus, under the broken light, smiling.

Does it make a difference?

And if it does, what then? She is still where we left her, on the floor, in that room, staring at that door.

The difference is whether a reader will care enough to turn the page or close the book. Which is to say, all the difference in the world. And whatever has changed has not been caused by the 'what happens next', but rather the 'what happened before' and the rippling out in the happenings of the woman's memory and mind. Or in other words, her character.

But what is character, and how do you write it? And how do you get away from the endless lists? *Give them interests, give them bodies, give them skills, give them worlds, give them conflicts, give them flaws, give them, give them, give them.*

There are plenty of characters I care about who are barely relatable. Without skills, hobbies or interests. More than that, I love them. And if any of them were in that room, I wouldn't want them to open that door. Even if the scene told me to.

Lists are helpful, but inherently limited. Because, in the end, what we are setting out to create is not characters, but people. A person in that room. A person who feels real because she embodies the invariable element of identity, not the accoutrements existence.

The question then becomes, 'what is a person?'

In the sixth century the philosopher Boethius declared, 'We have found the definition of Person, the individual substance of a rational nature' (Teichman 1985: 175). Upon which Thomas Aquinas expounded that the unity of these two things was 'the cause of identity', adding that essence – or soul – is 'not a body, but the act of a body' (Aquinas 2012: n.p.). Not exactly practical writing advice, but then came John Locke, who was nothing if not practical. For him it was a matter of what he termed *psychological continuity*, because identity depends on 'consciousness' not on 'substance' (Locke 1847: 210–11). Or in other words, what makes a person that one, single, unique person, or that character that one, single, unique character, is their ability to remember themselves. Or the 'what happened before?'

Character 31

Don't give them hobbies, then. Don't spin the wheel of attributes and interests. Rather, give a cause, a door to open, a reason to be or not to be. Give them psychological continuity. Memories and vagaries, yellowed and misremembered, washed in lavender and bleach.

Ask them who they are and listen with the page.

Ask: why haven't you opened the door yet?

And watch her stand, clutching that flare and gritting her teeth. 'I was a child!' The sound of her own voice startles her, and she stares at the crack beneath the door. It took him a few hours to bleed out, that's what they said. Took the beggar a couple of days though. Drooling, and mumbling, shaking and wetting himself. *You saw him fall, didn't you? Didn't you!* 'I was only a child', she whispers again, and thinks she sees movement through the crack. 'I saw him fall', she tells herself, 'I saw him fall'. She closes her eyes and imagines the beggar behind the door. Drooling and mumbling, urine and blood dripping on a Welcome-Home mat. Then she sees her uncle's face. In her mind. All blunt angles and rage. *Tell them*, she hears his voice. *Tell them how you saw him fall.* And she feels herself recoil. 'No', she says to herself as she begins to undo the locks. 'I saw you fall'. She whispers as she begins to turn the knob.

References

Aquinas, T. (2012), *Summa Theologica (Part 1)*, United Kingdom: Authentic Publishers.

Locke, J. (1847), *An Essay Concerning Human Understanding*, United States: Kay and Troutman.

Teichman, J. (1985), 'The Definition of Person', *Philosophy*, 60 (232): 175–85, Cambridge: Cambridge University Press.

SEE ALSO

Dialogue
Atmospherics
Listing

Chorality

MARTINA COPLEY

'Slippage between singular and plural in pronouns of the first person is not uncommon in ancient poetry; the traditional explanation is that much of this poetry was choral in origin, that is, performed by a chorus of voices who collectively impersonate the voice that speaks in the poem.'[1]

Writing choral is to see and follow the movement of thought around the organizing theme as it emerges and digresses. The choral (event as abstraction) is performed as 'a movement or passage through language, a spreading memory, drawing to itself an associated tangle of meanings'.[2]

Thoughts in motion become articulations – movement-becomes-thought and vice versa as an elastic almost, an incipient potential, a coming to language that is a moving-with-movement.[3]

This movement need not be thought.

'The point is to whisper at us weirdly from the trees, to make us hesitate.'[4]

.

Everybody

–

sings to-

gether.

Everybody

does

not

sing to-

gether.[5]

---

[1]Carson 2002: 365.

[2]Ulmer 1994: 227.

[3]Manning 2009: 6.

[4]Morton 2015: 349–51.

[5]Holder & Waterman 2015: performance script.

And the 'performances of the paratext have their own unruly potential'.[6]

Pointing to what lies outside, behind or beyond the text, to that whispered from behind the hand – the Ancient Greek chorus was both medium and commentator.[7] Onstage throughout, the choral presence imposed an openness on the space so that even the most secret exchange was conducted in clear public view,[8] in a public fictional space.

The Japanese *noh* chorus (*jiutai*) creates and makes use of the distance between actor and role to become multi-vocal – 'a shifting unidentifiable collective, able to speak for and about the character'.[9]

The recitation is transparent, so the lines belong to no one.

This 'strange and powerful plural-singular choric voice is also heard in prayer, children's games, pledges and protest, celebration and in the collective utterances of crowds'.[10]

'Chorality is the means whereby we allow ourselves the collective hallucination of collectivity.'[11] And 'every individual vocality has a connection to a phantasmal chorality.'[12]

In *How to Live Together*,[13] Roland Barthes focuses on the concept of 'idiorrhythmy', a form of living together in which each person respects the individual rhythms of the other. Barthes points to the self-regulating form of monastic practice of a small group of monks on Mount Athos, Greece in the tenth century who lived with few voluntary links to the collective life of the monastery and appear to have reconciled the extremes of solitude and sociability.[14] It should be pointed out that the Holy Mountain was a peninsula reserved for Orthodox monks, where no female, not even a cat, was welcome.

For Giorgio Agamben, living together is the product of rhythm. Agamben situates life in the affirmative conditions of thought and of communicability. Life constituted as action rather than as a quality that is defined by external prohibition or expectation.[15] Rhythm as a guide to practice.

The movement goes both ways.

This movement is a configurative poetics that engages different modes of attention. Attention to inklings, hesitations, curiosities, attractions that allow for beginnings which in turn stimulate thinking about possible structures and ways to proceed.

---

[6]Drucker 2013: 11.

[7]Bierl 2009.

[8]Slavey 2013.

[9]Smethurst 2013: 92.

[10]Connor 2016: 3.

[11]Connor, 'Choralities', *Twentieth Century Music*: 20.

[12]Connor, 'Choralities', *Twentieth Century Music*: 21.

[13]Barthes 2013.

[14]Barthes *How to Live Together*.

[15]Agamben 2013.

34   A to Z of Creative Writing Methods

A movement within a space, and a movement that creates a space and new spatialities,[16] the choral effects subtle disruptions of orthodoxies.[17] Think of the voices inside your head – a space of inner rhythm and monologue parsing the world of experience – and the 'delirious multiplicity' of the 'I'.[18]

The choral has a poetic function; it moves, dances, offers the privilege of distance onto language and works to recast awareness.

'What I'm interested in […] is observing the movement that takes place in me.'[19]

These 'inner movements […] hidden under the commonplace […] slip through us […] in the form of undefinable, very rapid sensations. They hide behind our gestures, beneath the words we speak, the feelings we manifest, are aware of experiencing and able to define.'[20]

An insistent poetics motions across different orders of experience.

'In place of a seamless continuity of argument/evidence, there is a *movement of thought* that again and again is interrupted and begins anew in order to approach the object over and over from different angles.'[21]

This 'practice of thinking through one's singularity, not in fear of it, is both aesthetic and ethical in nature and takes on a social dimension'.[22]

'The little matter of the "we".'[23]

'One is never synchronous. One is never simultaneous with the object […] about which one is thinking or writing. And the appeal of such activities lies not in eventually becoming synchronous but in increasing the paradoxes to attain a feeling for slowness and fastness […] It is precisely through visible discrepancies that the voice gains its poetic independence.'[24]

.

The above text including footnotes and asides is formed in a choral mode of collated quotation of text from the author's doctoral thesis, 'The Movement of the Aside' (2019).[25]

---

[16]Connor, 'Choralities': performance script.

[17]Ulmer 1994: 149.

[18]Carlin 2018: 6.

[19]Carlin, 'Essaying as Method': 4.

[20]Sarraute 2018: vi.

[21]Frey 1996: 140.

[22]Stefans 2001.

[23]Carlin, 'Essaying as Method': 4.

[24]Tawada 2009: 184–95, 193–4.

[25]Copley 2018.

Chorality 35

References

Agamben, G. (2013), *The Highest Poverty; Monastic Rules and Form-of-Life*, trans. A. Kotsko, California: Stanford University Press.

Barthes, R. (2013), *How to Live Together: Novelistic Simulations of Some Everyday Spaces*, trans. K. Briggs, New York: Columbia University Press.

Bierl, A. (2009), *Ritual and Performativity: The Chorus in Old Comedy*, Washington, District of Columbia: Center for Hellenic Studies.

Carlin, D. (2018), 'Essaying as Method: Risky Accounts and Composing Collectives', *TEXT Journal*, 22 (1): 6. Available online: www.textjournal.com.au/arpil18/carlin.htm (accessed 13 March 2021).

Carson, A. (2002), *If Not, Winter; Fragments of Sappho*, New York: Vintage, 365.

Connor, S. (2016), 'Choralities', *Twentieth-Century Music*, 13 (1): 3–23.

Copley, M. L. (2018), 'The Movement of the Aside', PhD Thesis, University of Melbourne. Available online: https://minerva-access.unimelb.edu.au/handle/11343/233173 (accessed 18 November 2021).

Frey, J. (1996), 'On Presentation in Benjamin', in *Walter Benjamin: Theoretical Questions*, ed. David S. Ferris, 140, California: Stanford University Press.

Holder, W. and A. Waterman (2015), *Yes, but Is It Edible? The Music of Robert Ashley, for Two or More Voices*, ed. W. Holder and A. Waterman, performance script, Paris: Hub Lafayette Anticipations.

Johanna D. (2013), *DIAGRAMMATIC writing*, Eindhoven, Netherlands: Onomatapee 97 / Cabinet Project, J. Drucker and Banff Art Centre, 11.

Manning, E. (2009), *Relationscapes: Movement, Art, Philosophy*, Cambridge, Massachusetts, and London: The Massachusetts Institute of Technology Press, 6.

Morton, T. (2015), 'From Things Flows What We Call Time', in O. Eliasson et al., (eds), *Spatial Experiments: Models for Space Defined by Movement*, 349–51, London: Thames and Hudson.

Sarraute, N. (2018), *Tropisms*, trans. M. Jolas, Surrey: Calder, vi.

Slavey, H. (2013), 'Seneca's Chorus of One', in J. Billings, F. Budelmann and F. Macintosh (eds), *Choruses, Ancient and Modern*, Oxford: Oxford University Press, 99–116.

Smethurst, M. J. (2013), *Dramatic Action in Greek Tragedy and Noh: Reading with and beyond Aristotle*, Lanham: Lexington Books, 92.

Stefans, B. K. (2001), 'Review: Paradise and Method and the Language of Inquiry', *Boston Review*, December 2001. Available online: http://bostonreview.net/poetry/brian-kim-stefans-review-paradise-method-and-language-inquiry (accessed 11 February 2021).

Tawada, Y. (2009), 'The Art of Being Nonsynchronous', trans. S. Bernofsky, in M. Perloff and C. Dworkin (eds), *The Sound of Poetry / The Poetry of Sound,* 184–95, 193–4, Chicago: University of Chicago Press.

Ulmer, G. L. (1994), *Heuretics; the Logic of Invention*, Baltimore and London: Johns Hopkins University Press, 149.

SEE ALSO

Listening
Queering
Listing

Code

BENJAMIN LAIRD

Coding as a writing method is a practice of formalizing an algorithm, usually as software but not always. Central to the practice is using a process to produce a result that aids the writer in the creation of a written work such as with computer-generated poetry, the realization of executed code as an interactive, spatial or kinetic work in a screen-based practice or in writing that is altered by codelike structures such as Mez Breeze's poetry language/process *mezangelle*.

As a method of producing writing, it shares a history with experimental practices. Tristan Tzara's 'To Make a Dadaist Poem' from 1920 contains instructions for creating a poem by cutting up a newspaper article and describes an algorithm for creating literature that foregrounds the process. Later, members of Oulipo (Ouvroir de Littérature Potentielle founded in 1960) created techniques such as N+7 which has the writer take a text and a dictionary and replace each noun (N) in the text with the seventh (7) following noun in the dictionary (Motte 1998). These simple processes are not time-consuming to do manually for short text, but as the source text grows in length so do these techniques. Turning these processes into code and executing them on a computer makes repeated experiments much faster. However, as the complexity of these processes increases, the time required to carry out the processes without computation exceeds any practical time. Other processes for generating writing include methods that use word-level n-grams (sequences) such as bigrams (two-word sequences) and trigrams (three-word sequences). By processing already existing texts and determining the frequency of trigrams (each three-word sequence), new texts can be created randomly and dependent on the frequency, a different work is produced in the style of the source text. This technique is commonly used to mix different source texts to produce a new work that has the style and language of its sources. This can also be achieved at the character-level, as with the software Break Down that John Tranter used to produce *Different Hands* (1998), which includes pieces mixed by Break Down and edited by Tranter (such as 'Neuromancing Miss Stein', which has William Gibson's *Neuromancer* and Gertrude Stein's *The Autobiography of Alice B Toklas* as its source texts [Mead 2008; Tranter 1998]).

Not all code-based works require complex algorithms. JavaScript is the most ubiquitous programming language, given its support by web browsers, and most contemporary, non-trivial websites will use JavaScript in some way. For example, Nick Montfort's electronic poem 'Taroko Gorge' written in JavaScript (and in combination with HTML, to structure it, and CSS, to style it) implements a simple process for producing a kinetic nature poem (2009). The JavaScript programme for the poem assembles each line from lists of words depending on conditions – some random and some dependent on where the line falls in a sequence – and these lines are added to the page in turn. After twenty-six lines are added, the first is removed with each addition, creating a sense of movement. The text of the poem, the lines generated by the programme, feature the descriptive aspects of the Taroko Gorge – the rocks, caves and forest – but the poem itself is dependent on the creation of the lines and movement.

While one form of description in the surface text might describe the gorge's nature in snapshots, another, the code – that allows the moving text – enacts the unfolding of the gorge through the kinetic behaviour. Writing code in works like this then, in combination with surface text, allows a paralleled multi-level text, which adds different elements to the final work. Like a play, the code is readable to understand but not realizable until performed (executed).

Kineticism is only one aspect that code allows; code also allows for the material playing with space. Spatial and temporal aspects are of course features of print-based poetry, but as John Cayley argues: '[in] print-mediated literature, our established literary cultures recognize these poetics in the special attention we pay to the time and space of a poem – the way in which the words and lines are arranged and then silent-implicitly or oral-actually realized in the temporal rhythms that are borne by the same arrangements' (2009: 183). With code, however, 'programmable systems allow us to […] embody this address to poetics as material practice' (2009: 183). Code allows an implicit space-and-time of literature to become explicit and writing code is to recognize this as part of the potential writing process. The potentiality in a code-based writing also allows moving some of this potential from the code-author to the reader. Rather than be dictated by the code-author in the programme, generative sequences of text, the kineticism within a work or narrative choices, can be moved to the surface of the text. Again, giving the choice to a reader in this way can add another layer of spatial, temporal or narrative meaning. The code-author still controls the meaning of the work, but at its potential level.

Historically, experimenting with code and the results it might bring was a difficult and time-consuming task. Contemporary access to technology and platforms enables experiments to be written and executed in a web browser. Online IDEs (Integrated Development Environments) like Glitch allow users to code directly via their browser and immediately see the results. For hypertext fiction or text-based games, software such as Twine allow a more accessible experience in producing works that are designed for the web.

While coding can seem to be writing against a set of machine values it is important to see that writing code is dependent on a broader sociality of software from the design of programming languages to the implementation of those programming languages. JavaScript, for instance, is based on the ECMAScript specification and then implemented by JavaScript engines in various environments (like Google's V8 which is the JavaScript engine used by Chrome and on servers through software like Node.js). People are involved in each step of developing the language: they develop the standards, and they create the software that implements those standards. The JavaScript written and run on a website remains the same, in terms of what is written, but the implementation is dependent on the browser it runs in, which in turn is dependent on how that implementation adheres to the standards and the values of those who defined the standard and produced the implementations.

38   A to Z of Creative Writing Methods

Writing code is much like other writing, although it encourages the author to hand over some of their authorial control to the potential that code can produce and the unexpected experiences the writing might not have otherwise created. The potentials in the code are in how words are arranged, how they move, how they appear in space, how a reader interacts with them and how the software the code is written for executes it.

References

Breeze, M. (2002), *data][h!][bleeding texts*. Available online: http://netwurkerz.de/mez/datableed/complete/ (accessed 16 September 2021).

Breeze, M. (2017), *Attn: Solitude*, Carlton South: Cordite Publishing Inc.

Cayley, J. (2009), 'Screen Writing: A Practice-Based, EuroRelative Introduction to Digital Literature and Poetics', in F. J. Ricardo (ed.), *Literary Art in Digital Performance: Case Studies in New Media Art and Criticism*, 178–86, New York: Continuum International Publishing Group.

Mead, P. (2008), 'It's Poetry Jim, but Not as We Know It!', in *Networked Language: Culture and History in Australian Poetry*, 338–98, North Melbourne: Australian Scholarly Publishing.

Montfort, N. (2009), *Taroko Gorge*. Available online: http://nickm.com/poems/taroko_gorge.html (accessed 16 September 2021).

Motte, W. F., ed. (1998), *Oulipo: A Primer of Potential Literature*, 1st Dalkey Archive edn, French Literature Series, Illinois: Dalkey Archive Press.

Tranter, J. E. (1998), *Different Hands: Seven Stories*, South Fremantle: Folio/Fremantle Arts Centre Press.

Tzara, T. (1977), *Seven Dada Manifestos and Lampisteries*, trans. B. Wright. London: Calder.

SEE ALSO

Experimentation
Erasure
Translation

Collaboration

QUINN EADES

When I think and write about collaboration, I am also always thinking and writing about collaboration as love.

It is impossible to think and write about love. As soon as the word 'love' is written and then read, we are smothered by what we and our world/s bring to this word. We link immediately to the word heart (not the heart itself all that bluered muscle all that blood), a word that stands in for strength or failure, health or sickness, wholeness or brokenness. There are no in-betweens in white cis-heteronormative ways of thinking and speaking about love. We are *in* love or we are *out of* love. We are loved or unloved. It is impossible to think and write about love but

I am a writer who falls in love with other writers.

It is rare, but it happens where I am, in the body, the ecstatic thrill of intellectual and textual attraction moving between me and other/s. It is this feeling I follow when I ask people if they would like to work with me. It is an intuition, an invitation, an advance. There are flirtations involved but eventually comes the question

Would you like to write with me?

If we think collaboration-as-love we can consider the ways we write with others as acts of love. If we say yes to the offer, or we make the invitation ourselves, we are saying yes to the im/possibility of being in love.

My dear friend Anna Poletti is someone I have always wanted to write with. The moment I met them I knew I wanted to work with them. In the first couple of years of knowing each other, we unknowingly went to the same exhibition, *Marina Abramović: In Residence* (2015). We had both found the experience uncanny and talked about it over coffee. The resulting essay, 'DystopiAbramović' (Eades and Poletti 2018), used cut-up techniques to develop a fragmented, lyrical consideration of forms of collective embodiment (see exercise below).

We didn't make anything else together for years, but instead talked about what we might make. What follows is an intimate portrait of our next collaboration/act-of-love in progress. We don't know what we're making together. There is no particular outcome in mind. It is a kind of journaling, but it is a journaling to a loved other, not to the self. I don't know the name for this. It is a conversation made possible by digital technology.

Anna and I were working on individual projects when the Covid-19 pandemic hit, and both experienced severe trauma during our respective lockdowns. Towards the end of the second wave in Australia I realized that my partner, who I was deeply in love with, was no longer in love with me. From out of the freefall pain one night on the phone with Anna I said:

I've been writing poetry to them for 5 years – they were my you
and cried. Anna said

You can write to me. I can be your you.

I told Anna on the phone that I simultaneously do and do not want to write. I told Anna I must write but I can't, that I am frightened (as always) of what writing will find.

I am always writing wounds.

An hour or two later I got an email with a link to a shared doc called 'Dear Quinn'. Anna had written to me in it, and I read about their afternoon, their PTSD cat, what they were working on, and some time later, I wrote back.

On another phone call I say that I am a dried husk of writing. I read from Marguerite Duras's *Writing* (1999), saying that she has never been afraid of the fear of writing. Saying too that 'if one has any idea what one was going to write, before doing it, before writing, one would never write. It wouldn't be worth it anymore' (19). Then I get self-conscious for reading aloud for too long, hear Anna say what a pleasure it is to be read to (we delight in each other like this often) and quietly blush.

This new *you* that I write to is infinitely patient, and the blank space that waits for me beneath their last entry is an invitation rather than a rebuke. In *A Lover's Discourse: Fragments*, Barthes when discussing the heart writes that 'you wait for me where I don't want to go: you love me where I do not exist' (1978: 52) and this is exactly what this *you* does. This you waits for me on the page and so this where I go.

We have been writing to each other now in that document for months. Entries are sporadic. Sometimes weeks or months go past before one of us adds another part of our lives. But each time one of us writes, our writing picks up and weaves threads from the other. Writing becomes a third body, one that holds us to each other, a body that extends into and through each of ours, pulsing desire. It is what holds me while I squirm and wrench from the person I thought I would be with for the rest of my life. What I realize as I write and don't write, as Anna writes and doesn't write, as we wait for each other on the page, that here is another love of my life. I realize that when I collaborate with and through love in all its thicknesses, pleasures and terrors, I let myself and my work open. I enter and am entered. I am in thrall, and it is here we find each other, where we do not exist.

Exercise

Writing art in fragments:

- Find and agree on an art exhibition or performance you and your collaborator/s would like to attend.
- Attend separately, on different days, and after attending write your experience, thoughts, recollections, descriptions and reflections.
- Prior to meeting in person or online to exchange your writing with your collaborator/s in its entirety, cut up your writing into fragments or smaller pieces.
- If you meet in person, bring your cut-up pieces of writing with you and play with the text and your collaborator/s – rearrange the order, find patterns you could not see when you were working with a single-authored piece and be willing to let go of time and expected narrative arcs as the primary ordering factors for your work.
- If you meet online, try similar sorts of play in a shared document. The experience will be less somatic and material but can still serve as a shared space for playing with text.

References

Abramović, M. (2015), 'Marina Abramović: In Residence', 24 June–5 July 2015, Pier 2/3, Walsh Bay, Sydney.

Barthes, R. (1978), *A Lover's Discourse: Fragments*, New York: Hill and Wang.

Duras, M. (1999), *Writing*, trans. M. Polizzotti, New York: Lumen Editions, Brookline Books.

Eades, Q. and A. Poletti (2018), 'DystopiAbramović: Marina Abramović: In Residence: Sydney 2015', *a/b: Auto/Biography Studies*, 33 (2): 279–84.

SEE ALSO

Hybrid
Camping
Chorality

Collecting

ANDER MONSON

I begin with my collections, of which I have quite a few: doll arms, doll heads, every bag of every chip I've eaten in the last five years including Rap Snacks, bizarro and possibly magical South Korean Bugles, several Canadian Ketchup chips, fried egg-flavoured chips from Spain and so forth (I want to also note the attenuation of a list is a kind of violence even if it's occasionally necessary), Spice Girls figurines and other paraphernalia, Spice Girls twelve-inch singles autographed by famous writers, gnomes, masks, fantasy miniatures, computer games on floppy disks from the 1980s, vinyl records (unoriginally), crystal gavels (more originally), a lot of disc golf discs, hundreds of cables (SCSI, USB, charging) for technology I no longer have, stolen telephone equipment I've kept for decades, *Dragon* magazines #118–166, a bust of Carl Sandburg, vintage stationery, it's too obvious to say books, but I have very many of those too as most writers do.

If these things are memorabilia, they don't all spark memory. Some are autobiographical artefacts; others are objects of beauty or desire. Listing them is lusting after them at least a little. Describing them, I lust more. That lust is intentional and part of the magic of collecting. The things we collect also collect us, or reveal us, or allow the dark interiors of ourselves to extend into the light.

Conjuring them all here becomes generative: it probably raises questions for you reading this: why all the Spice Girls stuff? I could answer but I won't (not now anyhow). That you have the question at all shows that you know there's method in collecting.

This week students in my undergraduate class on literary craft ask me how I handle writer's block. Don't start from nothing, I tell them. Start gathering and when you turn to the page, you'll have something to start with. Collect trinkets and doodads but also bits and images and ideas and strangeness and fragments of language. When you read, I tell them, you collect: angles, tonalities, strategies, language. I mean, you're doing it anyway. Let's make it more formal. Start a menagerie or a journal.

I cite Orhan Pamuk's 'A Modest Manifesto for Museums' from *The Innocence of Objects* (2012), in which he argues both for the importance of objects – saving and collecting and displaying them, especially those in danger of vanishing into the past (and this describes almost all objects almost all the time) – and that 'the aim of present and future museums must not be to represent the state, but to re-create the world of single human beings' (2012: 49). (We note this latter sounds like a novel or a memoir or a poem.) 'We don't need more museums that try to construct the historical narratives of a society, community, team, nation, state, tribe, company, or species. We all know that the ordinary, everyday stories of individuals are richer, more humane, and much more joyful' (Pamuk 2012: 48).

In sum: 'The future of museums is inside our own homes' (Pamuk 2012: 50). I add: and in our own books.

In his introduction to the *Best American Essays* 2007, David Foster Wallace defines the task of non-fiction as starting with everything and editing down. He compares it to the task of fiction: starting with nothing and building up (2007). As usual he's half-right. In non-fiction we do start from the collection of everything and select those things that have meaning to us. We erase the rest until what remains is connected, even if we can't yet articulate why. Wallace's error is claiming that fiction differs from nonfiction in its origination. He can't really believe it comes from nothing. Of course, it doesn't. All good fiction is as idiosyncratic and populated with collected things, pulsing with energy, as good nonfiction. The difference is that nonfiction is more explicitly documentary, and therefore tends to begin by telling us more about the world these things come from than fiction does.

And non-fiction is the more overtly collaborative literary art. Even autobiographical nonfiction collects others' stories: my brother dislocating his shoulder at forty-four trying to run Class IV rapids in kayaks with his son, or my friend Nicole teaching me how to make much better scrambled eggs (I assume everyone else knows this already, but if not, the key is to cook them much more slowly over a much lower heat; I didn't learn this until I was in my thirties, and if you didn't know this, now you've collected a real thing from this brief excursion; execute and enjoy). And with that sentence my brother and Nicole (and you) are selected and summoned and preserved, collaborated with, with or without their permission. Selah Saterstrom composes an essay consisting only of stories she was told by friends (2017). Svetlana Alexievich wins a Nobel for her polyphonic collections of others' stories (2017). The writing is the collection. The writing is the arrangement.

Collecting objects collects *our feelings about them*. When we collect (or write, or write about a collection), we see them again. We bring them into the light, put them on the shelf, notice something new about their oddnesses. When we pull them from one context into another, we perform their seeing, and this preserves the objects and their stories and our relationships with them. When we display a collection we reveal the self – in fact we often reveal it to ourselves – whether it's a narrator or a speaker or the I in essay.

The self is slippery. Shy thing, it emerges (is built, really) *only* when it faces something else, when it thinks nothing's looking at it. In looking and paying these things the compliment of our attention, the eye starts to project the I. How rarely do we understand just what our infatuation with these objects actually means or says about us until they are on display, until we think about them in relation to an audience.

But context matters too, perhaps even more than the object on its own. Though no object is ever on its own. Even the unloved have futures and histories. Back to Pamuk: 'If objects are not uprooted from their environs and their streets but are situated with care and ingenuity in their natural homes, they will already portray their own stories' (2012: 50). Collecting as method requires attention to context. Consider every object with its story in its place. All you have to do is recognize it. All you have to do is hold it. All you have to do is tell it.

References

Alexievich, S. (2017), *Secondhand Time: The Last of the Soviets*, New York: Random House.
Foster Wallace, D. and R. Atwan, eds (2007), *The Best American Essays 2007*, New York: Mariner.
Pamuk, O. (2012), *The Innocence of Objects*, New York: Abrams.
Saterstrom, S. (2017), *Ideal Suggestions: Essays in Divinatory Poetics*, Buffalo: Essay Press.

SEE ALSO

Keepsake
Notebooking
Vocabulary

Communitas

FRANCESCA RENDLE-SHORT

Communitas is a Latin noun referring to the making of unstructured communities where everyone is equal, also to the very spirit that is community, what it means, how it holds together and how it plays out. It is a loanword from Cultural Anthropology and the Social Sciences, and this is where it is most applicable to the discussion of creative writing methods, where coming together in some sort of (un) structure or ritual brings intense feelings and a sense of urgency, intimacy and connection; a strong bond is formed and with it a sense of belonging.

In her introduction to *Communitas: The Anthropology of Collective Joy*, Edith Turner (2012) refers to a key principle at the heart of *communitas* being 'the inversion of the structural order, and the abandonment of status and acquisition' (9), or 'loss of ego' (3): purposefully not taking sides (5), allowing *communitas* to unfold. How *communitas* is a condition of creativity, 'a readiness without preconceived ideas' (3). Turner writes: 'It comes unexpectedly, like the wind' (3).

I first heard the word *communitas* when performing together with a collective of writers – Mary Cappello, Ames Hawkins, Peta Murray and Peggy Shriner – at a performance-cum-panel at the NonfictioNow conference in 2018. This unpanelled performance of queer promenade-as-nonfiction was participatory, immersive, playful and performative (Cappello et al. 2018). It consisted of a community promenade, displays of selected objects on plinths at 'Stations of the (Very) Cross' amongst which the audience moved, such as keys, plastic bags, dinosaurs, photographs and egg timers, along with soliloquies from participant-performers, demonstrative choral responses from the gathered audience and radio sound bites from a panellist *in absentia*.

Everyone in the room was engrossed, listening, joining in; nobody wanted to leave. It was unexpected, à la Turner's 'collective joy'. There was a joint felt experience between participants, a common purpose of being together arising from that very fact of *being together*, of love. We were held as a group by and through story: 'the sense felt by a plurality of people without boundaries' (Turner 2012: 1). A perfect case of *communitas* in practice.

When I begin to extrapolate from the specificity of that first encounter with *communitas* to the usefulness of the idea for broader application, I get excited by possibilities.

What if we apply this *communitas* way of thinking or art of 'collective joy' to making work, creative writing, as method? What if we think about *thinking* as *communitas*, create a sense of belonging and attachment to ideas and writers we encounter on and off the page, what we read, what we hear when we listen, those ideas and experiences we collect along the way? What if we create spaces of encounter in our work and practice where the unexpected can happen, where we allow *unfolding* to occur, collective *satori* (Turner 2012: 1)? What if we ritualize the tiny movements of back and forth, across and between, stick with it, return and review – create invitational creative conditions for whatever it is that is gathering or has been gathered – allow the 'intensity of feeling' or joy to arise: '*communitas* is thus a gift from liminality, the state of being betwixt and between' (4). What if we give in to the spirit of thinking, singly and together, give equal weight to different components or different thoughts, pay attention, repeat, slow down, expand, allow.

What could/couldn't, might/might not happen?

Alongside the noting of the word *communitas* in my notebook, I read other notes from that nonfiction conference I could Velcro to this idea (in the gentlest of ways), such as Gretel Ehrlich's thoughts from a keynote: 'Don't be afraid of the mess, that's the manure, that's where everything grows. It will tell you what it is later.' Or notes from Nicole Walker and others talking out loud on a panel at the Association of Writing Programs Conference in Portland in 2019 that now in my thinking and in writing to this topic form a kind of litany-as-prompts, *communitas* 'readiness':

- look beyond what is in your own head to learn from others; exercise 'beyonding'
- be alert to *connective tissue* across distances through consonance and assonance
- attune to the 'experiencing writer', the different versions of writer as character
- dissociate yourself as writer in order to see yourself acting, speaking, thinking: 'to place yourself means you have to split from yourself to do the putting'.

Embedded in this word are practices of *action*, about how to create *communitas* encounters to enable and empower different kinds of cultural exchange. Here I'm thinking about what happens when writers and their writing come in close proximity to one another, how conditions for *communitas* might be created so that it 'fountains up' (Turner 2012: 1).

In retrospect, I can see now that an example of 'fountain-ups' happened around the table at WrICE (Writers Immersion and Cultural Exchange) residencies my colleague and I facilitated. WrICE brings writers from around the Asia-Pacific region together to share their writing and literary cultures. The generative exchange at these residencies draws on principles of gift exchange à la Lewis Hyde (1983), the potential of writing *in the company of*, and what we termed as 'acrossness': 'a prepositional space, where the relations-between is the key':

> We gather to disclose the in between. It strings us, and our writing together in composition and pattern. It is in the round, where the made is still being made, when anything and everything is possible [...] It is a place of all-in-company, a second person space – the you-you of interaction between writers, between storytellers, between intimate readers (Carlin and Rendle-Short 2016: 7, 8).

This is heart-work, love-work:

> If it does that, it's a miracle [...] what we are telling each other through these stories [allows] us to inhabit the insides of a pocket-exchange to dwell, to dream, to imagine, conjure up, and envision picture-to-oneself otherness (Carlin and Rendle-Short 2019: 280).

As Yankunytjatjara/Kokatha poet and WrICE alumni Ali Cobby Eckermann puts it:

> There is a shift in one's perception when the impact of cultural identity is shared, when the similarities are louder than the differences, when respect of each other creates an equal and safe environment (Carlin and Rendle-Short 2019: 281).

Still, a question arises: how might I practice *communitas*-as-method *in practice*? – thinking here (as an aside) of method or μέθοδος (*methodos*) as rendered from its Greek origins, where there is an 'always doing', a *without interruption* or unbroken whole, a together *with*, or more correctly *towards*, a hold (Ellis, pers. comm.). In response: here is my 'to-do (to-practice)' list of suggestions:

- Experiment *acrossness* with fellow writers
- Create a you-you space *all-in-company*
- Let go of ego and preconceived ideas – unfold yourself
- Engage in prepositional thinking with/near/around/beside/beyonding
- Do 'love-collaboration' as the new norm
- Practice deep listening as heart-work (love-work) as you would a new language
- Resist giving up and ready yourself for the unexpected
- Allow joy to fountain up
- Give and receive in equal measure
- Pay attention, repeat, slow down, expand, allow.

References

Cappello, M., A. Hawkins, P. Murray, F. Rendle-Short, and P. Shriver (2018), 'The Peripatetic Panel: Nonfiction as (Queer) Encounter', Digital Writers Festival, 2 November. Available online: http://2018.digitalwritersfestival.com/event/peripatetic-panel (accessed 11 February 2021).

Carlin, D. and F. Rendle-Short (2016), '*In the Company of*: Composing a Collaborative Residency Programme for Writers', *New Writing: The International Journal for the Practice and Theory of Creative Writing*, 13 (3), 21 July: 450–61.

Carlin, D. and F. Rendle-Short, eds (2019), *The Near and the Far: Volume II*, Melbourne: Scribe Publications.

Hyde, L. (1983), *The Gift: How the Creative Spirit Transforms the World*, Edinburgh: Canongate Books.

Turner, E. (2012 [2011]), *Communitas: The Anthropology of Collective Joy*, New York: Palgrave Macmillan.

SEE ALSO

Experience
Collaboration
Preposition

Dialogue

CATH MOORE

When we think about some of our favourite films, plays or books, it's often a line of dialogue that resonates more clearly than the story as a whole. Sometimes the delivery is persuasive and succinct, or a heated exchange between characters reveals true intentions. Effective dialogue speaks to character and plot but also sharpens our awareness of how stories reflect and comment upon the world in which we live.

From a functional perspective, dialogue is primarily understood as a conversation between two or more characters that drives the narrative forward. Such interplay allows both reader and writer to 'track and unpack' character behaviour, the shifting relationship dynamics and changing desires or attitudes that create story momentum and character dimension.

In addition to serving story, these verbal exchanges can also facilitate a writer's connection to the characters they are writing about. Screenwriters, such as Noah Baumbach, speak of using dialogue as a vehicle for finding story through scripted conversations between characters (Greens 2017). In my own screenwriting practice, I have often let characters 'free range' in my head, listening to speech patterns, verbal hiccups and mannerisms. It is only when I have a better sense of how characters communicate with the fictional world through language, that I have the confidence to write them onto the page.

Then too, the value of dialogue changes depending on where it sits within the unfolding story. Below is an excerpt from a novel I wrote, eight lines into the opening chapter:

> Fat spits onto his arm but Pat doesn't even flinch.
>
> 'Siddown.' Pat's not one for hairs and graces. Not at 6.00 am in the morning.
>
> There are fried eggs too. I break the yolk and watch as it runs the wrong way down my plate.
>
> 'From now on, you eat what you're given and ya don't play with your food,' Pat says real quiet.
>
> 'But it's moving south.' I knife the bacon rind off and put it under the runny yolk. It stops going any further, so I eat the bacon and leave the yellow puddle, even though it's the best part of the egg.
>
> 'You finish that plate. It's a long drive' (Moore 2020: 2).

This exchange highlights the multifaceted utility of dialogue. In this case I'm establishing the mood, inter-personal dynamics, peculiarities of character and hopefully, a sense of intrigue about where the story might be going. Dialogue can anchor storyworld time and space, offering clues as to the characters' place within them, in relation to what has come before and where the story is heading. At the conclusion of the novel, I've used dialogue to establish a shift in character dynamics. The exchange below takes place three pages from the end:

> Pat and I nod at one another.
> 'How you goin'?'
> 'I'm goin' alright' (Moore 2020: 249).

While the Australian vernacular remains, a shorter exchange and a more thoughtful tone highlight a quiet acceptance between the characters.

Aside from defining character relationships, dialogue can also be a useful device in creating a consistent 'voice', one that helps delineate between characters through distinct speech patterns, language preferences (such as slang or lingo) and use of the vernacular. A character's dialogue may also infer markers of identity such as class, culture, psychology, personality and value systems.

Dialogue can be seen as an architectural tool in the construction of character. Indeed, the values often ascribed to good dialogue reinforce language as a means to activate characters but also illuminate plot and conflict (Iglesias 2005). As a development tool, writing verbal exchanges as a way 'into' the narrative can often help writers understand the purpose of the scene or chapter. As part of the mechanics within story construction, dialogue can be viewed as both imperative and dispensable throughout different stages of development and drafts.

Prose dialogue may be indirect, a condensed or abridged version that infers rather than replicates a word-for-word conversation as is required in screenwriting. There are a number of questions writers often ask when formulating frameworks. Is the character part of the action or are they recalling/commenting on plot? Is vernacular language applicable? Is expression formal or casual, intimate or aloof? Is content implicit or explicit? Dialogue can also be explored as a conversational component of storytelling, shepherding dramatic action (unfolding plot) and/or thematic concerns (overarching story) through the text.

Dialogue can be used for subterfuge or disclosure. Dialogue is often revelatory in function, commonly employed to deliver *exposition* or information crucial to understanding the plot, character intention and emotion. It may reveal dramatic goals, conflicts and inter-personal dynamics between characters. However, dialogue may also be used to suppress, distract or conceal character motivation. The writer can activate the audience's puzzlement through ambiguity (Law 2021). Further, dialogue can be an important component of genre expression. As Moulton (2019) suggests, the interview scene, commonly used within the serial killer sub-genre of procedural crime, often reflects multiple dialogue typologies: 'the killer as a fount of wisdom, the investigator as an eager receptacle and the psychological boundaries between the two characters as disturbingly permeable' (195). Dialogue exchanges enact archetype and confirm genre convention.

Subtext is the implicit message or meaning of a verbal exchange. Subtext is often seen as a 'truth submarine' revealing genuine emotions, thoughts and intentions of character. For example, in a scene I wrote for a screenplay, older sister Layla makes an impulsive decision to let younger sister Bea use her beloved iPod as they walk home from school. This is despite fighting about the device in the previous scene:

50   A to Z of Creative Writing Methods

```
Layla slows and takes her headphones off.

                          LAYLA
                   You wear them.

This surprises Bea, who accepts hesitantly.

                          BEA
                   Thanks?

Layla turns the volume up and hands over her iPod.
```

Up ahead in the park, Layla has seen a boy prone to racist language. She gives her sister the iPod so she won't have to hear his taunts. The subtext to Layla's line is 'I'll protect you'. Bea won't understand this, but hopefully the audience will.

Genres such as melodrama shy away from subtext and use dialogue as a confessionary tool, through which characters proclaim their desires or reveal key plot points with little artifice. The terms *set up* and *pay off* can also relate to the use of dialogue to 'plant' strategic questions, statements or observations that are only given dramatic context later in the narrative. The reader/audience is a participant in the meaning-making process. Consequently, dialogue can be appreciated on another level as a series of exchanges, conversations and transactions between the text, reader/viewer and writer in the shared experience of storytelling.

At its most functional dialogue gives voice to character, revealing personality, viewpoint and agenda. However, as a distinct story-building block, the importance of dialogue extends beyond character-building and plot. Conversational exchanges often illuminate thematic concerns that underpin the text and anchor narrative time and place. Dialogue that works for story creates an indivisible pathway between all players involved: the reader/viewer, author and character alike.

References

Greens, R. (2017), 'Character over Concept; Writing Dialogue in Search of Story', *Journal of Screenwriting*, 8 (12): 39–54.

Iglesias, K. (2005), *Writing for Emotional Impact*, California: Wingspan Press.

Law, H. L. (2021), *Ambiguity and Film Criticism*, Reading: Palgrave.

Marotta, J. (2017), 'Diablo Cody Sets the Record Straight on Juno', *Vanity Fair HWD*. Available online: https://www.vanityfair.com/hollywood/2017/04/diablo-cody-sets-the-record-straight-on-juno (accessed 20 July 2021).

Moore, C. (2020), *Metal Fish, Falling Snow*, Melbourne: Text Publishing.

Moulton, E. (2019), 'Crafting an "Authentic" Monster: Dialogue, Genre and Ethical Questions in *Mindhunter* (2017)', *Journal of Screenwriting*, 10 (2): 196–212.

Nash, M. (2013), 'Uncertain Spaces and Uncertainty in Film Development,' *Journal of Screenwriting*, 4 (2): 149–62.

SEE ALSO

Fade out
Listening
Character

Drawing

SARAH LEAVITT

The first thing that most people think of when they imagine making comics is drawing. In fact, comics creation calls on a wide range of skills that are useful in all forms of writing, including, but not limited to, capturing and holding a reader's attention, organizing material into a clear structure, and paring down and focusing one's prose.

For the last thirteen years I have taught comics classes in the School of Creative Writing at the University of British Columbia. The students in our Bachelor of Fine Arts (BFA) and Master of Fine Arts (MFA) programmes are required to take courses in at least three different forms. This means that in every class I teach, some students are cartoonists and others are poets or novelists, essayists or screenwriters, who will use the course as cross-training to strengthen their abilities in their chosen forms. (There are always converts, too – students who unexpectedly find themselves falling in love with comics partway through the term and changing their specialization, but that's another story.)

A drawing exercise that I often recommend involves creating a one-page autobiographical comic using a nine-panel grid. The nine-panel grid is a classic layout for comics, with three rows of three panels, all panels being vertical rectangles of the same size. This layout works well not only as an introduction to thinking visually about story structure, but also as a way of learning how to craft raw material into a deliberately constructed form.

I offer writers a few ways in which to approach the grid: they can think about each tier (row) of panels as a sentence, or they can imagine that the three tiers represent the beginning, middle and end of the story. Like a line of poetry or a paragraph of prose, each tier is carefully composed, with first and last panels deliberately chosen. The first panel of the page hooks the reader into the story, and the last panel provides a definitive ending. The fifth panel, sitting in the centre of the page, can act as a focus or turning point.

As writers begin to shape their story to fit the grid, they realize how small the space is, and how economical their storytelling must be. They realize that when each panel is the same size it means that each contains about the same amount of information, and when they try to fit too much content into one panel the rhythm is disrupted, and the reader becomes confused or frustrated with the story. They learn to think of panels like beats in a story.

At the same time that they're thinking about which bit of story goes into each panel, they must also remember that comics is a visual form, and they need to think about how each panel will look, as well as the page as a whole. These questions can be useful starting points: Where do you want the reader's eye to focus? Which character do you want them to follow through the page?

We use exercises that explore the impact of different kinds of shapes and colours. What part of your story is spiky? Which part chaotic? Which part peaceful? Which part is darkest?

Brightest? Loudest? Fastest moving? Again, this exploration could be a productive part of the development of a short story, poem or film script.

When students in my classes share and discuss their comics with each other, the learning expands. In an exercise developed by cartoonist and educator Nick Sousanis, they pair up and tell each other a brief story about themselves. Each writer makes two comics, one about their own story and one about their partner's story. When they then share their comics, they observe how each approached the same story quite differently, choosing different parts to highlight or leave out (Sousanis 2020).

The way we approach drawing in comics class can be applied to other forms of writing. One of the barriers to working with the comic form is the belief that one 'can't draw'. In fact, my experience as a comics teacher has shown me that everyone has the ability to create drawings that communicate information and emotion, whether or not they are realistic or polished or pretty. Like many educators, I've been deeply influenced by the approach of Lynda Barry, who likes to point out that all children draw, but many or most stop around age ten, when the 'good artists' are identified, and the rest discouraged (2008: 80). This is a huge loss, as drawing is a way of thinking, as well as a way of making art. As artist and researcher Andrea Kantrowitz writes, '[t]he act of drawing can be understood as the creation of a physical space to play with our thoughts outside the confines of our minds, to see and manipulate our ideas and perceptions in visible form' (2012: 3).

Writers spend time drawing in every session of my comics classes – not only to create finished comics, but to discover and explore stories in the conception and planning stages. For example, in a quick drawing exercise, students might be prompted to invent a character by combining human and animal features. Some end up creating characters that inspire ideas for stories. Or they are asked to think about a childhood memory and make rough sketches of what happened. The act of drawing often unearths memories of events or details that haven't emerged in written explorations. Writers can continue to use drawing to find and research stories, even if the final form of those stories is poetry or prose.

I see comics as a valuable part of any multi-form or cross-genre creative writing programme and encourage instructors and writers of all forms to consider borrowing techniques from comics.

References

Barry, L. (2008), *What It Is*, Montreal: Drawn and Quarterly.

Kantrowitz, A. (2012), 'The Man behind the Curtain: What Cognitive Science Reveals about Drawing', *The Journal of Aesthetic Education*, 46 (1), Spring: 1–14.

Sousanis, N. (2020), 'Thinking in Comics: All Hands-On in the Classroom', in S. Kirtley, A. Garcia, and P. E. Carlson (eds), *With Great Power Comes Great Pedagogy: Teaching, Learning and Comics*, 92–116, Jackson: University Press of Mississippi.

SEE ALSO

Permission

Braiding

Phototextuality

Ekphrasis

SARAH HOLLAND-BATT

In a work of ekphrasis, a poet or writer responds to a work of art by describing or critiquing it, ventriloquizing its figures or evoking its mood, textures or palette through language. Ekphrasis is not a literary form: it has no set rules, nor a prescribed stance towards its subject matter, such as the elegy's mournful tone or the ode's celebratory one. Ekphrasis is best understood as an intertextual mode: one in which a piece of writing depends on an external artwork for a quotient of its meaning. While ekphrasis can take the form of prose – art criticism, for instance, entails extended ekphrasis – the preponderance of creative ekphrastic writing today occurs in poetry. As a poet writing within this tradition, I focus on poetic ekphrasis in this essay.

The practice of ekphrasis stretches back to Antiquity; from the Greek *ek* ('out') and *phrasein* ('to speak') (Barbetti 2011: 4), ekphrasis has been dated to at least the third century AD, when it denoted 'an extended and detailed literary description of any object, real or imaginary' (Webb 2003: np). In the classical world, ekphrasis was used to train rhetoricians to achieve fidelity in description; students wrote ekphrases about shields, pottery and other objects not only to learn how to express themselves vividly, but also to produce 'analogous work[s] of [their] own' (Webb 2016: 41).

Ekphrasis has entered into renewed popularity in the late twentieth and early twenty-first centuries, where the ekphrastic gaze has expanded to include not only traditional subjects such as paintings and sculptures, but also photographs, and non-static artworks including films, performances and installations.

Yoking together these diverse subjects is ekphrasis's central concern with 'verbal representation of graphic representation' (Heffernan 1991: 299). Historically, the balance of power between text and art has been figured as a hierarchical 'contest between rival modes of representation' (Heffernan 1993: 6), which seeks to determine 'superiority between visual and verbal arts' (Barbetti 2011: 3). This combative conception tends to emphasize the respective stillness of the artwork and the dynamic voice of the poem, figuring the work of visual art as subjugated by the verbal – yet paradoxically, the converse is also arguably true, as the ekphrastic poem is perpetually indebted to the artwork.

Ultimately, the old adversarial conception of ekphrasis – where art and writing are considered oppositional semiotic modes – is unilluminating. Ekphrasis is, at heart, relational rather than adversarial: it privileges exchange, interpretation, response and conversation. It is best understood as a metapoetic, symbiotic interchange of visual and verbal syntax and language.

This conversation between artwork and text necessitates excesses and deficits: the ekphrastic poet cannot fill all the silences of the artwork, but rather embellishes, refracts, adds, supplements, reflects and reinterprets it. The ekphrastic poem is also a site where multiple temporalities converge: the ekphrastic poet may comment on the artist's techniques or ideation or biography, as well as the passage of time since its construction, and the contemporary context in which the artwork now exists, disrupting any semblance of a unified art object, and drawing attention to its fabrication. Ekphrasis also implies a regression of viewpoints: first the artist's, then the poet's and then the reader's. Ultimately, it is a distinctly self-conscious, reflexive, metapoetic mode about the *act* of interpretation, as much as it is about the interpretation itself.

Historically, the impulse towards ekphrasis has been figured by both theorists and poets as a positive one, akin to a spell, longing, enchantment or seduction. Yet the apprehension of beauty is only one of many impetuses prompting an ekphrastic response. Contemporary poets write ekphrastic poems as a form of critique, argument or disagreement as often as they do out of admiration. Many contemporary feminist ekphrastic poems adopt a critical stance towards the male gaze, demonstrating that 'the patterns of power and value implicit in a tradition of male artists and viewers can be exposed, used, resisted and rewritten' (Loizeaux 2009: 122). Other poets are propelled by an adverse response to images of violence, trauma, war or other confronting subjects.

In addition to the plethora of critical perspectives a poet may adopt towards the artwork, ekphrastic poets adopt a range of speaking positions. While a classic ekphrastic poem such as Keats's 'Ode on a Grecian Urn' – wherein the poet meditates upon a single art object – typifies the most common form of ekphrasis, it is by no means the only type. The poet may write about an entire school of art while eschewing the particularities of an individual painting, as the Polish poet Adam Zagajewski does in 'Dutch Painters', a poem which evokes the tropes of the Dutch Golden Age still lives – spiralling lemon peels, gleaming oysters, chrome-like silver ewers, undulating linens – without explicitly naming an individual artist or work (2002). In this type of ekphrastic poem, the poet conjures the spectre of an imaginary amalgam by combining particularities from existing works; John Hollander defines this as 'notional ekphrasis' (1995: 4).

The ekphrastic poet may also write about a motif or subject running through an individual artist's entire corpus, as Wisława Szymborska does in 'Rubens' Women', a poem which draws upon a visual idiom associated with Rubens the ruddy corporeality of his female subjects – as well as pastoral imagery, such as the steaming baths, blushing wines and 'cloudy piglets' (2000: 47), which evokes tropes of the Baroque period as a whole.

The poet can also undertake ekphrasis by writing about a genre of art, such as the still life or portrait, or a motif or common subject, such as the odalisque, without making reference to any individual painter or period.

Ultimately, the conversations which take place within the ekphrastic mode are as varied as those which unfold within the art gallery and beyond; whether querulous, adulatory, perplexed, incensed, earnest or ironic, all suggest a generative interplay between the visual and the verbal.

Readers wishing to familiarize themselves with some diverse examples of contemporary ekphrasis may like to consult Kevin Young's *To Repel Ghosts* (2005), Pascale Petit's *What the Water Gave Me: Poems After Frida Kahlo* (2010), Ciaran Carson's *Still Life* (2020), Claudia Rankine's *Citizen: An American Lyric* (2014) and Cole Swensen's *Try* (1999).

References

Barbetti, C. (2011), *Ekphrastic Medieval Visions: A New Discussion in Interarts Theory*, London: Palgrave.

Carson, C. (2020), *Still Life*, Winston-Salem: Wake Forest University Press.

Heffernan, J. A. W. (1991), 'Ekphrasis and Representation', *New Literary History*, 22 (2): 297–316.

Heffernan, J. A. W. (1993), *Museum of Words: The Poetics of Ekphrasis from Homer to Ashbery*, Chicago: University of Chicago Press.

Hollander, J. (1995), *The Gazer's Spirit: Poems Speaking to Silent Works of Art*, Baltimore: Johns Hopkins University Press.

Loizeaux, E. B. (2009), 'Women Looking: The Feminist Ekphrasis of Marianne Moore and Adrienne Rich', in J. Hedley, N. Halpern, and W. Spiegelman (eds), *In the Frame: Women's Ekphrastic Poetry from Marianne Moore to Susan Wheeler*, 121–44, Delaware: University of Delaware Press.

Petit, P. (2010), *What the Water Gave Me: Poems after Frida Kahlo*, Bridgend: Seren Books.

Rankine, C. (2014), *Citizen: An American Lyric*, Minneapolis: Graywolf.

Swensen, C. (1999), *Try: Poems*, Iowa City: University of Iowa Press.

Szymborska, W. (2000), 'Reubens' Women', in *Poems New and Collected*, trans. C. Cavanagh and S. Baranczak, 47, Boston: Mariner.

Webb, R. (2003), 'Ekphrasis', in H. Brigstoke (ed.), *The Oxford Companion to Western Art*, Oxford: Oxford University Press.

Webb, R. (2016), *Ekphrasis, Imagination and Persuasion in Ancient Rhetorical Theory and Practice*, Oxon: Routledge.

Young, K. (2005), *To Repel Ghosts: The Remix*, New York: Knopf.

Zagajewski, A. (2002), 'Dutch Painters', in *Without End: New and Selected Poems*, 222–3, New York: Farrar, Straus and Giroux.

SEE ALSO

Archival-poetics

Juxtaposition

Metaphor me

Ensemble

SHUCHI KOTHARI

In 1990 when I asked my instructor if I could write an ensemble story for my first ever screen-play, he warned me against it saying (perhaps correctly) that they were difficult to write well and harder to sell. As a Master's student studying Screenplay Writing at the University of Texas at Austin, it was my first introduction to the 'Western' screenplay's conventions, format and history. During instruction and examples, the goal-driven single protagonist Hollywood narrative in three acts took precedence over other forms of organizing story. The character wants something; they go chasing what they want; overcome many obstacles, only to eventually realize that it is what they *need* that matters. In Christopher Vogler's terms, whatever the 'call to adventure' the hero must 'return with the elixir' (2007: 9).

Even though single protagonist feature films have dominated the film industry in the United States and offered a template to many other countries, sitting in the classroom eagerly absorbing the analysis of Syd Field (1994), Vogler (2007), Robert McKee (1999) and others (all white men), I found myself gravitating to films with multiple protagonists: an ensemble cast of characters that may or may not achieve their goals but give us more complex and indefinite views of the world. I also realized that despite Hollywood's predilection for single protagonist stories, it has produced ensemble films from the early days of features, such as *Intolerance* (1916) and *Grand Hotel* (1932). I couldn't pinpoint exactly what it was about the ensemble structure that drew me to it except that I grew up in an extended family in India with three generations in one big house. Many activities and tasks were shared. Consensus was not always possible, so one learned to navigate differences and competing desires to move forward. The community superseded individual gratification. The notion of being a solo protagonist in the centre of the universe in which one person could (let alone would) provide a panacea to its problems felt alien to me.

Ensemble screenplays seek to represent the community through multiple storylines and an array of subjectivities. They invite the audience to multiply and/or split their identifications with characters in different narrative situations. As Linda Cowgill (2003) notes, some of the plotlines conclude ambiguously and even unhappily, making this type of film structurally more open than the more common goal-oriented narrative of a single protagonist. David Bordwell labelled them network narratives in which there are 'several protagonists, but their projects are largely decoupled from one another, or only contingently linked' (2008: 192). In her discussion of organizing principles of the multi-protagonist film, Linda Aronson highlights the importance of dramatic unity (of action, time, place) in all subtypes, be they reunion films, siege films, quest films, tandem and sequential narratives. According to Aronson (2001), the ensemble screenplay has two aims: 'they explore versions of the same social role which display different approaches, concerns and solutions; and they study the dynamics and the story of the group itself' (222).

Both my feature-writing credits are for multi-protagonist films (*Firaaq* 2008; *Apron Strings* 2008). In *Apron Strings*, mothers and sons of two unconnected families follow their own storylines to ultimately arrive at a better understanding of familial love and boundaries. The dramatic unity in *Apron Strings* is neither an event nor geographical location. Instead, co-writer Dianne Taylor and I united the stories via the shared theme of mothering, nurture versus control. On the other hand, *Firaaq*, a 'character mosaic' (Tröhler 2010: 462) about the aftermath of the 2002 pogrom against Muslims, unfolds over eighteen hours in Ahmedabad in Gujarat, a month after the peak of the riots. Director Nandita Das and I co-wrote the screenplay to explore what lingers after the visible violence is over – the fear, the anger, the prejudice, the desire for revenge, the hopelessness and the need to have faith. The range of emotions engendered by such violence could not be captured through the experience of one central protagonist. Besides, when thousands were killed and displaced, one person's suffering seemed no more important, nor could it become the repository of everybody else's pain or mediate the social schism entirely on its own. Moving across neighbourhoods, ages, classes and gender, the ensemble form allowed us to explore distinctive feelings through six intercut stories: fear through the story of a Hindu-Muslim couple about to flee the city, guilt through the story of a middle-class Hindu woman who denied refuge to a Muslim riot-victim, revenge in the case of an Muslim auto-rickshaw driver whose house is looted and burned, betrayal in the story of his wife and her Hindu best friend: faith in the story of a Hindustani classical vocalist and his loyal caretaker and finally, the loss of innocence in the story of a six-year-old boy who is looking for his father after witnessing the slaughter of his family. Even within these six stories, we displaced the centrality of individual protagonists to explore relationships: married couples, a group of friends, a woman within a joint family, master and loyal caretaker, and two best friends.

Often, the cognitive mapping of the ensemble city film ends up offering a totality in its assemblage, which is what the audience finds pleasurable, but we risked the loss of this pleasure by not letting all *Firaaq's* stories intersect. The characters do not come together for a climactic finale, nor do twists and turns of the plot in the third act provide a shared resolution. While there is some change or movement in the characters' journeys, these shifts and transformations are not equally weighted. The decision to establish an ensemble structure was also grounded in research and the responsibility to represent authentically the experience of the pogrom. I conducted interviews, consulted testimonies, journalistic and documentary evidence. The research confirmed that the final film could never match the horror of what actually took place but, through crafting an ensemble screenplay, we could articulate the residual emotions of different people who lived through it. The ensemble structure allowed us to write 'a work of fiction based on a thousand true stories' and bring to the surface a longer history of Hindu-Muslim feelings about each other that have little promise of resolution. The open-endedness of some of the stories and their states of anxious suspension remind us that though the pogrom is over, 'normalcy' is not possible for everyone in the city.

There is no one way to approach an ensemble but it helps to lay down a rhizomatic road map, rather than a linear one. Let each story, or character explore a different facet or point of view on the theme to earn their place in an ensemble. Whether or not the stories converge at the end, a clear uniting principle (usually theme, geography or event) must bring together different stories/characters. The literary notion of the conceit is helpful while writing an ensemble. A sound guiding principle is that the whole is greater than the sum of its parts. Yes, they are hard to wrangle but when executed well, ensemble structures explore complexity of relationships between people and situations and offer various points of identification for increasingly variegated audiences.

References

Apron Strings (2008), S. Kothari and D. Taylor (wr.), Sima Urale (dir.), New Zealand: Great Southern Films.

Aronson, L. (2001), *Scriptwriting Updated*, New York: Allen and Unwin.

Bordwell, D. (2008), *Poetics of Cinema*, New York: Routledge Press.

Cowgill, L. (2003), 'Ensemble Films: The Gang's All Here', Plot's Inc. Productions. Available online: http://www.plotsinc.com/sitenew/column_art_10.html (accessed 10 December 2015).

Field, S. (1994), *Screenplay: The Foundations of Screenwriting*, 3rd edn expanded, New York: Dell.

Firaaq (2008), N. Das and S. Kothari (wr.), N. Das (dir.) India: Percept Picture Company.

Grand Hotel (1932), W. A. Drake (wr.), E. Goulding (dir.), USA: Metro-Goldwyn-Mayer.

Intolerance (1916), D. W. Griffith, H. G. Baker, T. Browning, A. Loos, M. H. O'Connor, F. E. Woods (wrs.), D. W. Griffith (dir.), USA: Wark Producing Corporation.

McKee, R. (1999). *Story: Substance, Structure, Style, and the Principles of Screenwriting*, London: Methuen.

Tröhler, M. (2010), 'Multiple Protagonist Films: A Transcultural Everyday Practice', in J. Eder, F. Jannidis, and R. Schneider (eds), *Characters in Fictional Worlds: Understanding Imaginary Beings in Literature, Film and Other Media*, 459–77, Berlin: De Gruyter.

Vogler, C. (2007), *The Writer's Journey: Mythic Structure for Writers*, 3rd edn, Studio City: Michael Weise Productions.

SEE ALSO

Juxtaposition
Hybrid
Camping

Erasure

NHÃ THUYÊN

nàng chỉ là một mảnh thư
đang cháy mà ai đó, hay chính tôi,
gửi cho người chết she is just a piece of a
burning letter that someone, or it is me, is sending to the dead.

the annihilating letters

'a pencil and an erasure scratch on me the story of their time-worn life', the page mumbles, 'until all the letters are annihilated and what remains, the traces, the unoccupied spaces, the dots, the commas, the inerasable, the unreadable, the unmendable, the unwritten-able, is what must be devoured with mouths, tongues, teeth and lips, must be handled with both hands, all ten fingers. i am not virgin' [1].

> he, once more, striving just to make me see my officially withered dreams, once more, striving to hurt me in a dream, but mornings come, i have forgotten the dream, i have forgotten the hurt, i have forgotten all of whatever i wanted to forget, i have forgotten all of whatever i meant to forget.

'the words catch fever,' the wind hums, 'self-immolating, their ashes desire the previous life, but the fire only exists as a symbol, and has no power.'

> the crying sounds now asleep, the wind gradually erases itself, the crumbling narrative of fire and paper and the whimsical life of an old dictionary that consists of only crossed out words

'the process of erasure: the process of remembering, of recalculating, of collecting the forgotten, a practice of the everyday, the every minute, the every second, the every non-existent, the art of counting the wind's breath and analyzing the cent', the reader murmurs, 'why does the wind efface my face or does the page efface the wind by receiving its breath?'

> then the falling rain having cleared
> out the smell of dust and mould deserted on the dry back of an old horse who nibbles wildflowers by the road to forget time waiting for the hour of death

> i throw hours of wretched reminiscence into the void and without end
> pursue a smell

> forever searching

'i make no attempt to write, not at all,' the writer's tongue tied, 'except to end the unendable, the unmendable, the unrecordable, and to drink the waters of lethe, to blank you and blank the contours of this earthly body. the memories cry, but they lost themselves.'

because called by that river.

our debate on words drags on until the end of this winter, as the flock of birds is finding new shelter.

i write, erase it and write again, until all this anguish and love lighten, a volcano's memory of being cold comes back, pebbles at the edge of sea disperse in the wave, i will invent a barren desert among crowds, envelope you in warm sand and we will be unseen

we bicker to fatigue, cackle in agreement on the notion of beauty we imagine the greatest dream is only written in air and we are entwined in deep sleep with the whispering angels.

i am not the storyteller. i am the story. i am not the story. i am the trace of a forgotten story, the trace of hazy sweat i wrote on your left cheek a shapeless scar the wind vaporized, of the dream only vague inconsequential details remain, the silhouette is gradually swallowed, a trap, a leap between frenzied thought and composed act, a page of biography written and rewritten and the eternal erasing of mistakes and fallacies.

questions and the great effort to answer them, stories that have died, meanings that have dried up, depth is a visual illusion, and my body is only the temporary substitute for an urn holding withered ashes of the dead, and i am the withered ashes of the dead, now i lie unmoving in that urn

'the storm must shake her,' the reader shudders, 'to not celebrate the wound and repeat the lesion, Hélène, don't be scared' [2].

whatever beats, whatever dies, whatever exhales except

in the head unfamiliar voices as autumn rain drops a block of dead rotting brain, the tip of a knife gently pierces an eye, a bird's melodious call, we should clench our breath to be drifting and forget the blood running

the page lies idle, the wind stands soundless, the pencil and the erasure hide, the writer sleeps, only the reader keeps counting.

----

the reader's note:
this poem traces back the whole book of Nhã Thuyên, *từ thở, những người la* (2015), and its English translation-body by Kaitlin Rees, *words breathe, creatures of elsewhere.* some words, some lines, some parts of several poems in the book are reused in different ways.
    and my memory asked to quote these lines without finding their origins.

Erasure 61

[1] Maurice Blanchot: 'The paper is white only if the page is virgin.'

[2] Hélène Cixous: 'All literature is scary. It celebrates the wound and repeats the lesion.

[My favourite erasure pieces: *Borges and I* (Luis Borges, 2019 [1960]), *Ghost of* (Diana Khoi Nguyen, 2018), *Vicious Circles: Two Fictions and 'After the Fact'* (Maurice Blanchot, 1985).]

in an idle summer, i collected a vocabulary of erasure, of remembrance, of forgetfulness and found nothing more meaningful than the Vietnamese word: *xóa* [*xóa dấu vết, gạch xóa, xóa bỏ, xóa mờ, xóa mù, xóa nhòa, xóa sổ*], *xóa* could bear all these traces of words: to erase, to cross out, to delete, to eliminate, to wipe out, to negate, to obliterate, to scratch out, to annul, to blank, to efface, to extirpate, to kill, to nullify and to be nothing], and without its rising tone, *xoa* [*xoa đầu, xoa tay, xoa dịu*], to stroke a baby's skin, to soothe the burning heart, to rub love of my right hand on my left hand, to console. their darkness read the antonyms in the dictionary, so somehow i can build, i can construct, i can create, i can ratify, i can allow, i can keep, i can retain, i can validate, i can add, i can insert, and i can hold and collect the forgettings, the erasure, the elimination.

hoping for an expanse of silence on pages, the writer puts more negated words, recycles her nullified selves, carries mistakes of translations. layers of letters abolished dive into the page. her hands chaotic on keyboard, her eyes hurt at the landscape of uncontrollable disappearances, and i saw her googling *how to overtype in google docs*, to hold the traces, to embody the traces, the forgotten infancy.

----

chỉ còn những dấu máu there only remains traces of blood

References

Blanchot, M. (1985), *Vicious Circles: Two Fictions and 'After the Fact'*, trans. P. Auster, Barrytown, New York: Station Hill.

Blanchot, M. (1993), *The Infinite Conversation*, trans. S. Hanson, Minneapolis and London: University of Minnesota.

Borges, J. L. (2019 [1960]), 'Borges and I', in *Collected Fictions*, London: Penguin.

Cixous, H. (2005), *Stigmata*, New York: Routledge Classics 2 Edition.

Nguyen, D. K. (2018), *Ghost of*, Chicago: Omnidawn Publishing.

Thuyên, N. (2015), *từ thở, những người lạ*, Hà Nội: Nhã Nam.

Thuyên N. (2016), *Words Breathe, Creatures of Elsewhere*, trans. K. Rees, Sydney: Vagabond Press.

SEE ALSO

Fade out

Vocabulary

Translation

Experience

KÁRI GÍSLASON

Drawing on personal experience is fundamental to storytelling. It has certainly been central to my own writing in memoir and other forms of creative nonfiction, such as travel writing (*The Promise of Iceland* 2011; *Saga Land* 2017). While the topics I have covered vary from cultural history to family life, they have been deeply connected by the heightened role of experience, memory and the process of recollection, be that through my own reflections, conversations with others or the discoveries that occur during the writing itself.

In writing memoir, the past does much more than provide story content alone. Autobiographical works have a profound impact on how we understand our lives, and one reason for this is that they are seldom just about *what* we remember, but also *how* we expand, order and examine our memories. They create methods for viewing the past at the same time as they narrate it.

The results can be as varied as memory itself. One of the most widely read memoirs of the past two decades, Karl Ove Knausgaard's six-volume collection *My Struggle* (2013–19), seems to perform the author's search for memory in front of us. As Knausgaard puts it, his autobiographic writing is about 'lowering thresholds – between what was in my head and what was on the page' (Rothman 2018). Consequently, he 'seems unable to leave anything out' (Wood 2012), because to do so would expand that threshold through selectivity. In J. M. Coetzee's autobiographies, on the other hand, selection is one part of how the narrator stands back from the events being described, and so allows him to interpret his boyhood and youth with the critical distance with which one might read sections of a text (see *Boyhood* 1998; *Youth* 2002).

Despite their very different styles, both Knausgaard's and Coetzee's works present questions through the ways in which they structure experience, and this is crucial in establishing their ethical framework. Autobiographical writing is often very intimate. It takes us into family lives and private situations and reveals secrets and problems that others will want left unsaid. It also turns the people we know and love into characters. The uneasy ethical position that follows is one reason many memoirs state or strongly imply the questions that drive the writing and inform the revelations that may come. Doing so provides an explanation for the necessity of the intrusions, as well as something akin to a research topic that is being addressed through personal experience.

In my view, one of the best examples of a memoir that develops these kinds of questions, both directly and impliedly through its structural devices, is Joan Didion's *The Year of Magical Thinking* (2006). In this work, Didion explicitly links the task of analysis to her understanding of the role of storytelling. She tells us that the memoir is an attempt to make sense of the period after her husband John Dunne's death, a sense-making that is joined by her explanation that, 'long before what I wrote began to be published, I developed a sense that meaning itself was resident in the rhythms of words and sentences and paragraphs [...] The way I write is who I am' (7).

As a result, Didion's book significantly contributes to the subject of grief by performing the changes of perception and understanding that occur during the period after loss. Early on, Didion warns the reader that the memoir will struggle to move beyond the moment of her husband's death and its implications for her. The result is that it also struggles to narrate that death scene conclusively. In this way, the memoir represents and at the same time performs the idea of the collapses, ellipses and denials that are part of her mindset. Dunne's death is, of course, just the sort of thing that happens after forty years of married life. But Didion's attempts to accept this are undermined by an inability to believe that he won't come back. As a result, the narrative collapses whenever it nears the moment of accepting the reality of his death, because that would constitute a narrative completion of it. While the work returns to the causes and nature of his death compulsively, it also does so inconclusively – otherwise, it's betraying the very 'magical' thinking it describes.

Joan Didion was one of the first exponents of the so-called New Journalism, a form of reporting that foregrounds personal experience as a way of accessing and incorporating different kinds of knowledge: embodied and perceptual. In other creative non-fiction forms that similarly incorporate memoir elements, their social and cultural discourses are developed alongside the author's self-characterization. Helen Garner's *This House of Grief* (2014), for instance, uses her attendance at a long murder trial as the basis for her examination of the criminal justice system and the kind of family violence being prosecuted in the case. Her perception, grounded by her physical attendance at court, becomes a key component of research that can only be performed through a long period of time and extraordinary emotional commitment. Garner's self-characterization is a technique for personalizing the story she will tell; it is also essential for the transformation of her singular experience into general observations.

The central role of personal experience as a method in autobiographical writing is also part of what makes it increasingly useful in other fields. Narrative medicine, or 'medicine practiced with the narrative competence to recognize, absorb, interpret, and be moved by the stories of illness' (Charon 2006: vii), is a new area of research that examines how the tools of narrative, including in literature and creative writing, can be applied in medical practices. Creative writing methods may well be part of 'what medicine *lacks* today – in singularity, humility, accountability, empathy' (ix).

This must, in part, be because of the ways in which creative writing raises and frames questions about the past through narrative techniques. In the case of my own writing, one goal has been to do so in a way that recognizes how the experiences that form story content are necessarily shared by the characters. How might the narrative voice and structure of a work reflect this? In the opening chapters of my first book (*The Promise of Iceland* 2011), my answer was to alternate between a narrative of my childhood and stories my mother told me about hers. This, I felt, was essential for a story that was about the complex inheritances of family life, migration and home. It allowed questions that we shared to be expanded in different ways, and, at the same time, for the way we talked about the past – over coffee, looking through old photographs, as I became a parent myself – to be represented in the exchange of our experiences on the page.

References

Charon, R. (2006), *Narrative Medicine: Honoring the Stories of Illness*, New York: Oxford University Press.

Coetzee, J. M. (1998), *Boyhood: Scenes from a Provincial Life*, New York: Viking.

Coetzee, J. M. (2002), *Youth: Scenes from a Provincial Life II*, New York: Viking.

Didion, J. (2006), *The Year of Magical Thinking*, New York: Alfred A. Knopf.

Fidler, R. and K. Gíslason (2017), *Saga Land: The Island of Stories at the Edge of the World*, Sydney: HarperCollins.

Garner, H. (2014), *This House of Grief*, Melbourne: Text Publishing.

Gíslason, K. (2015), *The Ash Burner*, St Lucia, Brisbane: University of Queensland Press.

Gíslason, K. (2011), *The Promise of Iceland*, St Lucia, Brisbane: University of Queensland Press.

Knausgaard, K. O. (2013–19), *My Struggle: Books 1–6*, London: Vintage.

Rothman, J. (2018), 'Karl Ove Knausgaard Looks Back on *My Struggle*', *The New Yorker*, 11 November. Available online: https://www.newyorker.com/culture/the-new-yorker-interview/karl-ove-knausgaard-the-duty-of-literature-is-to-fight-fiction (accessed 16 April 2021).

White, H. (1987), *The Content of the Form*, Baltimore: Johns Hopkins University Press.

Wood, J. (2012), 'Total Recall: Karl Ove Knausgaard's *My Struggle*', *The New Yorker*, 6 August. Available online: https://www.newyorker.com/magazine/2012/08/13/total-recall (accessed 16 April 2021).

SEE ALSO

Resistance

Character

Observation

Experimentation

COLLIER NOGUES

Literary experimentation orients us towards discovery: we want to move beyond the tools we already have, beyond what we already know how to say. But distinct from literary innovation or invention more broadly, experimentation is decidedly practical. It explores with a goal in mind, aiming towards a particular end even if (and perhaps especially because) that end is not fully imaginable. As Joan Retallack puts it, experiment turns on 'paying attention to what happens when well-designed questions are directed to things we sense but don't really know' (2007). Of course, any writer or biologist or amateur kitchen scientist knows that even brilliantly designed experiments are not guaranteed to turn out the way we plan them. But in the case of writing, the risk of failure is a strength; the most valuable experiments are those which cede control over the results, setting something in motion that can transform, develop, continue moving on its own, with a life of its own. These are the experiments which open language to new possibilities, and which open us to new understandings of what it means to live in language with each other.

Often 'experimental' has meant linguistically nonnormative, even anti-lyric writing; think of Language Writing or Conceptual Poetry. But as Dorothy Wang reminds us, what has counted as experimental, formally innovative or avant-garde has long been determined by the standards of High Modernism, with its often-racialized assumptions – Wang points to Amiri Baraka's jazz poetics as an example of experimental work often excluded from the 'experimental' canon (2014: 32). Poet and critic Erica Hunt offers a fruitful alternative way of thinking about literary experiment and its camps (1990). She points out that there is a spectrum of 'oppositional' poetic modes that have been misunderstood as mutually exclusive: from the speculative language-based thinking which views language as 'social artefact' and as 'art material' (read: Language Writing) on the one hand, to the more lyric, liberatory poetics characteristic of what have often been described as identity-based or minority poetries, on the other. What unites the different modes, Hunt argues, is not only their 'critically active stance against forms of domination' (1990: 3), but the crucial fact that no matter their style or approach, they are all subject to the 'limitations of the society which they reproduce, even as they resist' (6). Experimental writing, understood as oppositional in Hunt's sense, seeks to expose, examine, invert or renegotiate those limitations we are subject to by virtue of living and writing in our society, here and now. Experimental, oppositional writing calls another society into being, not only *imagining* a future world before us but also *building* that world so that we can enter it. Some of the best contemporary examples are Douglas Kearney's visual poetry (*Sho* [2021]; *Buck Studies* [2016]; *The Black Automaton* [2009]) and performance recordings (*Fodder* [2021]); Don Mee Choi's 'errorist' poems and self-translations in

Hardly War (2016) and *DMZ Colony* (2020); Lillian-Yvonne Bertram's computational elegies in *Travesty Generator* (2019); and Layli Long Soldier's quilt poems, whose structure allows for multiple points of entry and near-infinite readings of a single poem (2017). Across their very different approaches, all these writers share a method in common: they foster intimate encounters between the writer, the reader and what the writer lets in by relinquishing control, acknowledging and welcoming the power of what cannot be anticipated.

Experimental writing involving chance operations and similar constraints has been around for a long time – Oulipo and other procedural practices come to mind. But contemporary practitioners of experimental, oppositional writing tend to think more explicitly of formal experimentation and linguistic materialism as ways to let the world into their work. Retallack calls this orientation 'poethical' writing (2003). Poethics, she argues, involves the Aristotelian concern with pursuing the good life as a life in common with others, linking the individual with the public ethos. In her terms, 'poetics can take you only so far without an *h* […] a poetics thickened by an *h* launches an exploration of art's significance *as*, not just *about*, a form of living in the real world' (2003: 26; original emphasis). To practice poethics, then, is to understand the stakes of our literary experiments as undergirding a broad field of activity which includes the whole of our activism, collaborations, community and intimate relationships, and activities of our daily lives as those activities accumulate, in concert with the activities of others, in pursuit of a life worth living in each other's company.

That company is not only human. Kristin Prevallet, building on Édoard Glissant, names as 'relational' the poetics which keeps our interconnectedness with non-human others in mind. The relational writer recognizes 'that one's self and one's poetics are mutable forms, moving among the multiplicities that constitute the world' (Prevallet 2003: 24–5). She writes not *above* the environment, but *through* it. Ultimately, such an experimental, relational mode of writing recalls the literary materialism characteristic of historical avant-gardes but complements it with an ecocritical materialism that acknowledges the ways agency is distributed among human and non-human, even non-living, entities in an interconnected, interdependent world. This mode ideally suits our present moment, with our ever-growing awareness of how the future will be shaped by the interactivity of human and non-human forces.

And really, if we are to make a future worth welcoming, we'll have to find ways to avoid the imaginative paralysis of what Lynn Keller calls 'scalar dissonance', the 'cognitive and affective dissonance' caused by the vast gap between the enormous collective impact we have as humans and our seemingly miniscule capacity as individuals to change anything for the better (2019: 49). Keller argues that formal and linguistic experimentation is a crucial resource in poetic attempts to imagine new, human-decentring paradigms and new ways of thinking about climate crises (2017: 66). She cites the work of Evelyn Reilly, Ed Roberson, Forrest Gander and Juliana Spahr, among others. To her list, I'd add Will Alexander, C. S. Giscombe, Craig Santos Perez and CAConrad, as poets who approach writing as an experimental practice oriented towards a world lived in common. For example, Conrad's trademark (Soma)tic Poetry Rituals are collaborative poem-writing exercises designed to help both writer and reader access what Conrad calls the 'extreme present' through sensory awareness (2014: xi). For Conrad, it's only through the creativity borne of this awareness that we can rise to our responsibility to each other and to the world. This work, like the best literary experimentation, understands the practical value of experiment as encounter with ourselves, each other and our world. Key, too, is the pleasure this sort of experimentation

Experimentation 67

yields, for the writer and for the reader – to return to Retallack, a pleasure like that which the swimmer finds in the very act that keeps her from drowning (2007). Experimentation is how we, as writers and as humans, keep ourselves alive and thriving as we look together towards our common future.

References

Bertram, L-Y. (2019), *Travesty Generator*, Blacksburg, US: Noemi Press.

CAConrad (2014), *Ecodeviance: (Soma)tics for the Future Wilderness*, Seattle: Wave Books.

Choi, D. M. (2016), *Hardly War*, Seattle: Wave Books.

Choi, D. M. (2020), *DMZ Colony*, Seattle: Wave Books.

Hunt, E. (1990), 'Notes for an Oppositional Poetics', in C. Bernstein (ed.), *The Politics of Poetic Form: Poetry and Public Policy*, New York: Roof Books. Available online: http://writing.upenn.edu/epc/library/Hunt-Erica_Politics-of-Poetic-Form_1990-2.pdf (accessed 12 January 2020).

Kearney, D. (2009), *The Black Automaton*, New York: Fence Books.

Kearney, D. (2016), *Buck Studies*, New York: Fence Books.

Kearney, D. (2021), *Sho*, Seattle: Wave Books.

Kearney, D. and V. Jeanty (2021), *Fodder*, Portland: Fonograph Editions.

Keller, L. (2017), *Recomposing Ecopoetics: North American Poetry of the Self-Conscious Anthropocene*, Charlottesville: University of Virginia Press.

Keller, L. (2019), 'Twenty-First Century Ecopoetry and the Scalar Challenges of the Anthropocene', in J. Gray and A. Keniston (eds), *The News from Poems: Essays on the Twenty-First Century American Poetry of Engagement*, 47–63, Ann Arbor: University of Michigan Press.

Long Soldier, L. (2017), 'Quilts', *Poetry Foundation*. Available online: https://www.poetryfoundation.org/poetrymagazine/articles/146882/quilts (accessed 22 November 2021).

Prevallet, K. (2003), 'Writing Is Never by Itself Alone: Six Mini-Essays on Relational Investigative Poetics', *Fence*, Spring/Summer: 19–31.

Retallack, J. (2003), *The Poethical Wager*, Berkeley: University of California Press.

Retallack, J. (2007), 'What Is Experimental Poetry and Why Do We Need It?', *Jacket*, 2 (32), April. Available online: http://jacketmagazine.com/32/p-retallack.shtml (accessed 28 May 2020).

Wang, D. (2014), *Thinking Its Presence: Form, Race, and Subjectivity in Contemporary Asian American Poetry*, Palo Alto: Stanford University Press.

SEE ALSO

Zim

Code

Bricolage

Facilitator

ALI COBBY ECKERMANN

Writing is like a church. A church has many personal and varied denotations. People know its intended purpose, yet many people do not attend. When I was young, I was very influenced by the constant reading of bible stories, and I still respect the premise of the Ten Commandments, the considerations of good and bad. As an adult I seek my spiritual solace through the practice of my Aboriginal culture and its teachings. This is a fulfilling and lifelong journey. In Australia we often have to research our history, due to the ongoing impact of colonization of Australia and the government practice of minimizing our cultural presence. Visits to my traditional country where my grandmother was born are mandatory for me. The benefits of these times are private and so personally rewarding. So, in my journey the concept of *church* has become an everyday occurrence. The influence of the old still lingers interwoven with the new. Good and bad are of equal understanding in both precincts, and I needed to decipher this. In my poetry and writings, I have become the facilitator between those two religious thoughts. Many of my truest friends have a dual identity, or perhaps a dual purpose. I believe everybody has a lived experience that heralds the pinnacle of their shift between young and old, when they began to stand in their own identity as a singular role. I think this is something that everyone shares in life, more enjoyable for some than others.

On random days for the sake of my writing, I lie down in my bed. I imagine that I am young and that in the distance nearby, around the kitchen table or in another room, the murmur of voices that belong to my older generation is drifting into my listening. Quietly, I lie there under the blankets, in the safeness of that, and gently massage my remembering. Slowly, I will recall a situation and reimagine what that murmur would contain. I love to capture the writings that come from those faint murmurs because they are not actual realities, but realisms of memory that are caught in my recall, by my imagination, that become my ownership. That role is the facilitator. I own that role of telling my story, my version of thought.

In my experience and journey as a poet/writer the role of facilitation has become more and more important. Self-facilitation assists to remove the detriment of ego and unnecessary words of judgement or justification. A true story should simply be. A true story should be free, allowing each and every reader to benefit from its telling, respecting each individual response. The absence of ego allows gifts to be shared, however humble, however foreign from one's own reality. A genuine gift can overcome the debris of modern-day prejudices, revealing routes over social mountains to new views of thought. Facilitation also comes from reading widely. Please encourage reading wherever you can!

In my view, facilitation also arrives from deep inner listening. This requires a process of trust. As mentioned, I climb under the blankets to find my place of safety, as trust is often difficult for me. Constantly I am reminded that I live inside a dominant invasion society of derogatory self-regard. Too often I am coaxed to edit or reduce my story. Too often I have felt nervous to tell my truth. My early writings were cathartic and fell onto the page. These were the unspoken words I had held within me for decades. It was the reunion with my mother and Yankunytjatjara family and senior people that released this volume from within. These are the true storytellers from the oldest cultural continuum on this planet. How blessed to belong here! Storytelling is an honour.

My understanding of facilitation has been deepened by my time in the desert with my family and friends and wider community. In the desert, conversation ebbs with time. It is a gift of belonging to be able to feel this, to see this. It is an ephemeral facilitation, where all hearts and minds are respected. It is more difficult for this facilitation to occur in the mainstream with the volume of media interjecting. I need to constantly check myself to limit the presence of electronic input in my life. I challenge myself to read more, and it is a constant challenge to prioritize my time, even when time has increased through the public restrictions of the Covid-19 pandemic.

Outside, in the realm of festivals and marketing and promotions the role of facilitator continues. For me, the public role of facilitator is a crucial skill. In my experience, the act of facilitation at festivals during panels often borders on rudeness. I believe a facilitator's role is to introduce and guide the listening, without the harshness of self-opinion. Some facilitators answer questions that are directed to the panellists from the audience. Other facilitators risk overstating the obvious, adding commentary between poems (e.g. *awesome, powerful*), ruining those precious seconds as our spoken words suspend in the air before infusing into audience consciousness. Whenever this occurs, I feel reminded that I live inside a dominant invasion society of derogatory self-regard. Unconsciously this can act as a tool to alter the impact or influence of story. Everybody has an individual and unique path of experience and living. Once interrupted the murmur and trajectory of faint thought are changed. **Please do not override my story with yours**.

For me, listening is the equivalent to white space on the page. This is the gift from the writer to pause, to consider, to reflect and to learn. When the white space is filled with an outsider's opinion, the intended impact of the discussion or reading is diminished. Sit in quietness and listen for thoughts. Write and remember it is a humble act. Be the facilitator in your own field and interpretation of literature. Enjoy the listening.

SEE ALSO

Camping
Rites
Listening

Fade out

STAYCI TAYLOR

Here is the offer: make like a screenwriter. Write as if to FADE OUT, rather than enshrining your words for eternity. Write as if posting to Snap Chat, not Facebook. Aim not for literature, but for 'literature in flux' (Sternberg 1997: 29).

If this all seems like a trick, it is. If this essay could be reduced to one commanding line of dialogue it might be:

DR TAYLOR
Let go of the outcome.

High fives to the scribes whose journeys have already divested from the destination. Read on those of us for whom 'process over product' is easier read than done.

When I say, 'make like a screenwriter', I mean, write as if each of your carefully chosen words is destined to disappear, to be subsumed by a new medium. 'Once the film exists, the screenplay is no more', writes Jean-Claude Carrière, 'it is fated to undergo metamorphosis, to disappear, to melt into another form, the final form' (1995: 148). In this way, the screenplay fades through the processes of production until it is effectively erased, its relationship to the film a 'troublesome ghostliness' (Price 2010: xi). Yet those lean sentences and strong verbs of the screenplay are hard won and delicately arranged, to 'not only communicate the story of the potential film but also, more importantly, how it should be visualised on the screen' (Ingelstrom 2014: 31). Perhaps traces remain, although to watch a screen work and say 'I can hear the writing' is not usually a compliment.

In my practice, I have struggled with the disposable nature of my words. One enduring memory is of an actor's improvised joke, replacing my scripted dialogue, later quoted by a TV critic as an example of my bad writing. All screenwriters have these stories. We understand that the screenplay represents a collaboration, is 'a location for, and partial description of that shared idea, representing a framework within which others will work' (Macdonald 2013: 5). To achieve this, conventional screenwriting practice is enacted in several stages and expressed in a series of documents. The planning phase requires dexterity in various forms of prose – from the story expressed in one line, to synopses of various lengths and then to the full 'treatment' detailing the whole story from which, only then, the script or screenplay will emerge. At this stage a whole new raft of rules applies. 'Given the linguistic demands that the screenplay forces upon writers', writes Steven Maras, 'it would be natural to think of the screenplay as a literary genre in its own right' (2009: 48). While the debate continues in screenwriting scholarship as to whether the screenplay should always be 'compared to its "intended" media, rather than as a discrete form with its own literary and poetic properties'

(Sherry 2014: 102), I wonder if the screenwriter's lot has a wider application for all of us in the business of arranging our words to be read.

For screenwriters, the words FADE OUT come at the end of the draft, but to fade out is not to end, rather to vanish with intent. Brian Eno has said of a pop song's fade out that it 'gives the impression that somewhere the music is still going on' (cited in Anderson 2021: 42:26–3:06). I offer FADE OUT as a method of deliberate disappearance for those of us whose progress is stalled by compulsive self-editing. Poets and prosaists for whom pages are always performance and never practice. Screenwriters whose 'vomit draft' is secretly a polished turd. Stalled shut-up-and-write writers for whom others' unbridled typing is but the sound of tiny tappers interpreting your shame through the medium of dance.

Embracing the FADE OUT is not the same as relinquishing effort. It's risking effort for no reward, investing in the fine but transitory work of your sand mandala before releasing it back to the sea. It's busting out your best moves for no audience. In *The Virtue of Forgetting in the Digital Age*, Viktor Mayer-Schonberger reminds us that the evolution of writing, and then the societal reforms of the twentieth century, created an external, shared, societal memory (2009). I propose that writing to FADE OUT is an act of defiance against the 'demise of forgetting' (Mayer-Schonberger 2009: 17) in an age where everything is recorded for posterity.

How to FADE OUT:

- First, practice. Finish a sand mandala. Okay, finish a jigsaw puzzle. Dismantle it immediately. Show no one. Do not post a photo to Instagram.
- Compose a poem in wet sand when the tide's coming in. Let the sea wash your words away. Do not post a photo to Instagram.
- Befriend a whiteboard (or, depending on your vintage, an Etch-a-Sketch, or a Mystic Writing Pad). Write, erase, repeat.
- Give away the stationery you've been 'saving for good'. Replace with something tear-away or spiral bound. Fill pages with a story that plays with literal definitions of 'fade', an intransitive verb meaning 'to change gradually in loudness, strength, or visibility' (Merriam-Webster Dictionary). Write to achieve peak vividness and then to dissolve. The result will be brilliant, pun intended, yet you'll dispose of it responsibly.
- Write a story using pen and paper. Make no copies. Mail it locally to an imaginary address, created by counting the words in your first sentence, and scrambling together the letters of your name and the story's title. Allow me to demonstrate: Dr Fay Tait, 8 Youlac St.
- Set up a private Twitter account. Tweet daily. Accept no followers.
- Make a pact with an actor. You'll write a monologue, they will learn it, you will both permanently delete all written copies. Organize one unrecorded live performance.
- Make a pact with a writer, working in another mode, to both write to be rewritten. You'll each rewrite the other in a different form. You'll ritually and responsibly dispose of the original. You're invited to be creative with the ways in which the original will 'sink away'.

Once sufficiently liberated by these acts of wilful erasure, you will likely crave indelibility. This is, of course, the point of such interventions and you may even wish to invert them.

What might it mean to write to FADE IN? You also may have cheated and committed to memory a vital description or witty turn of phrase that was too good to lose. This is also to be encouraged. FADE OUT aims to create the conditions for forgetting in order to enhance the value of what's remembered.

References

Anderson, L. (2021), *Spending the War without You, Lecture 1: The River*, The Norton Lectures, Department of History of Art + Architecture, Harvard University, 10 February.

Carrière, J-C. (1995), *The Secret Language of Film*, trans. J. Leggatt, London: Faber and Faber.

Ingelstrom, A. (2014), 'Narrating Voices in the Screenplay Text: How the Writer can Direct the Reader's Visualisations of the Potential Film', in C. Batty (ed.), *Screenwriters and Screenwriting: Putting Practice into Context*, 30–45, Basingstoke and New York: Palgrave Macmillan.

Macdonald, I. (2013), *Screenwriting Poetics and the Screen Idea*, Basingstoke and New York: Palgrave Macmillan.

Maras, S. (2009), *Screenwriting: History, Theory, Practice*, London and New York: Wallflower Press.

Merriam-Webster Dictionary (n.d.). Available online: https://www.merriam-webster.com/dictionary (accessed 1 June 2021).

Mayer-Schonberger, V. (2009), *Delete: The Virtue of Forgetting in the Digital Age*, Princeton: Princeton University Press.

Price, S. (2010), *The Screenplay: Authorship, Theory and Criticism*, Basingstoke and New York: Palgrave Macmillan.

Sherry, J. (2014), *Teaching Adapting Screenwriters: Adaptation Theory through Creative Practice*, Basingstoke and New York: Palgrave Macmillan.

Sternberg, C. (1997), *Written for the Screen: The American Motion-Picture Screenplay as Text*, Tübingen: Transatlantic Perspectives, Stauffenburg Verlag.

SEE ALSO

Erasure

Observation

Memory work

Feelings

ERIK KNUDSEN

In proposing feelings as method, I seek to draw attention to the intimate and delicate creative practices that lie at the heart of the ideation process. With this in mind, I will share two anecdotal experiences related to feelings and ideation, each bookended by an inspirational quote and a practical working axiom that I have derived from these experiences.

> Stories are the secret reservoir of values: change the stories individuals and nations live by and tell themselves and you change the individual and nations (Okri 1995: 21).

For my first anecdotal story, it is important to note that I am what most people call 'black'; I was born in Ghana to a Ghanaian mother and Danish father and grew up in Denmark and the UK from the age of five. When I was around twenty-two, some years ago, I submitted a short screenplay to Southern Arts in the UK for production funding. This was a regular middle-class story with no particular reference to race or other protected characteristics. I was shortlisted and went for an interview. When I walked into the room of exclusively 'white' people, I so distinctly remember their confused faces when they saw me walk in. They were clearly having trouble reconciling my name (a very Danish name), the colour of my skin and the nature of the story in front of them. At the end of the interview, they went to great lengths to tell me how much they liked me and that they thought I had a lot of promise etc. They insisted that I work with the Film Officer to put in a new application, which they strongly hinted would be looked at very favourably, as they didn't feel the one I had put in was quite the right one for me. When I met the Film Officer for my first meeting, it quickly became clear that he was encouraging me to tell a story about 'black problems' and 'black issues'. Suddenly I started seeing around me 'black' people guided into cultural ghettos, segregated by arts policies of well-meaning elites, condemned to a career of storytelling rooted in other people's idea of them as victims. After this realization, I decided not to pursue the development of any project with them.

Axiom: Don't let yourself be enslaved by other people's stories about you – especially not as an entrenched victim – and have the courage to free yourself from the bondage of other (often well-meaning) people's definitions and expectations. Don't become a mascot for other people's political agendas and other people's feelings of social guilt. Find your own independent authentic voice that only you are capable of feeling.

> Things are beautiful where they are inevitable, that is, when they are free exhibitions of a spirit (Suzuki 1996: 281).

In 1995, I completed a film for Channel Four Television in the UK entitled Reunion. A creative documentary freely mixing fiction and non-fiction technique, the film explored themes of psychic and mediumistic spirituality. All of the documentary aspects of the film revolved around the work of the spiritualist medium, Mavis Pittilla, who was well known in the field and taught at Arthur Findlay College, a college of spiritualism and psychic sciences in Essex in the UK.[1] During the year I spent researching her, I sat in on many of the training sessions she would run for others who felt they might have the gift. In one of these sessions involving about forty participants, she insisted I participate in workshop activities like everyone else. One component consisted of relating to colours through sight, touch and blind sense and writing down associations related to these colours. In my case, I had associated the colour brown with wealth. A little later in the workshop, some of us were selected to sit at the back of the room with our eyes closed, hold out our hands and wait for an anonymous person to emerge from the crowd, hold their hands a short distance from our hands, without touching, and then disappear back into the crowd. We were then asked to open our eyes and say something about the person who had held their hands close to ours.

While I had felt the presence of someone standing in front of me, I had absolutely no idea what to say about that person. Pittilla kept pressing me and the forty or so people were looking at me, expectantly. The pressure was on, and nothing was coming to mind. Eventually, Mavis decided to help me. She asked me what colour came to mind. At first, I had no idea, but then I decided just to say the first colour that came to mind: brown. And what had I associated with brown? Pittilla asked. Wealth, I remembered. That was all I could come up with. Eventually, Pittilla asked the woman who had stood with her hands close to mine while I had my eyes closed to stand up. She asked that woman if the notion of wealth had any connection to her. The woman said 'no' and was asked to sit down again. Pittilla turned to me and kept pressing. She kept asking me simply to say the first thing that came to my mind; something I was fighting. Eventually, I gave in and decided to just feel and imagine something and say it out loud. I created an imaginary mental picture in my mind that felt right and described it. I described a long driveway in southern England, lined by tall trees leading up to a manor house set in beautiful gardens. It felt right. I described seeing an old woman through a ground floor window, probably around ninety, playing a grand piano, while another old woman of a similar age sat nearby listening. I had simply made it all up, but somehow it felt right.

Mavis Pittilla asked the same woman to stand up again. She asked her whether she recognized any of this. The woman said 'yes'. While she herself was not wealthy, she had an old aunt who was. What I had described was her ninety-two-year-old aunt in her home. She was a keen pianist and often played music for her ninety-year-old friend. I was shocked. Pittilla then went on to explain that the distinction between imagination and reality is a false one, a construct that often presents barriers to seeing. This experience was to profoundly change my approach to ideation.

---

[1] It is worth noting that 'psychic' for Mavis Pittilla relates to sensory qualities that everyone, to varying degrees of awareness, possesses, whereas 'medium' relates to communication with deceased third parties, which only a few people were capable of engaging with.

Axiom: Have the confidence to let your feelings guide you to a place where the stories and images are not constrained within walled concepts and definitions and where there are no judgements about right and wrong. This is where the stories are waiting for you, the stories that belong to us all, but that only you can tell here and now. 'Make visible what, without you, might never have been seen' (Bresson 1977: 39).

References

Bresson, R. (1977), *Notes on Cinematography*, New York: Urizen Books.
Okri, B. (1995), *Birds of Heaven*, London: Weidenfield and Nicholson.
Reunion (1995), E. Knudsen (dir.), UK: One Day Films Ltd.
Suzuki, D. T. (1996), *Zen Buddhism: Selected Writings*, New York: Image Books.

SEE ALSO

Sensing
Imagination
Uncertainty

Flow

MARY CAPPELLO

When a friend of mine was dying, she told another friend who called to visit her that her call had come too late. She was 'already in the flow', our friend had said from the bardo[1] of her deathbed, 'she had already entered the flow', so she couldn't accept a visit. When I heard this story, I pictured a telephone with a coiled cord stretched between the two friends – no passing of cell phones for this exchange, but a cord attached to receivers that couldn't possibly reach far enough, the cutting of a second cord already in progress and set to drift.

And I wondered about what my dying friend was telling us: if we enter the flow when we die, where is it that we live? On the shore, beneath the sky, at the table or the lathe, in interruption? Before the cup and saucer, at the casement window, ascending the hill? In the envelope of voice and mood, does writing anticipate the flow or work to staunch it? Run against its current or alongside it?

Pausing to interrupt the workshop vernacular of flow – as in 'I like the way it flows' – I screech to breaking point: 'Menstrual blood flows', I say, and 'milk is expressed. Let us dispense, therefore, with the application of these terms to discussions of writing'. You'd think I was averse to the female body what with my examples of its effluvia, glistening or matte. 'The poet writes the history of his body', Henry Thoreau pronounced (or uddered) one liquid day before the invention of a sharpener for his pencil (1993: 246). Is it the Oscar parade of flowing gowns and ramrod suits that makes me want to forget my body when I write, or at least get past it? Or past some hetero norm of flows and sticks that break my bones and words that ever hurt me?

Where did this phrase come from – 'it flows'? From music and the assumption that all writing be lyrical. From the idea of writing as a craft set to glide on still waters. From a romance with a several century's old Coleridgean attitude of waft – Wordsworth's poetry as the 'spontaneous overflow of powerful feeling' (2004: 6). From assembly line culture and factory output. From electricity and tears.

One kind of flow makes another sort of flow possible. Flow begets flow as when the stark O of my friend's absence floods and drenches me. ('To set the eyes at flow': to cause to weep).

---

[1]See Eve Kosofsky Sedgwick's *The Weather in Proust* on the 'bardo of the dying' in Tibetan Buddhism: 'A privileged instance, but not the only one, dying is one among a group of states – also including meditation, sleep, and dreams – that are called bardos, gaps or periods in which the possibility of realization is particularly available. *Bar* in Tibetan means in between and *do* means suspended or thrown' (2011: 210).

One night I dream that dying is a coming into and out of consciousness until you can't find the energy to come in: the energy instead becomes you. It could have been a dream of how to stay asleep without dying, or an image repertoire for the stuttered breathing of my snoring. On a busy street, I might add, because the setting was a city thoroughfare, thick with noise and people, and I remember thinking in the dream, 'Why am I trying not to die on such a busy street? Why did I choose such an impossible place to die?'

The day before I had run into a friend and colleague whom I hadn't seen in some time. Just before noticing her, I had been fighting a sort of autism I occasionally experience in grocery stores, when, frozen by the sensory overload of rows of stacks of aisles of pyramids of vegetables and fruits, labels and prices and shapes, I temporarily freeze and forget what I have come for. Seeing D in a periphery partly broke my trance, and I wandered towards her, brightening, 'It's so good to see you!'

D and I had been diagnosed with breast cancer in the same year, so whenever we saw one another there was always a degree of checking in to the land of our living. Though D 'looked great', and seemed to be about her daily business, she said she wanted me to know that her cancer had metastasized. Pain flowed into her hands from her sternum, she explained: a sudden sign of cancer in her lungs and bones. She wanted me to hear this, she said; she wanted me just to know that cancer follows the flow of a pre-determined path we can never know.

There was no time to suggest we plan to get together, and at a certain point in the deepening of our conversation, I realized we were probably seeing each other for the last time. 'I have really enjoyed knowing you all these years', D said, hugging me, while streams of shoppers flowed around us, bumping into us. This was clearly no place for such a conversation. 'You're in the way!' one woman blurted as, embracing, we blocked access to the tomatoes and the kumquats, the grapefruit and asparagus.

Strangely, we didn't cry; we laughed a lot. We were in the bardo of the dying, our thoughts and words even our bodies on a plain apart from the bustle and flow.

See how beautifully this paragraph misses the boat of its calling. Tune your intelligence to the drip drip drip of your favourite novel's leak. I won't refuse the compliment of a piece of writing being compared to butter – also said of a second-hand cashmere sweater by a store proprietor in Rhode Islandese, 'It's just like *buttah*!' Here's to prose-like-butter better to pull the wool over the reader's eyes, and breasts, and groins. We read to get lost in the flow.

We want the writing to flow because we want writing to complete or satiate us – *complementi*! We want it to flow because we want when we read to be met even though we know we will never be met, not ever fully, not really, that we will only be met halfway. I want writing to meet me as a cascade of swirls. I want writing to take me on board for fear that life is passing me by. I want writing's surface to shimmer rather than reflect.

Writing isn't flow. It is mood modulations, fine-tunings or coarse. Writing is not a flow but a vibration, not a pulse but a recombinant re-chording: the song we sing, orchestrate or divine, the duration of a here, and here, and here.

If it must flow, then why not praise it for its murmur, that low indistinct continuous sound as of a stream. No sullen discontent of a half-articulate voicing, why not say of writing, 'it murmurs well', 'I like the way it murmurs'. I like the octave of its murmur, the hollow, hum and buzz. I love its bumbled hovering between spoken-ness and flight. The way I have to strain to hear it, like the sounds we have to bend to hear beneath the surface of audible flow: on the thither side of complaint, a joyous murmuration.[2]

References

Clive, W. and L. Smith, 'Murmuration', 2 December 2011 [video]. Available online: https://www.youtube.com/watch?v=iRNqhi2ka9k (accessed 16 May 2021).

Sedgwick, E. (2011), *The Weather in Proust*, Raleigh: Duke University Press.

Thoreau, H. (1993), *A Year in Thoreau's Journal*: 1851, London: Penguin Classics.

Wordsworth, W. (2004), '"Preface" to the Second Edition of *Lyrical Ballads* (1802)', in M. Kwasny (ed.), *Toward the Open Field: Poets on the Art of Poetry, 1800–1950*, 3–26, Middletown: Wesleyan University Press.

SEE ALSO

Atmospherics
Preposition
Paragraphing

---

[2]Thanks to poet Talvikki Ansel for introducing me to murmurations of starlings with Sophia Windsor Clive and Liberty Smith's beautiful Youtube video, *Murmuration* (2011).

Ghost Weaving

PAOLA BALLA

Ghost Weaving is a methodology I named in collaboration with Professor Tracey Bunda, Ngugi/Wakka Wakka scholar, to describe how I weave visual art, writing, family and community relationships, lived experience, community work, stories and bodies of work together. It speaks back and *Blak* (Perkins and Williamson 1994)[1] to patriarchy and colonialism, towards healing and epistemic justice, acts of resistance and repair, recovering and remembering.

In Ghost Weaving, I work from my standpoint as a Wemba-Wemba and Gunditjmara woman, in weaving story, art and writing in practice as research. I weave this with, for and through my matriarchal herstories and celebrate Blak women's resistance and sovereignty in and through art, community work, activism and writing. Ghost Weaving holds my art and stories in speaking Blak to the so-called white arts world and academia, and weaves legacy practices of Aboriginal women's sovereign research methodologies across diverse methods and the 'everywhen' (Gilchrist 2016: 19). I *ghost weave* to disrupt stale white colonial readings of Aboriginality and urban and rural white binaries with Blak continuous cultures of Country, as I come from the bush, live in the city/Naarm and traverse these spaces continuously.

By writing my intimate connections between these places I write myself into spaces from where my Peoples and I were and are erased. By writing and making art, I practice 'survivance' (Balla 2016: 32) named by Anishinaabe Chippewa scholar, Gerald Vizenor (2008: 1): not just surviving colonialism but thriving and making space for Indigenous sovereignty. I ghost weave memory spaces to hold the personal as political. I float back across time into memories and stories told to me and write them out urgently. I make art that is unapologetically Blak, sovereign, nostalgic and beautiful, that I want critiqued by Blackfullas (and anti-racist, educated non-Aboriginal settlers).

My matriarchs gifted me with stories, and these stories sit within my spirit like ghost memories waiting to be woven into the present. They require me to remember and assert my sovereignty with loving urgency because I have come to know that, 'to be sovereign is in fact to act with love and resistance simultaneously' (Balla 2017: 15). I have always 'researched' my survival and my matriarchs by observing them, listening to them, trying to

---

[1] In the catalogue for the 1994 exhibition, *Blakness: Blak City Culture* at the Australian Centre for Contemporary Art (ACCA), in collaboration with Boomalli Aboriginal Artist Co-operative, curators Clare Williamson and Hetti Perkins write, 'The term "Blak" was developed by Destiny Deacon as part of a symbolic but potent strategy of reclaiming colonialist language to create means of self-definition and expression' (1994: 20).

soak in everything about them because I was taught that respect and listening are central to our lives, and that time was fleeting for Blak women.

When I was unsure how to name this process, I made art. It made representable my experiences of colonial violence and traumas because the colony continually erases them. I make art and I write because, like Gloria Anzaldúa, I am 'more scared of not writing' (1981: 187) and express my sovereign voice in these practices. Asserting sovereign processes in practice-led research requires us to know our Blak knowledges and scholarship legacies, and challenge ourselves as researchers and artists and, to be open and grateful for Blak critique. Our relationships with our families, communities, Elders, children and Ancestors are embedded with ethics that colonial institutions fail to comprehend. We name and enact these ethics in our languages and ways of 'being, knowing and doing' (Martin and Mirraboopa 2003). Making art that responds to racism, violence and oppression requires the weaving together of multiple practices because racism functions across all spaces and places. I write and make art through a lens that responds to the functions and injuries of racism, sexism and classism; and I celebrate our Blakness in doing this.

Without romanticizing, healing, writing and story work is restorative, as opposed to wounding, as happens in institutions: 'Giving voice to our stories creates a healing, a knowing that our voices weave back into age-old traditions, enabling our bodies to thread seamlessly with the veracity of our spiritual selves' (Phillips and Bunda 2018: 107).

We are practised at dancing with genocide, resisting and disrupting the ongoing colonial project, and dedicated to sovereignty that can never be destroyed, as this is ontologically who we *are*.

The global pandemic and ongoing climate traumas are not new. They are repetitious disruptions experienced by Indigenous Peoples everywhere and 'everywhen' since colonizations.

Creating and practising Ghost Weaving has been a series of intimate revolutions. It has given me critical insights about my practice. Realizing more deeply that as Aboriginal Peoples, our Families and Ancestors have always been practice-led practitioners has been empowering. Going into story, with my Elders and mother in particular, has guided my ethics, processes and ability to share stories that I am part of, but don't own. I am responsible in not replicating harm, or exploiting my own People in telling stories, especially of trauma.

Naming myself, my people, family and standpoint in this process is central to grounding my work and being responsible for it. Being known and claimed by family, community and Mob means everything to me. Our genealogy as Aboriginal People is central to our 'ways of knowing, being and doing' (Martin and Mirraboopa 2003) and has to be protected from those attempting to replicate, appropriate or steal it.

In adapting 'practice-led research' for Ghost Weaving, as both art praxis, and the critical-analytical in writing, I bring my academic work into the service of Blak women's erased experiences. I don't want to have to constantly respond to and critique the western art canon, white exploitation, violence, appropriation and dominance in community and art institutions. But its unrelenting presence means I am required to.

In Ghost Weaving art and writing, I create rites of resistance in text and spaces to exist and honour the joy in Blakness and to embody unconditional love, Blak solidarity and express our sovereignty.

References

Anzaldúa, G. (1981), 'Speaking in Tongues: Letter to Third World Women Writers', in C. Moraga and G. Anzaldua (eds), *This Bridge Called My Back: Writings by Radical Women of Colour*, 163–72, Watertown, Massachusetts: Persephone Press.

Balla, P. (2016), 'Disrupting Artistic Terra Nullius, The Ways in which Aboriginal Women Artists and Activists Speak Back to Colonial Australia through Art', PhD thesis, Victoria University.

Balla, P. (2017), '*Sovereignty: Inalienable and Intimate*', in P. Balla and M. Delany (eds), *Sovereignty*, 13–17, Melbourne: Australian Centre for Contemporary Art, 17 December 2016 – 26 March 2017.

Gilchrist, S. (2016), *Everywhen: The Eternal Present in Indigenous Art from Australia*, Cambridge, Massachusetts: Harvard Art Museums.

Martin, K. and B. Mirraboopa (2003), 'Ways of Knowing, Being and Doing: A Theoretical Framework and Methods for Indigenous and Indigenist Re-search', *Journal of Australian Studies*, 27 (76): 203–14.

Perkins, H. and C. Williamson, eds (1994), *Blakness, Blak City Culture*, Melbourne: Australian Centre Contemporary Art.

Phillips, L. and T. Bunda (2018), *Research through, with and as Storying*, Oxon, New York: Routledge.

Vizenor, G. R. (2008), *Survivance: Narratives of Native Presence*, Lincoln, Nebraska: University of Nebraska Press.

SEE ALSO

Archival-poetics
Feelings
Ensemble

Hybrid

MARION MAY CAMPBELL

Hybrid, or cross-genre works characteristically present the writing of resisting subjects. It's not surprising that contemporary practitioners are usually culturally and politically marginalized, feminists or non-cis gender-aligned, identifying somewhere along the LGBTQI+ spectrum. For Kaplan (1992), the hybrid work is an 'outlaw': frequently within autofictional practice, traversing and mixing genres, modes and registers, in an overtly citational fabric. Many hybrid practitioners refuse to mystify representation as a reflection of a pre-given reality, but draw the reader into co-production, a process as intersubjective as it is inter-textual. Generally, hybrid works refuse closure, eschewing the tidy ending, contesting the teleological fix of, say, novels continuing the nineteenth century realist tradition. Relativizing perceived 'events' through the generic mix, the hybrid work offers no sure position from which truth or secure knowledge can be guaranteed. It's anti-authoritarian and the stable omniscient narrator is thus antithetical to its ethics and politics. For instance, Kathy Acker's hybrid novels (1984, 1986) and essays (1997) flaunt carnivalesque parody and wild cross-genre traffic. Acker draws on myriad texts from de Sade, Foucault, Bataille, to Burroughs, Genet and Deleuze, raiding them 'plagiaristically', parodying the family romance (through literalization of incestuous possession) and in particular, the *Bildungsroman*, in a sustained attack on patriarchal capitalism and its endless sexualized sites of consumerism.

Often, in hybrid work, suffering generates tropes that 'open holes which representational constructions of the subject would elide' (Hulley 1992–1993: 33). In fact, the poetics driving a hybrid text implies an unstable or even splintered subjectivity, in imperilled emergence from the trauma of patriarchal capitalism. Another remarkably potent hybrid work is Austrian poet and novelist Ingeborg Bachmann's *Malina* (2006 [1971]). The range of genres, through which *Malina*'s 'I-persona' is refracted and splintered, includes epistolary, libretto, playscript, philosophical dialogue, questionnaire, folk fairy tale, dream narrative and terminal echoes of *Antigone*. This tessellation of multi-generic fragments performs a protest against the pre-occupation of the 'writing I' ('*das schreibender Ich*' Bachmann qtd in Paul 2009: 75) by the violent phallocracy informing Nazism that is re-enacted in familial and intimate relations.

The poetics of formal fragmentation through cross-genre montage is intimately linked to a crisis in witnessing. Subjects who endure extreme trauma do not survive intact. They are, so to speak, para-sited, thrown alongside themselves and it is especially in the navigation of the interstices or fault lines between the cross-genre fragments that the implications of traumatic experience can be read. In the hybrid text, if there's *jouissance* or pleasure for the reader, it is usually coterminous with the shipwreck of identity.

Possibly one of the most influential 'outlaw' works of fictocritical autofiction has been Gloria Anzaldúas's *Borderlands/La Frontera: The New Mestiza* (2007 [1987]), whereby she formally performs 'in-betweenness', or her lived liminality, as both exile and enablement – in language (Spanish and American English), in geopolitical space (between Mexico and the United States), in gender (Lesbian identification 'outlawed' within Chicano culture) and, of course, through the oscillation between feminist, postcolonial and cultural theory and a practice of poetry, running the gamut from the fragmented and 'holed' inscription of traumatizing erasure to the jubilatory assertion of resistance.

Other outstanding hybrid and highly influential works are Roland Barthes (2010), Nicole Brossard (2006 [1982]; 2010), Marguerite Duras (2008 [1991]), Maggie Nelson (2015) and Zimbabwe-born Lesley Stern (1999), whose stylish navigation of different genres within the one work crosses several continents.

In Australian Quinn Eades's *all the beginnings* (2015), the traumatizing *rupture* within the sexual self, foreshadowing his transition, is written though abject leakages and enacted through genre-hopping: theory, lyric, prose poetry, auto-fictional account. The generic mosaic is somatized or troped as the abject *outing* of the inside: 'Ruptures where [they] learn to stop fearing the leak that is the body, to let what is inside be out; to step, anatomically disordered, remapped, into the next day' (204). Here, the writing from the wounded and endlessly reinscribed body is never just a narcissistic adventure of one. The reader is addressed always as intimate other, as if born again and again differently in the fold of the writer's ear.

From her first book *Writing* (1980), Polish-born Australian Ania Walwicz's experimental prose poetry has continued to make huge impact, repurposing a variety of discourse genres and modes for carnivalesque critique and resistance, in defiance of the marketplace of consumable story. In her *horse* (2018), the subject-in-process pushes consumption to its bulimic limits in protest against violence incarnated in a tsar figure, both father figure and rapist. Later, *horse* is pitched against the very theorist of *Nachträglichkeit*, or belated traumatic memory, Sigmund Freud, whom Walwicz triumphantly unseats at the end, pronouncing, 'I am the writer, actor, and director now. I am the supervisor. I am the Doctor' (Walwicz 2018: 159). Throughout *horse* Walwicz jostles registers and citations from cultural and literary theory, psychoanalysis, high literature, folk fairy tale, cinema, pop music and news media accounts.

Still in the Australian context, the works of Kathleen Mary Fallon (2000 [1989]), Dominique Hecq (2020), Peta Murray (2017) and First Nations Gomeroi poet Alison Whittaker (2020 [2018]) provide brilliant examples of hybrid poetics. Fallon and Whittaker, in particular, deploy fiercely parodic takes on a range of misogynist, homophobic, racist and nationalistic discourse genres to lay bare – with hilarity and rage – the smooth and often murderous rhetoric of whitefella entitlement.

It's through such trans-generic, self-interruptive tactics that the hybrid text can write back, performing radical resistance to internalized oppression, or what one can call intimate gaslighting. If it offers no solutions – beyond radical un-settlement, along with *jouissance* – poetically, hybrid inventiveness can perform unforgettably searing acts of defiance and critique.

References

Acker, K. (1984 [1978]), *Blood and Guts in High School*, New York: Grove Press.

Acker, K. (1986), *Don Quixote*, New York: Grove Press.

Acker, K. (1997), *Bodies of Work*, London: Serpent's Tail.

Anzaldúas, G. (2012 [1987]), *Borderlands/La Frontera: The New Mestiza*, San Francisco: Aunt Lute Books, 25th Anniversary 4th Edn.

Bachmann, I. (1990), *Malina*, trans. P. Boehm, afterword M. Anderson, Teaneck, New Jersey: Holmes and Meier Publishers.

Bachmann, I. (2006 [1971]), *Malina*, Frankfurt am Main: Suhrkamp Verlag.

Barthes, R. (2010 [1975]), *A Lover's Discourse: Fragments*, trans. R. Howard, New York: Hill and Wang.

Brossard, N. (2006 [1982]), *Picture Theory*, trans. B. Godard, Montréal: Guernica Editions.

Brossard, N. (2010), *Selections*, Jennifer Moxley, ed. and intro, Berkeley, CA: University of California Press, Poets for the Millennium Series.

Duras, M. (2008 [1991]), *The North China Lover*, trans. Leigh Haffrey, New York: New Press.

Eades, Q. (2015), *All the Beginnings: A Queer Autobiography of the Body*, Melbourne, Australia: Tantanoola, Australian Scholarly Publishing.

Fallon, K. M. (2001 [1989]), *Working Hot*, Sydney: Viking.

Hecq, D. (2020), *Kaosmos*, Melbourne: Melbourne Poets Union, Blue Tongue Poets Series.

Hulley, K. (1992–3), 'Contaminated Narratives: The Politics of Form and Subjectivity in Marguerite Duras' *The Lover*', *Discourse* 15 (2): 39–50.

Kaplan, C. (1992), 'Resisting Autobiography: Out-Law Genres and Transnational Feminist Subjects', in S. Smith and J. Watson (eds), *De/Colonizing the Subject: The Politics of Gender in Women's Autobiography*, 115–38, Minneapolis: University of Minnesota Press.

Murray, P. (2017), 'Essayesque Dis/memoir: w/rites of elder-flowering', PhD Thesis, School of Media and Communication, RMIT. Available online: https://core.ac.uk/download/pdf/83608312.pdf (accessed 11 November 2020).

Nelson, M. (2015), *The Argonauts*, Minneapolis: Graywolf Press.

Paul, G. (2009), *Perspectives on Gender in Post–1945 German Literature, Part II*, Woodbridge, UK: Boydell and Brewer.

Stern, L. (1999), *The Smoking Book*, Chicago: Chicago University Press.

Walwicz, A. (1980), *Writing*, Melbourne: Rigmarole Press.

Walwicz, A. (2015), *Horse*, Crawley: University of Western Australia Publishing.

Whittaker, A. (2020 [2018]), *Blakwork*, Broome, Western Australia: Magabala Books.

SEE ALSO

Bricolage

Erasure

Juxtaposition

Imagination

PAULA MORRIS

In a talk she gave in 1998, to a writers' conference in Manoa, Hawai'i, Patricia Grace spoke of writing fiction as an 'attempt to push out the edges of understanding what we know'. Fiction, Grace said, 'can't just have a head […] There has to be a body so it can have a head. There has to be a body so there can be heart, gut and soul' (2021: 201–2). Yet too often fiction writers prioritize the head over the body: the idea for a piece of work, or the ideas informing that work, rather than the work itself.

An idea suggests thinking, a break-through moment when something nebulous within a writer's unconscious surges into the clear, clever, conscious world of the mind and transforms into concrete thought. Thought leads to action, and seems more formed, and therefore useful, than dreaming or daydreaming, our sensory experience of the world, or memory – which may be flotsam or jetsam, or both. The question 'where do you get your ideas?' assumes that ideas, or their prompts, are lying about in public places or featured in shop windows. They are something to be acquired, and possibly borrowed, even stolen.

Writing does not depend on expressing feelings or having ideas, though both these things may be useful in our actual lives. More useful to the writer is the daydream. When 'we sit down to write', contends Orhan Pamuk, 'it is our daydreams that breathe life into us [… We] surrender to this mysterious wind like a captain who has no idea where he's bound'. The captain will still retain a 'general sense of direction' but can embrace both changes of course and 'moments of mist and stillness' (2007: 6–7).

Sometimes emerging writers talk about an 'idea' for a story when really, they mean they have a subject, as Chekhov described *Three Sisters* while he was busy writing it, or a premise – which is a 'what if?', and therefore an opening question rather than an idea (1973: 359).

When we valorize ideas, we place thinking, rather than instinct and imagination, at the centre of our creative practice. If we believe we can think our way into, and through, a work of art, we're informed by the approach of a critic rather than the art of a creator. Our manuscripts may execute or explore an idea, but they will be all head and no body – a body formed with language and drawing on experience and imagination.

What may be lost is an overall artistic vision, a sense of the work as a complex whole, a body of disparate parts that works in a three-dimensional way on the page. Ideas are not enough in a creative work that depends on words on the page.

'Remember that mediocrity', Nabokov warned, 'thrives on "ideas"' (1973: 66).

Inspiration is something we're supposed to have, in order to write something in particular, or to write at all. First, we must find it. It's often described as celestial, descending from on high to bestow its gift. 'Waiting for inspiration to strike' suggests it's a thunderbolt or flash of lightning hurled by some violent deity.

In reality, inspiration is an aspirational notion, like 'quality time' or 'self-care'. An urge to write sometimes translates as motivation, sometimes desperation. It requires action because thinking about writing is not the same as writing the words themselves. The urge to write something in particular may take hold of us at work, on holiday, at the super-market. It rarely illuminates the garret in which we sit holding our quill pen, in a green haze of absinthe, because contemporary writing lives rarely conform to the romantic writer-in-garret dream. Writers' residencies are the closest we get to a room of our own, and they are for a set amount of time: this cannot be idled away waiting for inspiration to materialize.

The belief that inspiration is a necessary first step – hand-in-hand with an idea, skipping about together, smug and elusive – stops a writer from getting on with work. An absence of inspiration is blamed for writer's block, for procrastination, for lack of progress. But inspi-ration if we must use that term, exists within us, all the time. On a walk or daydreaming, at home or somewhere distant and new, something within us will coalesce and we'll experi-ence an urgent desire to write. Once we're writing, the spark may seem more like a squib, but that doesn't matter. The main thing is to write, and to allow our instincts as writers to lead the way.

We develop the instinct for narrative as small children, listening to stories. We grasp the shape of a tale, the tension, the twists, the need for some kind of resolution.

Some writers talk about instinct as writing from the gut. It's a sense that's developed through listening, reading and writing. Too often we focus on the external – the lightbulb of an idea, the lightning-flash of inspiration, the feedback of peers and editors – and shut out the internal: instincts, memories, the subconscious. Notice the bright imagery around ideas and inspirations. The internal is darker and murkier. Instinct is almost an ache, a warning twisting in your stomach.

Waking and dreaming, Witi Ihimaera writes, are 'worlds that balance each other. One is an ordinary world and the other, by virtue of its amazing dimensionality, is the extraordinary world' (2014: 357). The imagination is part of our dream selves, a surge from the uncon-scious. Like dreaming, it's extraordinary in its scope and possibilities, and the way it feeds on and subverts our waking lives. 'I make the new world', says Pamuk, 'from the stuff of the known world' (2007: 5). Our imaginations are contained inside us despite their vast size and endless potential to transform, transcend and grow.

Without imagination, the fiction writer is doomed to banality. Research may be helpful, but no substitute. 'What I do in the writing of any character is to try to enter the mind, heart, and skin of a human being who is not myself', Eudora Welty wrote in the preface to her *Collected Stories*. '[The] primary challenge lies in making the jump itself. It is the act of a writer's imagination that I set most high' (1998: 829).

Our imaginations must leap. It is not always easy. This is the crucial work of the writer, and demands we are prepared to embrace the dream worlds of our stories, with all their uncertainties. We imagine our work into being, and when there are flaws to address in revision, our imaginations devise other possibilities. Without imagination our work will never soar – or, as Pamuk would have it, cross the sea, sails filled 'with a wind from an unknown quarter' (2007: 8). Both images, of soaring and sailing, suggest travel and its

Imagination 87

uncertainties. Words map the route, and record what cannot be known, only imagined, in advance.

References

Chekhov, A. (1973), Letter to V. I. Nemirovich-Danchecnko [November 24, 1899], *Letters of Anton Chekhov*, ed. Avrahm Yarmolinsky, New York: Viking Press.

Grace, P. (2021), *From the Centre: A Writer's Life*, Auckland: Penguin New Zealand.

Ihimaera, W. (2014), *Māori Boy: A Memoir of Childhood*, Auckland: Vintage New Zealand.

Nabokov, V. (1973), *Strong Opinions*, New York: McGraw Hill.

Pamuk, O. (2007), 'The Implied Author', in *Other Colours: Essays and a Story*, trans. M. Freely, New York: Alfred A. Knopf.

Welty, E. (1998), 'Preface to Collected Stories', in *Stories, Essays and Memoirs*, New York: Library of America.

SEE ALSO

Flow

Feelings

Hybrid

Iterative thinking

AMES HAWKINS

Iterative thinking, as artistic practice, involves the repetition of creative processes, approaches and methods. The repeated practice accumulates in/as a series of exercises, actions, activities, works, movements, pieces, images, postures, possibilities and/or objects, thereby allowing the writer and/or artist and/or poet to see, create and/or reveal something a/new.

Iterative thinking involves embodied, meditative practices intended to build knowledge about the relationship between the artist's body and their body of work. The repetition of any particular artistic practice accumulates both as body-knowledge and as the writing/work.

An iterative artist – an artist that purposefully engages in iterative thinking as a part of their practice – often focuses on form and/as their content. The work created evolves as a study of the repetitive process itself. Think Wayne Koestenbaum's trance writing (2015) and Ray Johnson's letter art (2014).

Iterative thinking, as a term, is a bit misleading because the artist and/or writer and/or poet doesn't merely turn ideas over, under, around and through their mind, though this sort of elliptical thought often occurs. Iterative thinking always involves some sort of 'doing' that allows the individual to process and consider a term, topic, idea, image, sensation, colour and/or mood in a methodical way. Examples of the repeated practice include, but are never limited to: walking, dancing, yoga and drag performance; journal writing, automatic writing, asemic writing and letter writing; painting, sketching, drawing and illustration; knitting, stitching, macramé and embroidery; pottery, photography, beading and mosaic; poetry.

Iterative thinking is one's creative process understood as research methodology. It is both a practice of discovery and the means by which we come to discover how our own processes of writing and making work.

Iterative thinking is not the same as magical thinking, though they share a belief in the power of serendipity as catalytic force. With magical thinking, a person may draw fantastical conclusions from a single pair of unrelated moments. *I saw five yellow bikes and five yellow finches, so this is a good day for writing.* They may attribute success or failure based upon ritualized superstition. *I only have success submitting work for publication when wearing my green underwear.* The conclusions are oftentimes completely inaccurate and unreliable, but magical thinking reveals the possibility for body-knowledge-as-self. Iterative thinking pushes into such possibility through repeated disciplined embodied practice which accretes as an aperture through which writer and/or artist, may come to recognize new possibilities for the same image, object, set of facts, objects and/or self.

Iterative thinking is not the same as Heidegger's meditative thinking, though they both share a foundational belief in creative processes that allow us to remain open to mystery.

Meditative thinking, Heidegger argues, 'demands of us not to cling one-sidedly to a single idea, nor to run down a one-track course of ideas. Meditative thinking demands of us that we engage ourselves with what at first sight does not go together at all' (1966: 57). Iterative thinking returns repeatedly to a similar set of practices that anticipate nuance as data, unexpected combinations as future illuminations we will know at first sight/site.

Iterative thinking is not the same as design thinking, though there is some overlap. Design thinking, in its broadest sense, engages in ideation and the testing of different iterations for the purpose of problem solving. Artists, poets and writers may be interested in addressing large-scale social problems, but the notion of offering a solution is rarely the point. Their creative practice is usually employed to challenge, defy, explode, explore, reveal, translate, transmogrify and offer apocalyptic framing (i.e. a great unveiling) for any usual, standard or straightforward understanding of the problem itself.

I engage in iterative thinking through a constellation of artistic and writerly practices that allow me to investigate the wonder and limits of intimacy, and the mercurial alchemical power of the line. Among my iterative practices are mosaic, needlepoint and *vox pop* audio editing. The repetition of stitching single pixels of thread on a canvas, practising *andamento* with tesserae, placing bits of recorded audio in a series of juxtapositions are all embodied artistic practices that allow me to think through what it means to bring words together in sentences, sentences into paragraphs, paragraphs into transgenre forms. As I select, juxtapose and organize squares of rock and glass, individual linear stitches, abrupt and isolated seconds of recorded audio into visual and audio art, I better understand the syntactical and grammatical and aural movement of prose, the secrets of (my) line.

Central to my practice of iterative thinking is letter writing. I wrote letters to three other individuals during the course of writing this entry on iterative thinking. I didn't talk much about iterative thinking in these letters. It was the form, the connection to language and love that I could access through the letter writing that was most important. I wrote to them as a way of opening myself an imaginative space in which I could most easily write this piece for you.

Iterative thinking is visible in many poetic definitions. My two favourite ones are 'Uses of the Erotic: The Erotic as Power', by Audre Lorde (2007), and 'Trans Poetics Manifesto', by Joy Ladin (2013). Random iterative thinking exercise: read these pieces and then write a letter to each author; read the pieces and then write a letter to me.

Iterative thinking is not the same as queer thinking, though they both constellate inside my queer body through the practice of letter writing.

Iterative thinking is the catalyst for alchemical writing. Alchemical writing transforms syntax into sensation, translates grammar into goddess, transmutes punctuation by design.

Dear Audre, Thank you for your gift of revealing to me the power of the erotic in my iterative thinking.

Dear Joy, Thank you for revealing the ways trans poetics allow us me to constantly reimagine my writing in/as my cells and/as my-selves.

Dear Iterative Thinking, Thank you for practice and process. I had a ton of fun! Let's make sure to do it all again sometime very soon!

xo

Ames

References

Heidegger, M. (1966), *Discourse on Thinking*, trans. J. Anderson and E. Freund, New York: Harper and Row.

Johnson, R. (2014), *Not Nothing*, ed. E. Zuba, Los Angeles: Siglio.

Koestenbaum, W. (2015), *The Pink Trance Notebooks*, Brooklyn: Nightboat Books.

Ladin, J. (2013), 'Trans Poetics Manifesto', in T. Tolbert and T. Peterson (eds), *Troubling the Line: Trans and Genderqueer Poetry and Poetics*, 306–7, Brooklyn: Nightboat Books.

Lorde, A. (2007), *Sister Outsider: Essays and Speeches*, Berkeley: Crossing Press.

SEE ALSO

Zim

Bung wantaim

Yoga

Juxtaposition

WENDY S. WALTERS

Juxtaposition is the act of placing literary elements in a work side-by-side or in rapid succession for the sake of emphasizing them in comparison. The effect is complex as it brings attention to similarities and differences at the same time.

Two persons enter a cafe at the same moment. There is one table and one chair still available. A bluebird also enters the cafe. The radio plays a song, but the bird sings more loudly. One person grabs the radio and turns the dial up. The other person winks at the bird, provoking it to sing louder. The bird and the radio are perfectly matched in volume.

Juxtaposition creates multiple trajectories in a narrative, even one based on facts, by directing attention to outcomes that are beyond the scope of the work at hand. The space between ideas may come across in the larger work as a pivot, a bridge, a leap in logic, or other manifestations of connection on a material or conceptual level.

Our persons now find themselves in an argument about volume in the cafe. The argument grows heated then turns into a fistfight. The fistfight turns into an embrace. Our two persons are suddenly weeping in each other's arms. They whisper to one another that they have a secret to share. Or perhaps, this is not what happened at all. Maybe, instead, as their argument grows, each person storms out of the cafe. One turns right. One turns left. Their rage dissipates with every step they take away from each other.

Juxtaposition is one way an objective, for example 'the desire to uncover the truth', might stand beside a suggestion, for example 'the truth is obvious to those who pay attention' that implies shared purpose and introduces the nuances of understanding. In this context, viewpoints that vary or contrast within a broader idea help express its complexity.

A person might whisper to themselves, under their breath, 'I am the winner', only to follow with statement that negates it, such as: 'Even if I am the loser'. This tight sequence of antithetical statements charges the reader with the task of imagining conditions in which both statements might be true. This may require the reader to temporarily suspend disbelief or engage their imagination so that the two statements can be held aloft simultaneously.

The mechanism of juxtaposition is proximity, and its impact should not be underestimated especially when a lyric or narrative requires the writer to marshal literary elements of a story that might be unfinished, irresolute, or fulgent with mystery.

A person walks to the bus stop, dejected and alone. On their shoulder sits a small blue bird that sings loudly. A car pulls up. Someone with a familiar face rolls down the window. The radio is blasting. 'Get in', they shout. Followed by, 'Please'.

Juxtaposition is also the act of arranging or moving literary components or actions next to each other. It is gesture of compression through placement and design. It can amplify the abstraction of the literary elements.

One person sits next to another in a car. Two persons travel on a blacktop road. They hardly know each other, but they want to impress the other. They stick out their chins, puff out their chests. Ahead, a fork in the road. One path winds up the mountain. The other ends at its base. A song plays on the radio, 'This is not the only island. This. Is. Not. The. Only. Island'.

Juxtaposition can also collapse time.

One person will run up the mountain. The other will fall down the mountain. Or will it be the other way around? This is how they might be linked in time – sequentially or synchronously – and in that relatedness they impact how realistically their actions are perceived.

Juxtaposition may also happen as a list, which creates a progression of ideas in a closed set that is the list itself. A list indicates the design of a system of related actions, objects, or ideas though without arguments or explanations that detail why they are so. A list also can suggest progress or evolution, though again without including the incidental steps to rationalize the associations. This does not mean that juxtaposition lacks or represents a failure in logic, rather it is a means for establishing logic where it might not be intuitively apparent to the broadest audience. In this way, it is a kind of formal insistence that there is an abstract connection between literary elements.

> Person. Person. Cafe. Chair.
> Table. Bluebird. Bus stop. Care.
> Blacktop. Bluster. Mountain. Air.

Outside of plot, juxtaposition can bring disparate actions, objects or ideas together to form a picture that can only exist as the sum of its components. This is another way it functions to inspire conceptual thinking alongside concrete examples.

A voice on the radio says, 'The Bluebird Cafe, one of the oldest businesses on the South Island, is where one can purchase a ferry ticket. It sits at the foothills of an ancient volcano frequented by tourists and locals alike. But travel has been down between the islands in the last few months due to the unpredictability of an active volcano on the North Island. The good news is that the warm waters of the strait have become a nursery for sharks, whose population, now growing, suggests there is an overall improvement in the conditions of the water.'

Juxtaposition can put actions, objects or ideas in line of sight with each other, which can imply or suggest collaboration or the eventual possibility of it, even if it is not likely, even if there is no established reason for those bits and pieces to come together. Suddenly another way of seeing the world is possible and come together those bits and pieces do.

SEE ALSO

Bricolage

Braiding

Preposition

Keepsake

FIONA MURPHY

Keepsakes became a part of my writing process while working on my memoir about deafness (Murphy 2021). I found myself creating spreadsheets, timelines and mind maps. I constructed detailed outlines of each chapter. I discussed at length with my editor the 'key turning points' of my narrative. But still, I couldn't shepherd my manuscript towards any kind of chronicity. My brain buckled and resisted the task; eventually even my grasp of tenses became tenuous. From sentence to sentence I skidded from the past to present to future. I had become lost in time.

Sociologist Barbara Adam suggests that time is never straightforward, but rather it is a force that acts upon us, within us and is wielded by us. Time is visceral and hot-blooded. It is far messier: 'Humans are time binding, time transcending and time controlling beings' (Adam 1990). Scientific research backs this up, with neuroscientist Dean Buonomano taking these ideas beyond the philosophical towards physics, physiology and evolutionary biology in his book *Your Brain is a Time Machine* (2017).

We continuously slip through time, daydreaming in Zoom meetings or reminiscing at the kitchen sink. How our brains travel through time is quite startling. Whether we are recalling the past or imagining the future, the process is the same. We even engage the same neural networks. Perhaps it is no wonder my sense of time had become increasingly tangled during the writing process. I spent hours recalling events in exquisite detail and equally as much time contemplating unrealized fears and desires.

Adam writes that while we cannot control time, historically humans have always sought to harness time through storytelling, ephemera, institutions, pleasantries and protocol (Adam 1990). In wanting to please my editor, I too, began to seek control. But now, instead of looking at Excel spreadsheets, I cast my gaze around my home looking for artefacts.

I gathered together a series of small commonplace objects to mend and reorientate my brain. Objects that I could hold. Objects that could release a wellspring of feeling. Objects that could transport me cleanly and quickly to the past or future. Each object was like a timestamp, imbued with feeling, memory and intention.

Soon I had amassed a series of unintentional keepsakes: a milky glass bottle, a blue button, a lightly gnawed biro a tea-stained mug, a travel journal containing only four pages of notes made eight years earlier, a fleecy jacket. They weren't anointed with the qualities of amulets but had quietly accrued as the slow debris of living. And this is what made them exceptional. Each item was a link to a previous version of myself.

The glass bottle: picked up from the street kerb whilst walking home after a devastating hearing test. The tea-stained mug: filled and drained every morning following my diagnosis of otosclerosis. The pen: teeth gnawing, nervous and fretful about how I would write about my deafened body. By keeping these everyday objects within reach, I could simply touch them and slip backwards in time.

I suspect that the best keepsakes aren't selected but recognized. In every instance they carry a quality, a feeling of residence within an idea or experience. Emily Maguire, author of the novel *Love Objects*, believes that 'most people do have some kind of real attachment to things that isn't about the usefulness of those objects' (James and Ashley). This relationship is as much with oneself as it is with the object. Maguire suggests that this is because '[o]bjects don't change. They don't contest your version of events and your memories' (James and Ashley).

Our brains, however, can distort and trouble our sense of time, for instance they can edit and erase trauma in an act of self-preservation. Traumatic memories have, as trauma therapist Judith Herman explains, 'a kind of "frozen wordless" quality to them. They lack context, they lack narrative. They are pure sensation or image. Traumatic memories are fragments, not fully formed stories. How then do you write about trauma? How do you write about trauma and time?' (Carey 2020).

Before setting out to write my memoir, I hadn't considered my experiences of deafness as traumatic. But it would take months, if not years of recursive writing, for me to realize that these were the only memoires within my purview. In attempting to construct a clear narrative thread, I discovered how skittish my brain behaved, how many memories had retreated from view.

In writing her memoir, *No Matter Our Wreckage*, Carey imagined her life like a deck of cards, with each card representing a different memory or sensation. The physicality of this approach, transposing thought onto and into physical objects, allowed her to gain a sense of control over time: 'Place them on the table and take one off the top, then another and another until the table is scattered with them [...] you might see patterns, connections – a story emerging. But they don't come out in a neat order' (Carey 2020). Carey discovered that externalizing the events of her life, safeguarding them within playing cards, allowed her to control time.

I followed a similar approach, but instead of cards, I looked through my wardrobe. A navy blouse, covered in blue buttons, resulted in a sudden shock of sound – I had been wearing it the day I first slipped hearing aids on. A fleecy jacket that a police officer asked if it could be sent for forensic testing following a sexual assault. Terrible truths appeared, filling in the gaps of my narrative.

To come to the page armed with keepsakes offers me a sense of security – consciously and unconsciously – I am no longer entering a vast, empty space but rather I am ready to springboard into a memory or feeling. With that 'mess' of seemingly mundane objects, I could re-enter my memoir regardless of how tired or wired I was feeling.

Now, for each new project, regardless of its length, I identify and catalogue the slip-streams – symbolic language, technology, artefacts: keepsakes – that will pull me back to *that* feeling of safety and potential on the page.

References

Adam, B. (1990), *Time and Social Theory*, Cambridge: Polity Press.

Buonomano, D. (2017), *Your Brain Is a Time Machine: The Neuroscience and Physics of Time*, New York: Norton.

Carey, G. (2020), 'Writing about Trauma Is Hard, but Not Always in the Ways You'd Think', *Canberra Times*, 19 September. Available online: https://www.canberratimes.com.au/story/6924026/writing-about-trauma-is-hard-but-not-always-in-the-ways-youd-think/ (accessed 23 November 2021).

James and Ashley Stay at Home (2021), 'Love and Hoarding with Emily Maguire, Author of *Love Objects*', [podcast], Ep 27 (27 April), https://jamesandashley.libsyn.com/27-love-and-hoarding-with-emily-maguire-author-of-love-objects (accessed 29 April 2021).

Murphy, F. (2021), *The Shape of Sound*, Melbourne: Text Publishing.

Sentilles, S. (2021), '11 Things I Wish I'd Known about Writing 11 Years Ago', *BookPage*, May. Available online: https://bookpage.com/behind-the-book/26179-11-things-i-wish-id-known-about-writing-11-years-ago-nonfiction#.YlqVaX0zZhB (accessed 22 April 2021).

Westerman, D. L., J. K. Miller, and M. E. Lloyd (2017), 'Revelation Effects in Remembering, Forecasting, and Perspective Taking', *Mem Cogn,* 45: 1002–13. Available online: https://doi.org/10.3758/s13421-017-0710-7 (accessed 29 April 2021).

SEE ALSO

Collecting

Rites

Experience

Listening

MARJORIE EVASCO

The embodiment of the act of listening is expressed in the Cebuano Visayan language by two words which are synonyms: *pamínaw* and *památì*. While both terms denote the hortatory form of the verb for listening, their connotative nuances evoke the affective response of the listener's consciousness in relation to that which is being attended to. The roots of *pamínaw* suggest clarity and quietude as conditions for listening, while the mycorrhizae of *památì* suggest the emotive resonances of the listener with the object of her attention.

This is how sentient beings – writers, most of all – radically listen to the living world: not with their ears only, but with their entire bodies. And sometimes, when the conditions are right, the tuning fork of her body can be struck to a pitch of full attention by a wild wonder breaking through the sheer pelter of sensory stimuli: a sliver of light in a mangrove swamp catching a kingfisher's wings just taking off from a branch, a horizon note of a blues song carried by the breeze caressing the skin of twilight, a damp scent of midnight wafting from the balcony as the Dama de Noche raises a tendril, an infant's prehensile fingers circling one's index as if for dear life itself.

Listening is the body's leaning into silence and hearkening towards the nascent sounds of words. These acts are moments in a rhythmic continuum, like the cadence of the heart, the opening and closing of a Luna moth's wings. This kind of listening senses the cadences of the vital dance of life, the cosmic flow in its particular shapes, sounds, smells, tastes, textures, motions: death-life-death-and-life yet again, over and over in the daily round of things which are all already here, in the open of one's 'brightening glance', as W. B. Yeats put it (1996: 48).

In this skilful practice of radical listening, a writer needs her aides-memoire: a writing pad and pencil. Like the naturalist and the anthropologist, she takes her daily 'field notes', where the things that animate her imagination are described just the way they are, without the consciousness hastening to use filters of self-projection and egocentric appropriation. These field notes of one's reciprocal attention to the marvellous in the everyday may become the imagination's material, resurfacing from the depths of the writers' consciousness in the crucial moments of composing a literary work. How this happens, one can never fully explain, as a large part of the creative process resides in the mysterious workings of the subconscious.

Aside from committing some time for listening during quiet reflective pauses within a day, one actively looks to writing mentors: other writers whose practice and literary works show one how to listen. The quality of a writer's attention is inevitably wrought into the body of the literary work. The work's corporeality can show us how it pays close attention. One who practises creative writing learns how to listen to literature this way, taking specific instructions from, say, the poems themselves on how to awaken, how to attend to the 10,001 things of beauty and terror in the universe and how to hear the sounds arising from the world's dreaming.

A mentor of skilful listening is Mary Oliver. She had the daily habit of walking early in the morning into the woods near her house in Provincetown, accompanied by her dog, Percy. In her back pocket would be a small hand-sewn three- by five-inch notebook and a pencil for her field notes, where she would jot down descriptions of her sense impressions. In her state of receptive porosity, her intently listening body lingered through the woods, open to the vibrance of the living world and ready to heed the inner stirrings of the desire to find words with which to correspond with the things that she absorbed and transformed. Her poem 'Mindful' is replete with luminous details of this lingering: 'Everyday/ I see or hear/ something/ that more or less// kills me/ with delight,/ that leaves me/ like a needle// in the haystack/ of light. It was what I was born/for –/to look, to listen// to lose myself/ inside this soft world –/to instruct myself/ over and over// in joy, and acclamation' (2005: 58–9).

Creating this space of mutual resonance in one's creative work is probably what poet Pattian Rogers means when she speaks of 'writing as reciprocal creation' (1999: 3). One of my favourite poems by Mary Oliver speaks precisely of this reciprocity between the world and the writer. In 'In Blackwater Woods' a persona actively gives instructions on how to be present to the presences here, how to embody listening, beginning with the sense of sight and proprioception, then moving on to the sense of smell, of movement and fulfillment: 'Look, the trees/ are turning/ their own bodies/ into pillars// of light,/ are giving off the rich/ fragrance of cinnamon/ and fulfillment' (1983: 82–3).

Elaine Scarry in *Dreaming by the Book* speaks of how these instructions to the senses are embedded in the formal practices of literary writing. They are the 'steady stream of erased imperatives' without which authors of poems, stories, plays, memoirs and other literary forms cannot make us imagine (1999: 35). The good reader listens carefully to these instructions to do the work of looking, smelling and tasting with the imagination, to truly perceive in the mind's eye every particular image that is configured in language.

The metaphoric imagination of a writer is trained to listen for the whisperings of a new way of looking at things in the dynamic act of creative synthesis. Denise Levertov's 'O Taste and See' ends with the imperative of tasting and seeing to transform the world into our very own flesh and our very own deaths (1964: 53).

Writers learn from each other how to practise widening the gyre of their listening to give space for wonder. In my poem 'In Baclayon, Reading Levertov's "For Whom the Gods Love Less"', the room of attention is huge enough for paradoxes:

> Perhaps it is now the other way around,
> and I have become an almost-perfect lover,
> caring little that the Gods love poets less.
> I am begun again, anew, listening
> from the open window to the old tambis tree
> drop red bells of fruit onto the grass and roof.
> In this humid May afternoon in Baclayon,
> the guava redolent on the branch meets the sun-
> bird's praise, both scent and song passing through me,

as though I have turned into all-embracing air
in this keep of grace, Levertov's radiant wings
decanting shadows, urging the only way to let love (2020).

References

Evasco, M. (2020), 'In Baclayon, Reading Levertov's "For Whom the Gods Love Less"', in *The Margins: Transpacific Literary Project*, New York: Asian-American Writers Workshop. Available online: https://aaww.org/a-turtle-poet-dreams-given-time-three-poems-by-marjorie-evasco/ (accessed 10 October 2020).

Levertov, D. (1964), *O Taste and See*, New York: New Directions Publishing.

Oliver, M. (1983), *American Primitive*, London: Little, Brown and Co.

Oliver, M. (2005), *Why I Wake Early*, Massachusetts: Beacon Press.

Oliver, M. (2010), *Swan: Poems and Prose Poems*, Massachusetts: Beacon Press.

Rogers, P. (1999), *The Dream of the Marsh Wren: Writing as Reciprocal Creation*, Minneapolis: Milkweed Editions.

Scarry, E. (2001), *Dreaming by the Book*, New Jersey: Princeton University Press.

Wolff, J. U. (1972), *A Dictionary of Cebuano Visayan*, Ithaca, New York: Cornell University, Southeast Asia Program and the Linguistic Society of the Philippines.

Yeats, W. B. (1996), *Sailing to Byzantium*, London: Orion Books.

SEE ALSO

Facilitator
Yoga
Resistance

Listing

DAVID CARLIN

1   To list is to *lean*. To lean is to tilt. To tilt is to joust, but before that, as *tyltan* in Old English, it meant 'to be unsteady', and, as *tyllast* in Old Norse, it was 'to trip', while as *tylta*, in Norwegian, 'to walk on tip-toe'. In Swedish, *tulta* signified 'to waddle', and in Middle Dutch if you said *touteren*, it meant 'to swing' (*Online Etymological Dictionary* 2021). *Tyltan, tyllast, tylta, tulta, touteren*. To be unsteady, trip, walk on tiptoe, waddle, swing. Two unexpected lists, each with its own music of associations.

2   This is a pleasure of the list: an arrival sideways at a small, marvellous conjunction.

3   A list might seem to offer order, containment and efficiency with its powers of collection, but every list is also by its nature endless (even a Top 10 list implies the endless set of numbers beyond ten). A list is a catalogue of the infinite, as Umberto Eco tells us in his phantasmagoric catalogue of catalogues, *The Infinity of Lists* (2009). Eco finds lists in Homer, the images of Hieronymus Bosch and Albrecht Dürer and a hundred other places. Lists abound in the hodgepodge accumulations and post-facto orderings of European *wunderkammers*, museums and botanic gardens: these are lists haunted by fantasies of seizing and hoarding all of the world's infinite worlds and bringing them into a single order.

4   Caution: every list fails at being comprehensive; every list excludes.

5   Essays can be lists: Mary Ruefle's 'Twenty-Two Short Lectures' (2012); Janet Malcolm's 'Forty-One False Starts' (2013); Peta Murray's 'Glossolalalararium Pandemiconium' (2020).

6   Alejandro Zambra's novel, *Multiple Choice* (2016), is structured as a list of questions from the Chilean Verbal Aptitude Test of 1993.

7   As exquisite literary use of listing, Claire-Louise Bennett's *Checkout 19* (2021).

8   For a writer the list opens up grounds for fertile strangeness in the accrual of differences: the loose amassing of the apparently ill-fitting, the non-parallel, the differently pulsed, scaled and calibrated, the nonsensical, the nonsequiturial (and non/secre-tarial), the ungainly and gainly, alike and unlike. Witness Borges's list, fictitiously discovered in 'a certain Chinese Encyclopedia', of types of animal:

> those that belong to the Emperor, embalmed ones, those that are trained, suckling pigs, mermaids, fabulous ones, stray dogs, those included in the present classification, those that tremble as if they were mad, innumerable ones, those drawn with a very fine camelhair brush, others, those that have just broken a flower vase, those that from a long way off look like flies (Foucault 2002: xvi).

9   As Foucault wrote in *The Order of Things*, this list of Borges, by means of laughter, opens up a space of radical possibility, shattering

> all the familiar landmarks of my thought – *our* thought that bears the stamp of our age and our geography – breaking up all the ordered surfaces and all the planes with which we are accustomed to tame the wild profusion of existing things, and continuing long afterwards to disturb and threaten with collapse our age-old distinction between the Same and the Other (Foucault 2002: xvi).

10   Some writers collect paragraphs and form them into lists. Maggie Nelson has said that she arranged the fragments that make up the non-fiction book *Bluets* (2009) in countless different orders – until she found the list that also made a story, a linear path along which to lead her reader. Roland Barthes's most poetic, dreamlike works, like *Roland Barthes by Roland Barthes* (2010)*,* are strings of paragraph/ fragments, ordered by titles through the arbitrary logic of the Roman alphabet. They are lists in so far as each item both carries on from what has come before and starts anew (just like: *toilet paper, bananas, cornflour, soap*). But in between each item, in the gap made by the comma or the paragraph break, there is a leap which, whether large or small, is somehow *wonderful;* as in, it jolts you into wonder, even if only micro-wonder, at its unexpectedness.

11   Fun fact: *parataxis* is the literary device of arranging side by side, without subordination or causation. But lists are often vertical.

12   Perhaps what I am drawn to in playing with list as method is the suspension of grammar. The move towards the unresolved ambiguities of *and.*

13   And –

14   A list over runs itself with difference. Across its free fall of items, it can invoke what Edouard Glissant calls a 'poetics of relation'. For Glissant 'there's no likenesses and differences; there's only differences. And the rhizome of these differences forms the weave of the living and the canvas of cultures' (Diawara 2011: 19).

15   To follow on, what about the list gone feral, so to speak? Digital forms allow for lists to splinter in all directions, and these are fertile grounds for collaborative and ecocritical practices of creative writing intermingled with other arts and disciplines. Witness the example of the *Feral Atlas* (Tsing et al. 2021), a digital publication curated and edited by three anthropologists and an architect. Therein we find a plenary list of field reports from contributors around the world that catalogue the 'feral effects' of the more-than-human 'ecological patches' observable in the Anthropocene (from *Antifouling Paint* and *Cats* to *Radioactive Blueberries* and *Styrofoam*). This list can be located in a gridded 'Super Index' (found at https://feralatlas.supdigital.org/index); there, it is cross hatched with other lists of 'Feral Qualities', 'Tippers' and 'Anthropocene Detonators', each suggesting different ways to navigate the rhizomic, multimodal text and assemble a version of its story.

16   Listing can support other processes of collaborative writing and regenerative practice. For example, a list of my 'random' associations on some agreed 'matter of concern' (Latour 2010: 478), if tossed in with a list of *your* associations, and

yours, and *yours*, could land us all together on unexpected footings. From here, embracing and celebrating Donna Haraway's seriously wry notion that 'we are all compost' (Haraway 2015: 161), we could begin, through 'the slow process of composition and compromise' (Latour 2010: 478) – for instance, by essaying and editing in a shared document (see Ballard et al. 2020) – to knit together something new.

17 And –

18 Feel free to add more items, and cross out any that you're done with.

References

Ballard, S., H. Brasier, S. Buck, D. Carlin, S. Langley, J. Lobb, B. Magner, C. McKinnon, R. Michael, P. Murray, F. Rendle-Short, L. Strahan and S. Taylor (2020), 'We Thought We Knew What Summer Was', *Axon: Creative Explorations* 10 (2). Available online: https://axonjournal.com.au/issue-vol-10-no-2-dec-2020/we-thought-we-knew-what-summer-was (accessed 23 September 2021).

Barthes, R. (2010), *Roland Barthes by Roland Barthes*, London: Macmillan.

Bennett, C. (2021), *Checkout 19*, London: Jonathan Cape.

Diawara, M. (2011), 'One World in Relation: Édouard Glissant in Conversation with Manthia Diawara', *Journal of Contemporary African Art* (28): 4–19.

Eco, U. (2009), *The Infinity of Lists*, New York: Rizzoli International Publications.

Foucault, M. (2002), *The Order of Things: An Archaeology of the Human Sciences*, London: Routledge.

Haraway, D. J. (2015), 'Anthropocene, Capitalocene, Plantationocene, Chthulucene: Making Kin', *Environmental Humanities*, 6(1): 159–65.

Latour, B. (2010), 'An Attempt at a "Compositionist Manifesto"', *New Literary History*, 41(3): 471–90.

Malcolm, J. (2013), *Forty-One False Starts: Essays on Artists and Writers*, New York: Macmillan.

Murray, P. (2020), 'Glossolalalararium Pandemiconium: A Meaningfully Irreverent, Queerelously Autoethnographic Essamblage for Trying Times', *Qualitative Inquiry*, 24 September. Available online: https://doi.org/10.1177/1077800420960144 (accessed 4 September 2021).

Nelson, M. (2009), *Bluets*, Seattle: Wave Books.

Online Etymological Dictionary (2021). Available online: https://www.etymonline.com/search?q=tilt (accessed 17 July 2021).

Ruefle, M. (2012), *Madness, Rack, and Honey: Collected Lectures*, Seattle: Wave Books.

Tsing, A. L., Deger, J., Keleman Saxena, A., and F. Zhou (2021), *Feral Atlas: The More-Than-Human Anthropocene*, Redwood City: Stanford University Press. Available online: http://doi.org/10.21627/2020fa (accessed 23 September 2021).

Zambra, A. (2016), *Multiple Choice*, trans. M. McDowell, New York: Penguin Books.

SEE ALSO

Bricolage

Juxtaposition

Flow

Memory work

MARIA TUMARKIN

Memory work doesn't have to involve digging.

In *Giving up the Ghost*, Hilary Mantel looks away from the metaphors of burial and excavation towards a vision of memory as 'a great plain, a steppe, where all the memories are laid side by side, at the same depth, like seeds under the soil' (2003: 25). You walk the steppe, bend over and look, maybe scratch the soil lightly with your fingernails. An older past, a traumatic past does not occupy deeper sediments of the soil; memories are laid next to each other companionably rather than being buried underneath each other in some kind of inverse hierarchical entombment. The archaeological and geological metaphors for memory work have been so culturally dominant in the West for the past century that Mantel's image produces a jolt – what do you mean *a great plain, a steppe*?

Say to yourself 'memory work' and the mind, always ready to spatialize abstractions, will call up basements, boxes in the furthest parts of the attic, thick-to-impenetrable forests, buried cities – what is concealed, near-impossible to get to, in the shadows, disallowed. Not a large, walkable sway of flatness as Mantel asks us to imagine. A torch, a candle: in the archaeological paradigm (let's call it that), the source of light is always finite and precarious. A *plain*, on the other hand, is just there, in plain sight. So: the jolt.

Perhaps it was Walter Benjamin who gave us the most legendary distillation of memory work as an act of excavation: 'He who seeks to approach his own buried past must conduct himself like a man [sic] digging. Above all, he must not be afraid to return again and again to the same matter; to scatter it as one scatters earth, to turn it over as one turns over soil' (Benjamin, 2005: 76). For Benjamin, writing over a century ago, the site of excavation itself was more important than whatever got unearthed and whatever resisted unearthing, because memory was 'not an instrument for exploring the past' (76), but its medium. It was the soil in which the past was buried or scattered – not the spade with which the soil was dug up.

Benjamin's figure of a person turning over the earth as if possessed in search of their (and their family's and their community's) buried past – let's say this person is an artist who is also, as all artists are, a historian – should feel antiquated, except it doesn't. Mining, digging, uncovering, unearthing, bringing out of the shadows and into the light – this is how memory work is routinely described in the field of life writing today, as if this language of burial and excavation, which inevitably takes us back to Freud and psychoanalysis, is the self-evidently factual representation of what writers do when they work with memory.

Freud, whose passion for archaeology is well-known, is not exactly the darling of the current moment and yet the entanglement of psychoanalysis with the common conceptions of memory work persists. In psychoanalysis, like in archaeology, the lost past is recovered; in psychoanalysis, like in archaeology, the power of the past is both undeniable and explosive. The repressed, buried, unconscious past impinges on the present. Doggedly haunts it yet cannot be *caught in the act.*

Metaphors get naturalized and become ways of thinking and doing – writers who work with memory are well-served to remember just how historically specific those go-to metaphors for memory work are. Don't swallow any of it, wholesale: even the fact that memory is a link between the past and the present, even that. Belgian philosopher Berber Bevernage (2008, 2015) argues that the reproduction of the conception of linear time always favours those who have inflicted violence with impunity (and who are likely continuing to do so), because it fails to capture the experience of the dissolution of the chronological time so defining of survivors' experiences and, I would add, of the lived experiences of minoritized groups more broadly. Bevernage suggests we reject the idea of past, present and future as discrete ontological entities and mutually exclusive categories (2015). What would it mean for our understanding of memory work if we were to take seriously, as I believe we must, the view that the separation of the past and the present is an act of epistemic violence and that, as Marie Draz writes, 'temporality is a central mechanism of power in racial and colonial formations' (2017: 376) Who is digging, excavating what now?

Memory work as a form of meaning-making which pushes against the notion of irreversible historical time is something we can see full-flight in the work of so many First-Nations poets/artists/intellectuals. 'The relationship between past-present-future is not linear nor limiting', writes Narungga poet-scholar Natalie Harkin, 'as we are already the re-telling of the past, always transforming it, and our stories are without end' (2014: 6). Memory work is always ethically charged and philosophically grounded.

I've been saying memory as if it is a noun, but of course it is not. Memory scholars remind us that there is no such thing as a memory – an object, an archive, a container, a place (unlike what Benjamin imagined). Instead, when we talk about memory, we are in fact talking about affectively charged acts and practices of remembering and transmission, voluntary and not, individual and shared. Memory (like love) is always a verb, not a noun.

Recently a new kind of orthodoxy has emerged around theorizing individual acts of remembering: how each act of remembering is an act of creation and self-narration, mutable, unreliable, selective, liable to mould itself to a current cultural moment. It all sounds so dynamic and sophisticated but be careful. All conceptions of memory work, no matter how radical they feel, can become prisons of our own making if we allow them to ossify.

Sometimes the work of memory is also the work of mourning. Sometimes it is the work of truth seeking and justice seeking; sometimes it is the quietest, most private free fall into your family history. Memory work can be a way of creating or consolidating communities and, as Joan Didion wrote once about her notebook-keeping habit, of staying 'on nodding terms with the people we used to be' (2006: 106). Memory work's greatest gift is, perhaps, to take the burden of remembering and testifying off the survivors' shoulders – to make remembering histories of violence and loss a shared, collective responsibility.

References

Benjamin, W. (2005), 'Excavation and Memory', *Selected Writings*, 2 (2): 1931–4.

Bevernage, B. (2008), 'Time, Presence, and Historical Injustice', *History and Theory*, 47 (2): 149–67.

Bevernage, B. (2011), *History, Memory, and State-Sponsored Violence: Time and Justice*, New York: Routledge.

Bevernage, B. (2015), 'The Past Is Evil/Evil Is Past: On Retrospective Politics, Philosophy of History, and Temporal Manichaeism', *History and Theory*, 54 (3): 333–52.

Didion, J. (2006), 'On Keeping a Notebook', in *We Tell Ourselves Stories in Order to Live. Collected Nonfiction*, 101–8, New York: Alfred A. Knopf.

Draz, M. (2017), 'Born This Way? Time and the Coloniality of Gender', *The Journal of Speculative Philosophy*, 31 (3): 372–84.

Harkin, N. (2014), 'The Poetics of (Re)Mapping Archives: Memory in the Blood', *JASAL: Journal of the Association for the Study of Australian Literature*, 14 (3): 1–14.

Mantel, H. (2003), *Giving up the Ghost*, London: Fourth Estate.

SEE ALSO

Erasure

Archival-poetics

Ghost Weaving

Metaphor me

SELINA TUSITALA MARSH

As a poet-scholar, I know the power of metaphor. I know it as an award-winning poet. And I know it as an academic who, like other artist-scholars, has transformed her arts practice into her research methodology. This knowledge (taken-for-granted application) became wisdom (internalized ways of being) when I not only discovered the power of the metaphor to describe who I am, where I'm from, and why I do what I do, but *who* I might become, and *how* I might become it.

For the past seven years, I've been guiding others to do the same, using a method I call 'metaphor me'. I've taught it to students of all ages, to Pacific Island corporate leaders who yearn to bring their cultural selves through corporate doors, to workshop participants who want to write poetry and who leave marvelling at the poetry of their lives. I've developed the following exercise to particularly help people stand in their identities of difference. I offer it here as a method for creative practice researchers to do the same. It is based on the Samoan proverb:

E pala le ma'a, a e le pala upu
(stones rot but not words).

Given the power of words, and the negative stories we might absorb from society or tell ourselves when we are 'different', my method helps people find new words and is designed to be practised in a group, although it could be adapted for individual use too. The method is as follows:

1 Choose a metaphor (allow two minutes): Think of an object or phenomenon (a sunrise, a tsunami) that energizes you, that you are drawn to, or that has followed you around over the years. Don't over-think it. Often the object or phenomenon is right under your nose. It's your grandmother's quilt on your bed or a carving from your village. It's the kind of shell you always collect at the beach. It's the garland of flowers you were taught to make by your aunties. It's your favourite black pearl earrings. It's the waterfall you seek out when hiking. It's dawn or dusk that gives you energy. It's the ocean or a lake or an island. First choice is often best choice.
   - Black pearl
2 Feel and visualize: Share a physical example or an image of your chosen object. Describe your object/phenomenon using all five senses of touch, sight, smell, sound and taste. Be as concrete and detailed as you can. In a circle, take takes turns showing your object or image. What's your connection with it?

3 Verbal word dump (allow one minute for each participant): Person A reminds every-one what their object/phenomenon is and when the timer begins everyone randomly calls out words associated with it and with any other words called out. This is a high energy, chaotic time where people shout words as they come to mind. It's helpful to assign a scribe to Person A in order to help write down all the words spoken out loud. At the end of the minute, Person A will have a sheet of words associated with their object/phenomenon. Go around the circle until everyone has had a turn.

- Black pearl: dark, precious, gem, valuable, round, grit, oyster, shell, sea, salt, deli-cacy, flesh, succulent, lemon, living, filter, imperfect perfection, ebony, gleaming, string, legacy, tradition, cutting, razor edged, round, hollow, light, sea emerald.

4 Choose what resonates (allow five minutes): Read through your collected words. Quickly circle twelve words that appeal to you. On new paper write your object/phenomenon at the top. This is your title. Transfer the twelve-circled words to the left side of the paper, one word per line, numbering each line.

- Black pearl
    i.   Dark
    ii.   Grit
    iii. Oyster
    iv.   Salt
    v.   Delicacy
    vi.   Ebony
    vii. Legacy
    viii. Razor-edged
    ix.   Flesh
    x.   Succulent
    xi.   Living
    xii. Imperfect perfection

5 Lean into metaphor (allow two minutes): What does the object have to say about you? Write 'I am' in front of each word. It doesn't need to make grammatical sense. Which ones resonate?

- Black pearl
    i.   I am dark
    ii.   I am grit
    iii. I am oyster
    iv.   I am salt
    v.   I am delicacy
    vi.   I am ebony
    vii. I am legacy
    viii. I am razor-edged
    ix.   I am flesh
    x.   I am succulent
    xi.   I am living
    xii. I am imperfect perfection

6   I am poem: version 1 (allow five minutes): Choose six 'I am' lines that attract you. Write them out. Read your poem out loud. What speaks to you? What challenges you? What wisdom surfaces?

- Black Pearl
    i.   I am dark
    ii. I am grit
    iii. I am legacy
    iv. I am delicacy
    v.   I am razor-edged
    vi. I am imperfect perfection

7   I am poem: version 2 (allow ten minutes): Now place a comma after your 'I am' phrase. You have until the end of line (and no more) to explore it. Lean into the material world of the metaphor. What does it look, sound, smell, feel and taste like? Use discarded words from your early drafts if they appeal. Evoke; don't explain. Choose concrete and specific words and phrases over abstract ones. Cut out unnecessary words. Play with rhyme, assonance and alliteration. Try and keep the lines roughly the same length.

- Black Pearl
    i.   I am dark, an ebony inner glow
    ii. I am grit, turning sand into gold
    iii. I am legacy, born from adversity
    iv. I am delicacy, fine succulent flesh
    v.   I am razor-edged, sharpened and pressed
    vi. I am imperfect perfection, tenacious grip on rock

8   Form is freedom. Play with form. Take your lines and select words to make several haiku following the form of three lines of poetry with a five, seven, five syllabic count. I love haiku because they condense the elements that mean the most to you. Shorten words, change their tenses, massage them into place.

- Black Pearl
    Dark ebony glow
    Grit, turning sand into gold
    Imperfect perfect

The process is fun, random and purposeful, a collaborative creation between you and your metaphor, and the people around you. It has been a joy to witness people discover, write and articulate the beauty and power of the story that was there all along. The story of You that rises when you fall into the Me in Metaphor.

Further reading

Marsh, S. T. (2009), *Fast Talking PI*, Auckland: Auckland University Press.
Marsh, S. T. (2013), *Dark Sparring: Poems*, Auckland: Auckland University Press.
Marsh, S. T. (2017), *Tightrope*, Auckland: Auckland University Press.
Marsh, S. T., ed. (2020), *Pasifika Niu Leaders in Aotearoa: Collected Poems*, Auckland: Capability Group.

Marsh, S. T. (2020), 'Why I Use a Poem in Every Single Classroom', in Fitzpatrick, E. and K. Fitzpatrick (eds), *Poetry, Method and Education Research: Doing Critical, Decolonizing and Political Inquiry*, 223–5, Taylor and Francis Abingdon, Oxon; New York: Routledge.

SEE ALSO

Speculation
Aswang
Bung wantaim

Nonhuman imaginaries

DEBORAH WARDLE

Storytelling with nonhuman imaginaries means entering simulated worlds where human viewpoints blur and slide towards other-worldly illuminations. Refusal to separate or bifurcate nature and culture, nonhuman and human is an increasingly important challenge to traditional dualisms. Rejecting the Cartesian idea that humans are inalienably distinct from animals and plants, no longer seeing ourselves as the controllers of the natural world, opens possibilities of recognizing a vast diversity of nonhuman voices. Humanist viewpoints traditionally separated human from nonhuman beings and entities – culture and nature were seen to be composed of different realms of thought. Unsettling human-centred thinking implies pushing writers to shift gears from anthropocentric binaries towards imaginings of other-than-Anthropocentric connections (Braidotti 2013). Writing with the nonhuman world, and here I include nonhuman animals, vegetables and minerals, opens wide and slippery terrains.

But writers have always written animal stories, haven't they? How do we think like, or with, a cat, a bat, a mat, a mountain, a giant rainforest or woodland eucalypts feeling rumbling bulldozers approach? Intra-relational or interlaced perspectives are foundational to the research and writing practices that imagine nonhuman animals and entities. Writers and theorists such as Rosie Braidotti, Simone Bignall (2019) and Karen Barad (2013) are among many now engaged with these ideas. Writing fiction that embarks towards nonhuman imaginaries, that engages with the relationships with and between human animals and nonhuman animals and with supposedly non-living entities, such as weather, oceans, rivers, mountains, stones, changes the stories that emerge. It's more than personifying the rage of fires, the stump of forests or the steadfastness of mountains. It's closer to the resonances of metaphor. My fiction focuses on the voices of water, both surface and subterranean flows. It explores the conundrums in expressing human connectedness to non-anthropocentric ecologies.

A plethora of ecocritical scholars contribute to our understanding of how to write beyond the confines of human-centric viewpoints. Ecocriticism is a way of analysing literature through a lens of critical ecologies (Chakrabarty 2009). It asks: how does fiction deepen understandings of sustainable, interactive environments? Connecting human writers and readers to more-than-human worlds entails bold and imaginative ways of thinking, backed up by thorough and scrupulous research.

There are several pitfalls and difficulties in the processes of writing with/from/into nonhuman imaginaries, especially at a time when human responsibility for global climate catastrophes is being slated home. The generic *anthropos* in the term *Anthropocene* obscures considering exactly which humans are causing the damage and who/what is bearing the consequences. Expressions such as the 'natural world', which is almost impossible to define, tend to emphasize human-centred pursuits, reflecting the dominance of Western, capitalist or colonial human viewpoints and experiences. Such limits to human imaginative capacities are shackles to be broken.

Expressing the deteriorating resilience of complex ecosystems in response to the effects of increasing carbon in the atmosphere and associated global warming invites the agencies and interconnectivities of places and entities that move beyond immediate human scale and time zones. Impending ecosystem collapse, escalating plant and animal species extinctions, may invite writers into speculative arenas. But these are real lives lost. Limited human knowledges are the troubling foundations from which our imaginations are asked to flourish, and from which writers stretch new, innovative stories (Haraway 2016).

Being in the skin of nonhuman animals risks speaking *for* another species. Writing the lives of nonhuman animals is not just creating talking creatures; it entails acknowledging the sentience, the agency and the resistances of nonhuman animals to human-centred meaning.

Dealing with nonhuman timescales unsettles the 'this, then that' approach to writing. Nonhuman imaginaries bleed from deep time through the recent past, through the plethora of present catastrophes, into speculative futures. Story options thrive as illustrated in the recent New Zealand and Australian climate fictions anthology, *Scorchers* (Mountfort and Proser 2020). What remains 'real' when time spans are either enormous or minuscule?

Climate fiction writers invoke global stories through the localized experiences of human and nonhuman characters. Adam Trexler (2015) and Gregers Andersen (2021) survey a wide range of climate fictions that address the problems of slippages in timescales and the implications of the 'butterfly effect'. The smallest of events in one place cascades to climate induced catastrophes in another. Nonhuman imaginaries test scale and locale to the max.

Writing activities:

1   Try writing 'with' aspects of the material, natural world, not just *about* it. Try writing with awareness of multiple nonhuman viewpoints. Consider the inherent interconnectedness of living and non-living matter. Imagine how you might portray a murderous stone, giving the stone the capacity to kill. How was the stone formed geologically, how can you express the agency of a non-living entity? For example, see Alexis Wright's *Carpentaria*, where a rock lying untouched for millennia kills a man, 'as if it had planned to do this incredible thing' (2006: 405–6).

2   Find the interactions of science and literature – explore the placement of science in fiction. List the different ways you can express the known facts of science into your fictional story. For example, have a scientist as a protagonist who tells the reader their knowledge, as with Laura McKay's *The Animals in That Country* (2020), James Bradley's *Clade* (2016) or Barbara Kingsolver's *Flight Behaviour* (2016). Insert imagined 'media' coverage in the story that portrays current scientific knowledge. Share information through spoken dialogue between credible scientists.

3   In fifty words place a nonhuman character on the immense island of plastic pollution floating in the Pacific Ocean.

Writing with and through nonhuman imaginaries has endless possibilities. Nonhuman imaginaries mean taking the leap into contemporary science, philosophy and innovative narrative technique. The precipice beckons (Bradley 2017). Be bold as you merge and unsettle human and nonhuman interactions alongside any of the other writing methods offered in this book.

References

Andersen, G. (2020), *Climate Fiction and Cultural Analysis: A New Perspective on Life in the Anthropocene*, Milton Park: Routledge.

Barad, K. (2012), 'On Touching: The Inhuman That Therefore I Am', *Differences: Feminist Theory Out of Science*, 23 (3): 206–23.

Bradley, J. (2015), *Clade*, North Sydney: Hamish Hamilton.

Bradley, J. (2017), 'Writing on the Precipice', *Sydney Review of Books*. Available online: http://sydneyreviewofbooks.com/writing-on-the-precipice-climate-change/ (accessed 22 March 2017).

Braidotti, R. (2013), *The Posthuman*, Cambridge: Polity Press.

Braidotti, R. and S. Bignall (2019), *Posthuman Ecologies: Complexity and Process after Deleuze*, London: Lanham, Maryland, Rowman and Littlefield International.

Chakrabarty, D. (2009), 'The Climate of History: Four Theses' in *Critical Inquiry*, 35 (2): 197–222.

Cohen, T., Colebrook, C. and J. H. Miller eds (2016), *Twilight of the Anthropocene Idols*, London: Open Humanities Press.

Ghosh, A. (2016), *The Great Derangement: Climate Change and the Unthinkable*, Chicago: University of Chicago Press.

Haraway, D. (2016), *Staying with the Trouble: Making Kin in the Cthulucene*, Durham: Duke University Press.

Kingsolver, B. (2012), *Flight Behaviour*, London: Faber and Faber.

McKay, L. J. (2020), *The Animals in That Country*. Melbourne: Affirm Press.

Mountfort, P. and R. Proser (2020), *Scorchers: A Climate Fiction Anthology*, Auckland: Team Press.

Plumwood, V. (2009), 'Nature in the Active Voice', *Australian Humanities Review*, 46: 113–29.

Trexler, A. (2015), *Anthropocene Fiction: The Novel in a Time of Climate Change*, Charlottesville: University of Virginia Press.

Wright, A. (2006), *Carpentaria*, Artarmon: Giramondo.

SEE ALSO

Xenos
Imagination
Listening

Not-knowing

JULIENNE VAN LOON

Not-knowing is a motivating factor in much research and creative practice: but how might we re-think it in a way that acknowledges its possibilities as a method? Conventionally, research comes into being when we see a 'gap in the knowledge' but how might we approach the state of not-knowing as a mode of practice in its own right? Practice is understood here in Donald Schön's sense, as knowing-in-action, knowledge that is to a significant extent 'tacit, spontaneously delivered without conscious deliberation' (1987: 28).

To think about methods is to think about the processes rather than products of research, especially those processes – and by association the skills, conditions, spaces and habits – that most often enable or afford us a kind of shift we might otherwise call progress with our research and creative practice. In proposing not-knowing as method we foreground emergent, immersive forms of practice that are less systematic and transferrable and more inclined towards the playful and the iterative (van Loon 2014; Webb and Brien 2008). We look towards a being-with not-knowing that is paradoxically deliberate, a state of trickery perhaps, but one we seek as researchers to fruitfully maintain.

The way in which experienced creative writers emphasize situated, tacit and embodied forms of knowledge, and tend to underline and value the roles of failure and non-knowledge (Japp 2000) in our approaches to research practice, creates for us a particular research and practice culture. Many of us are so familiar with the feeling of not knowing that we recognize it as a kind of dwelling place for our practice, especially in the early to middle stages of developing a major work of imagination such as a literary novel. There are plenty of examples of novelists speaking about this. The American writer E. L. Doctorow has often been cited for his observation that 'writing is like driving at night in the fog. You can only see as far as your headlights, but you can make the whole trip that way' (1986). More recently, the New Zealand novelist Emily Perkins echoed this sentiment in an interview about her own writing methods with Charlotte Wood:

> Being vulnerable to the mistake-making is part of the process, and you need to be prepared for it – but the stuff that feels awful is the stuff you can't prepare for, it's the stuff that's bad in new, unexpected ways. But I do think that the more you write, the more you recognize that feeling and go 'Oh, it's alright, I'm going to get through it' (2016: 307).

Creative writing privileges both experiential knowing and knowing in and through iterative and imaginative creative practice, and because of this our approach to knowledge can be said to be deeply emergent. Often, we 'sense we have some kind of "know-how" which is not yet manifest knowledge' (Gibson 2018: 30). We move towards communicating knowledge explicitly to others through a series of practices as well as through theoretical, historical and analytic processes, but ultimately, we understand our contributions not so much as a simple addition to a stock of knowledge but as shifts in understanding, sometimes quite subtle, and sometimes in a direction counter to conventional interpretations of knowledge (Gibson 2018).

Australian writer and multimedia artist Ross Gibson describes this experimental and iterative method of 'not-knowing' as inherently dynamic. It is a shift in understanding that is:

> Inside – but also outside – but also inside – but also outside – but also inside. The rhythm of this narrative acknowledgement is restless. And it's necessary. Because the world of lived experience and discovery-based research is restless like this, not simple, static or stable (2010: 10).

When we think about creative writing as research, we sometimes feel like an exceptional discipline, that is, we might feel that the methods we practice are markedly different to methods employed in other fields, and that they are not legitimate, perhaps because they're not often listed in the standard guides to methods in the social sciences and humanities. But it's helpful to be reminded that all research leading to new knowledge is 'marked by the legitimacy of its indeterminacy' and research outcomes are *supposed* to be contingent (Malaby 2009: 214). The sense of permeability and restlessness that comes with not-knowing as method may feel crucial to those engaged in immersive forms of creative practice, but it is also present in the research practices of the many of the world's most innovative thinkers, including those working in the so-called hard sciences. In researching states of uncertainty and doubt in research practices across other disciplines, I once interviewed an engineering professor who specializes in recycled steel. She described to me the huge role uncertainty had played for her in the months leading up to one of her major breakthroughs, where she'd chosen materials for her enormously expensive experiment intuitively. 'Even now,' she told me, 'when we get new furnaces and new devices built, there's a huge degree of uncertainty' (Sahajwalla qtd in van Loon 2014: 133). When I shared with her E. L. Doctorow's observation about the creative writing process being like driving at night in the fog, she recognized this as very good analogy for key phases of her own research practice.

I contend that *not-knowing as method* privileges ways of doing research that recognize and value uncertainty, play and experimentation. Not-knowing as method facilitates uncertainty in our practice, deliberately extending productive states of doubt. This can require us to acknowledge and dwell with periods of practice replete with discomfort, failure and risk. Here are some examples of how some researchers and creative artists from a range of disciplines have foregrounded not-knowing in methods:

1 Freefall Writing, a method led by Canadian author Barbara Turner-Vasselago (2017), foregrounds the idea that you 'let the writing teach you what you need to know' and in doing so strive to set aside ideas of your own selfhood/subjectivity and let go of your 'internal' censor. Principles include writing what comes up for you, not changing anything, providing all the sensuous detail, going where the 'energy' is.

2 Fuzzy Interventions. This method requires us to recognize when our thinking is 'underpinned by problem-solving and techno-centric tendencies that foster[ed] oversimplification' (Kushinsky 2017: 34). The *fuzzy intervention* – 'fuzzy because of the

ambiguity and chaotic nature that characterize it' (Sanders and Stappers 2008: 7) – involves applying a toolset not normative to our discipline – and improvised in a fashion that emerges out of the project's particular context.

What happens if we incorporate these exercises into regular research practice? What kinds of knowledge (or non-knowledge) might follow?

References

Doctorow, E. L. (1986), 'Interview: The Art of Fiction No. 94', *Paris Review*, 101 (Winter). Available online: https://www.theparisreview.org/interviews/2718/the-art-of-fiction-no-94-e-l-doctorow (accessed 7 August 2020).

Gibson, R. (2010), 'The Known World', in D. L. Brien, S. Burr and J. Webb (eds), *TEXT Special Issue 8: Creative and Practice-Led Research – Current Status, Future Plans*. Available online: http://www.textjournal.com.au/speciss/issue8/Gibson.pdf (accessed 7 August 2020).

Gibson, R. (2018), 'The Arc of Research', in J. Oliver (ed.), *Associations: Creative Practice and Research*, 19–23, Carlton: Melbourne University Press.

Japp, K. (2019), 'Distinguishing Non-Knowledge', *Canadian Journal of Sociology*, 25 (2): 225–38.

Kushinsky, S. (2017), 'Fluency in Uncertainty: Finding a Way into and through Participatory Design Practice', Masters by Research Thesis, RMIT University, Melbourne.

Malaby, T. M. (2009), 'Anthropology and Play: The Contours of Playful Experience', *New Literary History*, 40: 205–18.

Marina Abramović Institute (2020), *The Abramović Method*. Available online: https://mai.art/abramovic-method (accessed 7 August 2020).

Sanders, E. and P. J. Stappers (2008), 'Co-Creation and the New Landscapes of Design', *Co-Design*, 4 (1): 5–18.

Schön, D. (1987), *Educating the Reflective Practitioner*, San Francisco: Jossey Bass Publishers.

Turner-Vasselago, B. (2017), *Freefall: Writing Without a Parachute*, London: Jessica Kinsgley Publishers.

van Loon, J. (2014), 'The Play of Research: What Creative Writing Has to Teach the Academy', *TEXT: Journal of Writing and Writing Courses*, 18 (1). Available online: http://www.textjournal.com.au/april14/vanloon.htm (accessed 7 August 2020).

Webb, J. and D. L. Brien (2008), '"Agnostic" Thinking: Creative Writing as Practice-Led Research', *Working Papers in Art and Design*, 5. Available online: http://sitem.herts.ac.uk/artdes_research/papers/wpades/index.html (accessed 7 August 2020).

Wood, C. (2016), *The Writer's Room*. Milsons Point: Allen and Unwin.

SEE ALSO

Uncertainty
Iterative thinking
Experience

Notebooking

SAFDAR AHMED

I would like to start by resisting the idea of the notebook as an extension of our brains and bodies: like an old-fashioned counting tool, or a new-fashioned smartphone. Yes, notebooks can be likened to a form of technology. Yes, they augment, or substitute for, our reliance on memory. They are good for putting down lists, bullet-points, appointment times, phone numbers, addresses and other scraps of information. They are effective pedagogical instruments.

But all these things are secondary to their ideal function, which is to deepen our process of creative thinking. The notebook is best used as a storehouse for all the fleeting, unstable, tangential, transgressive, contradictory, stop-start lineaments of our daydreams and reflections.

Before print capitalism notebooks were rare (as rare as paper, or animal hide) and functioned as a type of palimpsest in which the languages of science, philosophy, mysticism, medicine and art were explored and integrated. Premodern scholars of the Graeco-Arabic translation movement under Abbasid patronage (eighth to tenth centuries CE) integrated Aristotelian ideas with Islamic theology in a milieu that was intellectually promiscuous. This epistemic syncretism would now seem unfamiliar to the intellectual silos of our disenchanted world. We currently exist on a monological register so shaped by neoliberal market forces and secular-rational categorization that to be 'cross-disciplinary' possesses a rare and exotic value.

Without labouring the comparison, the notebook is unique in its potential to aggregate information of every register and type. A place where all stripes of knowledge commune in a non-hierarchical, a-centered structure – where every thought (meaningful and irrelevant) has its place.

The notebook is a descendant of the list, of the eighteenth century 'common book'. It is a close cousin to the sketchbook and personal diary, and may share the latter's emphasis on self-reflection, keeping in mind that subjective writing only emerged alongside new ideas about the self-observing individual in the eighteenth century. Jean-Jacques Rousseau had some inkling of this when he wrote: 'I conceive of rendering a new kind of service' which would offer readers 'a faithful image of one among them so they will learn to know themselves' (qtd. in Shklar 1988: 161). In this sense the very form of autobiography is an outgrowth of our changing notions of self and the subjectivities they validate.

Notebooking, or what Samuel Beckett called the 'demon of notesnatching', is an idiosyncratic ritual that might take almost any form according to your whimsy or inclination (1999: xiii). It is helpful to think about it as a verb, as something we do, rather than as a concept or abstraction. It is where we jot suggestions, vent our anger, rehearse important speeches, scrawl intimate confessions, pursue dead-ends and exclaim fresh insights. A place for song lyrics, nonsense verse, quotations, collage, Burroughsian cut-ups (Burroughs et al. 1968) and absent-minded phone doodling – the latter being our most common experience of what otherwise passes for 'automatic drawing' (Maclagan 2013). It's where fragments are pulled together, where marginalia and non-marginalia become indistinguishable, in the work of collection and memory-gathering.

The creative person can wander, echoing Walter Benjamin's 'archiving' of even the smallest ephemera – a cataloguing of thoughts preserved on scraps of paper, train tickets, library request forms and all of what otherwise goes unremarked in the time poor bustle of our late capitalist work schedules (Esther and Marx 2007). The process can be likened to a state of *irrkunst*: of drifting around, getting lost, discovering things by chance and realizing you were mistaken about something in the first place (Gleber and Rollins 1989).

The notebook is an intimate space in which difficult thoughts can be held. Its privacy is never guaranteed but then is any format entirely secure? Books can be opened just as phones are lost, data is stolen, computers hacked. I am speaking, then, for an ideal. I'd like to imagine pages on which no self-monitoring exists, just as there are no boundaries on our brain-muddled thoughts. Robert Crumb wrote to himself in a sketchbook in late 1996: 'Free associate like when you're sick and have a fever. Be spontaneous – let go!' (2012: 155).

There's the risk this will end up sounding like the blueprint for a new life-hack, which is how things are so often commodified and sold back to us these days, so let me dispel any such expectations. Just as the notebook is not a tool for the problem-solving brain, nor is it a platform for journeys of 'self-improvement' or 'self-help'. Of course, it is useful for many things, but transcending our present condition is not one of them. There is no escape from the self, just as there is no new self to unlock. If all this talk about the absence of formulae or process could be visualized, I would picture a lonely stick figure (Giacometti-like) walking into a radically open, epistemic field.

The notebook is anterior to processes of 'serious' writing, which is what makes it so valuable. It is a place to daydream, to be so careless and roaming in your attention as to embody the creative process at its freest. Notebook jottings on other people's work, intertextual references and borrowed ideas are a necessary prelude to our own emerging thoughts, to ideas in process.

The best notebook should make sense only to the person who scrawled it. It should form a sort of time capsule whose content might become less resonant or meaningful over time. Its handwriting should be messy, and guided by restless curiosity, chance encounters, a snippet of conversation, a stimulating idea. The notebook should embody serendipity whilst denying the conventions of teleological (purpose-driven) thought.

These are jottings which I hope will motivate your own notesnatching. The notebook's potential to reach every corner of thought and experience makes it vital for creative processes, even if (*especially* if) it serves no practical end.

References

Burroughs W., G. Corso, S. Beiles, and B. Gysin (1968), *Minutes to Go*, San Francisco: Beach Books.

Crumb, R. (2012), *R. Crumb Sketchbook*, 10, Los Angeles: Taschen.

Gleber, A. and B. Rollins (1989), 'Criticism or Consumption of Images? Franz Hessel and the Flâneur in Weimar Culture', *Journal of Communication Inquiry*, 13 (1): 80–93.

Leslie, E. and U. Marx (2007), *Walter Benjamin's Archive: Images, Texts, Signs*, London: Verso.

Maclagan, D. (2013), *Line Let Loose: Scribbling, Doodling and Automatic Drawing*, London: Reaktion Books.

Pilling, J. (1999). 'Beckett's Dream and the "demon of notesnatching"' in J. Pilling (ed.) *Beckett's 'Dream' Notebook*, Reading, UK: Beckett International Foundation, pg. xiii.

Shklar, J. (1988), 'Jean Jacques Rousseau and Equality', in Ritter, A. and J. Conaway Bondanella (eds), trans. J. Conaway Bondanella, *Rousseau's Political Writings*, 260–1, Norton, New York: W. W. Norton & Co.

SEE ALSO

Braiding
Listing
Reading

Observation

STEPHEN CARLETON

I realized recently that the only time I keep an observational diary anymore is when I'm travelling. There's something about being the outsider-in-transit – the looker-in upon strangers' lives – that activates my powers of observation in a way not activated in my routine, everyday life. Walking down O'Connell Street in Dublin for the first time in 2010, for instance, it jolted me to observe that a solid majority of people waiting for buses in the morning as they headed to work were still smoking cigarettes instead of tapping away on smart phones. That taught me something immediate about that city, and something I didn't realized I'd noticed about my own (Brisbane) at that time.

A second discovery is that I only seem to write about my home city, Darwin, Australia – that city whose every bone and sinew and undercover flaw and scar I align with my own psychic-body map, and vice versa – when I'm away from it longest and missing it the most. It's almost as though I need to feel a stranger in relation to it to rediscover its patterns, rhythms, dirty habits and secrets all over again in a writerly way. I see it most clearly when I'm looking at it from the outside in.

There's something of the Russian formalists' notion of defamiliarization, or *ostranenie*, at work for me here. Viktor Shlovsky is talking about observing the differences between poetic and everyday language when he writes that:

> The most important thing for a novice writer is to have a personal relation to things, to see things as if they hadn't been described before, to place them into a previously undescribed relation. Literary works very often deal with a naïve man or foreigner who enters a town and understands nothing. A writer doesn't need to be this innocent, but he does need to see things afresh (Shlovsky qtd in Berlina 2018: 10).

For me, the same principle applies to writing about character and location. It is the making strange of the everyday world so that, through observation, we might recreate it as representational or theatrical space. Probably, as a playwright, I should be looking to Brecht and his *Verfremdungseffekt* (distancing effect), a metatheatrical kind of way of making performance strange to audiences through making-us-aware-that-we-are-watching-theatre-with-a-message. But that is not quite what I am talking about here. I am talking about writerly observation of time and place that might apply to those working in any medium.

There's a kind of a trick I find I have to play on myself in order to achieve this observational distance in everyday life – to recreate the sense of outsider-in-transit I describe above. If the Covid-19 pandemic and isolating experience of lockdown taught us nothing else as writers, it has highlighted the need to seek substitutes for long distance travel in the local.

I developed an outwardly simple exercise as a way of playing this trick on myself. It is an exercise I also set my students, to get them thinking about location through observation. I take myself to a bar or a cafe I've never been to, in a part of town I don't normally hang out in. I take a notebook, order a drink and sit and look and feel and listen to the atmosphere and activity in the room. I notice and absorb – observe – not only its characters, but its unique rituals, and I parse this through my own lens on the writing project I might be working on at the time. It helps to be pregnant-with-idea, by which I mean, to come loaded with a receptivity that allows you to apply the strangeness you might be observing in the environment around you. Or, perhaps as with Dublin or Darwin, above, it's a matter of just letting image and observation wash over you and bower-birding them for future use. Sue Woolfe describes this state of neurological receptivity to creative ideas as 'the lull', which, as Stephen Sewell parses it, she talks about:

> in almost contradictory terms as a consciously induced mental state of inattentiveness. Or in other words, a wilfully sought carelessness. 'When I teach,' [Woolfe] writes, 'I insist that students "lull" their minds, rather than writing down the first, often the most obvious, thing that occurs to them. Students are usually intrigued and inspired by the associations they discover. Lulling the mind is a basic first step to being creative' (2017: 6).

In my strange bar/cafe, in my lull state of attentive inattentiveness, I am asking myself some basic play-writerly questions:

> *Who are the other people here?*
> *Why are they here?*
> *What do they seem to be preoccupied with?*
> *What does their body language or conversation reveal about who they are and why they're here?*

But what I am ultimately looking for is subtext, or, as British playwright Noël Greig describes it, a 'true meaning' that is delivered 'under the surface' of the text, rather than through what is literally said or done (2005: 92).

The strangest example of this observational venture that has most recently found its way into my own writing came from a visit to a suburban RSL (Returned Services League) club in Brisbane, with its compulsory ritual one-minute silence at 7.00 pm to honour and remember the war fallen. Patrons are instructed to fall silent and stand – mid-meal, mid-mouthful, mid-game of darts, mid-click on the pokies. Everything stops. The instructions are delivered through piped, pre-recorded message. The ritual occurs, the silent minute lapses and then transmission recurs to normal as though nothing strange has just happened. This encounter and its subtext of collective subliminal cultural programming found its way into my latest play *New Babylon* in the following scene. Our characters are on a sinister cruise ship full of wealthy preppers and first world climate change evacuees:

> VIVIEN   I should return to my quarters.
> OLYMPIA   Yes, you should. Wolfgang, I think it's time for us to turn in too. Leave them to it …
>   *[Another squirt of vapour over the audience.]*

The muzak increases in volume but appears to get stuck on a particular phrase. It's not necessarily that this is what everyone else is hearing, but it's how it sounds to VIVIEN (and to us). She falls into a sort of trance as the music distorts, sours, echoes, fades to be replaced by a high pitched, ultrasonic hum that the others can't hear. She delivers the following robotically, on a single note:

VIVIEN　　　　　We are witnessing one of the great collapses. We are witnessing one of the great external shocks. One paradigm breaks down as another one rises to take its place. We are witnessing the inevitable conclusion of the capitalist cycle. The end of supply and demand. The end of insatiable consumption. In the postcapitalist paradigm there will be no more scarcity. In the postcapitalist paradigm sunshine, wind and water will replace – In the postcapitalist paradigm – In the postcapitalist paradigm – !

And the effect abruptly switches off. Everything resumes to normal. The muzak is soothing and innocuous once more. Vivien is her old self and doesn't seem to be aware that anything weird just happened.

VIVIEN　　　　　　　　　　　　　　*(smiles warmly)* Good night.
WOLFGANG/OLYMPIA/ASTRID　　Good night (Carleton 2021: 37).

The stranger-in-a-bar observation pushed me through a block in the writing process, providing me with an odd, disruptive ritual that might seem peculiar to the audience/observer, but perfectly normal for the character involved – an unexpected gift from the Yeronga RSL Club. And unexpected gifts are what we're hoping for in our writerly lull-observation states.

References

Berlina, A. (2018), '"Let Us Return *Ostrenenie* to Its Functional Role": On Some Lesser Known Writings of Viktor Shlovsky', *Common Knowledge*, January, 24 (1): 8–25.
Carleton, S. (2021), *New Babylon*, Brisbane: Playlab.
Greig, N. (2005), *Playwriting: A Practical Guide*, London: Routledge.
Sewell, S. (2017), 'The Creative Leap: The Science and Philosophy of Creativity', PhD Dissertation, University of Sydney, Sydney.
Woolfe, S. (2007), *The Mystery of the Cleaning Lady*, Perth: UWA Publishing.

SEE ALSO

Reading
Taxonomy
Experience

Paragraphing

DELIA FALCONER

A new breath. A macro-punctuation mark. A flash of lightning showing the landscape from a different aspect. A collection of sentences with a unity of purpose. The rules for creating paragraphs in the formal essay may be clear but, as these descriptions by Isaac Babel and others suggest, paragraphing in creative prose is a more instinctual business. For Australian author Anthony Macris (2007: 4), paragraphs are 'small neighbourhoods' made up of 'streets' of sentences, within the organizational units of chapters. For modernist author Gertrude Stein paragraphs were 'emotional' in a way sentences were not: this, she explained, was not because they expressed an emotion, but because they registered or limited it (Stein 1975: 36). And yet, Stein wrote, 'Rationalize it how you will but you make a paragraph when you feel like it' (17).

As Macris notes, few analyses pay much attention to the materiality of either sentences or paragraphs. Yet the paragraph's history is deeply material. Designer Jason Pamental (2015) traces it back to the ancient Greek *paragraphos*, a physical mark on the page within a solid text block denoting a change in speaker or passage. Scribes in the Middle Ages would standardize this mark into a symbol similar to the pilcrow – a reverse-facing double-stemmed P, with a solid head, which editors use today to mark up text. (This 'blind P' appears in desktop publishing programmes, in ghostly blue, each time we hit return.) When the printing press was invented, printers developed the convention of beginning each para-graph on a new line, leaving a space for illustrators to fill in with an ornamented capital; when these embellishments were abandoned, the indent space remained, which draws our attention to the new purpose of each paragraph. In his *Elements of Typographic Style* (1992), Robert Bringhurst would standardize this indent space as one em.

It is the Victorians, those great builders of paragraphs into mighty sequences, whose books of prosody offer the most fulsome analysis. In his *History of the English Paragraph*, published in 1894, Edwin Herbert Lewis wrote that the paragraph is complete in itself, 'but also a unit of composition' (1894: 22). When thinking of para-graphs, one must consider the larger whole they organize and divide as well as the sentences that comprise it. For rhetorician A. S. Hill, the paragraph was distinct but also marked the natural divisions of a composition: 'something more than a sentence and less than an essay' (quoted in Lewis 1894: 10). A 'paragraph is to a sentence,' wrote Barrett Wendell, 'what a sentence is to a word' (30). Yet this does not help the writer to know when to bring a paragraph to a close. Even a single sentence can count as a paragraph, Lewis notes, if it obeys the rules of unity and coherence. (Though this remains contentious, even today; in 2008, novelist Philip Hensher [see Champion 2008] would take Adam Thirlwell to task for his reliance on single-sentence paragraphs beginning with prepositions while Edward Channing would come to his defence). If nothing else, paragraphs offer the reader small moments of relief. 'The advantage of at least one paragraph indentation on almost every page of a printed book,' noted Lewis, 'is felt by every reader' (1894: 23).

If paragraphs are smaller building units within the whole, running on one after the other, a double-line break marks, in Lewis's words, an 'unusual break' (15). Such a break, which disrupts the organic flow of the whole, must also, logically, indicate a shift or cessation of feeling. What are we to make, then, of a growing trend in prose towards floating paragraphs without indents, each separated by a double-line break? This floating or fragmentary quality is a distinctive feature of the lyric essay, a form described by John D'Agata as 'in-between the two worlds of poetry and essay' (2015: 6) but it is also becoming increasingly common in novels, such as those by Jenny Offill (2020), Kevin Barry (2019), or Patricia Lockwood (2021).

Does the growing prevalence of non-indented paragraphs, each floating in space like a tiny stanza, have something to say about our times? David Carlin has suggested that contemporary essays are reacting ethically and affectively to the 'complicated material realities' of the Anthropocene by embracing particularly plastic forms that test the limits of human subjectivity and of critique (2017: 2). This may be one motivation for the floating paragraphs in the writing of essayists like Wayne Koestenbaum and Eula Biss, who, instead of following the traditional associative flow of the essay by tracing threads of thought and emotion, offer instead assemblages of paragraphs that are also sections in essays such as 'My 1980s' (Koestenbaum 2013) and 'Time and Distance Overcome' (Biss 2009), which refuse closure in favour of ambivalence and inconclusion.

Some novelists also appear to be abandoning the novel's organic imperative and promise of rationed feeling by writing in unindented, floating paragraphs that offer small bursts of intensity. In Jenny Offill's *Weather* (2020), the novel's fragmentation into tiny, startled text-bricks is implicitly a response to the terrors of the Anthropocene – our new era, in which human activity has become a geological force – in which the humble gestures of ordinary domestic life are haunted by the yawning void of planetary annihilation. Although these unindented paragraphs, separated from one another by a double carriage return, are organized loosely into sections, they radiate the angst and jumpiness of the narrator, who finds herself working in the Anthropocene field; meanwhile, the segments of blank page between them exert their own material force as a series of tiny voids. Perhaps, in this new age of terror and beauty, Offill infers – and reinforces formally – there is no place for the longueurs that once characterized the great novels. Her tiny paragraphs-as-sections go as far as suggesting that in this this age of catastrophic and rapid change, an older ecology of feeling in which human emotions unfurled across longer timescales may itself be under threat. As her narrator notes:

My #1 fear is the acceleration of days. No such thing, supposedly, but I swear I can feel it (Offill 2020: 18).

Notes

Richard M. Coe describes the paragraph as a 'macro-punctuation mark' in *Toward a Grammar of Passages* (1988: 90). Isaac Babel describes paragraphs as changers of rhythm and flashes of lightning in Konstantin Paustovsky's, *The Story of a life: Years of Hope* (1969). Alexander Bain describes paragraphs as 'a collection of sentences with a unity of purpose' in *English Composition and Rhetoric: A Manua*l (1867: 142).

References

Bain, A. (1867), *English Composition and Rhetoric: A Manual*, New York: D. Appleton and Company.

Barry, K. (2019), *Night Boat to Tangier*, Edinburgh: Canongate Trade.

Biss, E. (2009), 'Time and Distance Overcome', in E. Biss (ed.), *Notes from No Man's Land: American Essays*, 3–11, Saint Paul, Minn: Graywolf Press.

Bringhurst, R. (1992), *The Elements of Typographic Style*, Point Roberts, WA: Hartley and Marks.

Carlin, D. (2017), 'The Essay in the Anthropocene: Towards Entangled Nonfiction', *TEXT Special Issue 39: The Essay*, April: 1–13.

Champion, E. (2008), 'The Long and the Short of Paragraphs', the *Guardian Books Blog*, 2 January. Available online: https://www.theguardian.com/books/booksblog/2008/jan/02/thelongandtheshortofpara (accessed 15 December 2020).

Coe, R. M. (1988), *Toward a Grammar of Passages*, Carbondale: Southern Illinois University Press.

D'Agata, J., ed. (2015), 'Foreword', in *We Might as well Call It the Lyric Essay*, 6–10, Seneca: Hobart and William Smith College Press. Available online: https://www.theguardian.com/books/booksblog/2008/jan/02/thelongandtheshortofpara (accessed 15 December 2020).

Koestenbaum, W. (2013), 'My 1980s', in W. Koestenbaum (ed.), *My 1980s and Other Essays*, 3–14, New York: Farrar, Straus and Giroux.

Lewis, E. H. (1894), *The History of the Paragraph*, Chicago: University of Chicago Press.

Lockwood, P. (2021), *No One Is Talking about This*, London: Bloomsbury.

Macris, A. (2007), 'Words and Worlds', *The And Is Papers: The Refereed Papers of the 12th [AAWP] Conference, Held in Canberra During November* 2007. Available online: https://www.aawp.org.au/publications/the-is-papers/ (accessed 15 December 2007).

Offill, J. (2020), *Weather*, London: Granta.

Pamental, J. (2015), 'The Life of <p>', *Print*, New York, 69 (4): 24–6.

Paustovsky, K. (1969), *The Story of a Life: Years of Hope*, New York: Pantheon Books.

Stein, S. (1975), *How to Write*, Mineola, New York: Dover Publications.

SEE ALSO

Preposition
Chorality
Play

Permission

TINA MAKERETI

'It's such a confidence trick, writing a novel. The main person you have to trick into confidence is yourself' (Smith 2009: 101).

Let me preface this by saying I come from what must be the most self-deprecating nation on the planet, and that within this community who make a veritable competition of refusing credit and accolades, writers have the additional handicap of being, well, writers, which makes us even less likely to allow affirmation than practitioners of other artforms. New Zealand writers are the worst. I've seen writers fall into a tailspin of sleepless nights and self-flagellation for winning prizes; I myself have engaged in a battle of wills with my own poor British publisher who in an interview attempted to talk my work up while I batted it down. It was, I told him, my obligation as a New Zealand citizen to refuse all compliments.

So this advice stems from a particular cultural environment. While there is the odd arrogant and/or entitled New Zealand writer out there, for the most part we're not very good at giving ourselves permission to do anything. It's not necessarily seen as great to do anything better than anyone else, or to stand out in any way. This stems from our egalitarian roots, which are something to be proud of, but can hold us back when we actually want to create something new. And yet we do create new things all the time, so what gets us there?

The other place I come from, which is also important to this discussion, is te ao Māori, the Indigenous New Zealand world. This complicates the question of permission exponentially. I have observed the assumption amongst non-Indigenous folk that status as Māori somehow gives me automatic rights to write on certain subjects. This is true and also not true, so here we step into the world of paradox: I can write about and as Māori without asking for permission because that is who I am, yes, but the onus on us to get the nuances of our rights and obligations to each other and our ancestors right is far more complex and nuanced from inside than from out. Belonging to a group does not confer permission to write about them; it complicates permission.

I should be clear that this piece does not address the question of whether you can write of other cultures and how. That question has been discussed at length elsewhere. But I can offer two possibly conflicting perspectives: one, the worlds we write should reflect the worlds we live in, including the multiplicities who people them; and two, if we choose to write characters from cultures that aren't our own, we must be equipped to do so. If we are not, we must equip ourselves, but all the research in the world cannot make us see what it is to walk in another person's sandals. Sometimes we can imagine our way there. Sometimes.

Sometimes not. So this piece is not about that kind of permission. The permission I discuss here is the kind that we can only grant ourselves in order to write anything at all.

Writing well requires self-doubt – if it didn't, we wouldn't do it particularly well because we would assume all our first drafts are genius. But how do we continue to write if we doubt every step? For me, this involves a number of confidence tricks.

1 You may have noticed my first 500 words on this topic were basically me giving myself permission to write about permission. I do this in part by defining a position. Recognizing my positionality reflexively means placing all my cards on the permission-giving table. I recognize where I am weak and where I am strong, where I might fail or succeed, where my knowledge and impetus come from. I note the gaps. I embrace my fallibility. It's easier to accept our own imperfections if we make them part of the process.

2 Along these lines, I put not-knowing, uncertainty and discomfort at the centre of what I do – companions to the process rather than something to be vanquished. This doesn't mean I'm any less vigorous about the research: I have a responsibility to know as much as I can about a topic before I write about it. But what does 'as much as I can' mean, and how do I recognize when I have reached the border of that territory? How do I know when to stop researching? There is never any certainty that enough has been done, so discomfort naturally comes and makes a home here. It helps to know, whether I research for two years or ten, I will never reach a moment where I can know everything.

3 Further to this, we can put our troubles, our uncertainties, our imperfections, into the work. Recognize them directly. Pass them on to our characters, write them into our plots. The more we recognize our own flaws, the easier it is to write complex, conflicted, flawed characters. Write into our not-knowing.

4 When the discomfort becomes too much, I think about why I'm doing what I'm doing and who I'm writing for. Invariably, I reach the conclusion that my work is more important than I am. Stories are more important than I am. My ego is the part of me that struggles most with the risk that I might get it wrong on any level. That's the part of me that wants to be seen to write the perfect book. But the stories are too important to me as an Indigenous person who, like all other Indigenous people, has lost so much. And I'm not representing anything more than that lost Māori kid who needs to see the stories of other lost Māori kids like her. I'm writing for her.

5 In creative non-fiction, an immeasurable weight was lifted when I fully understood that even the 'I' voice is a construction; a version of me built out of symbols on a page, intimately connected to the real person, but not her. As I continue to practice, the space between us grows both more capacious and more intensely intimate at the same time. This paradoxical space is a safe place to write: like my identity, my writing sits in between several junctures, occupies a number of positions and doesn't know what it is until it gets there. Sometimes it's not so much giving myself permission to write but giving myself permission to be who I really am on the page. Sometimes the writing gives *me* permission.

And when all of this isn't working, it helps that I often forget that anyone ever reads what I write. My kiwi brain swoops in to tell me no one knows, and no one cares – self-deprecation can be useful, then, in the end.

Permission 127

Reference

Smith, Z. (2009), *Changing My Mind: Occasional Essays,* London: Penguin Random House.

SEE ALSO

Not-knowing
Radical effrontery
Experience

Phototextuality

KAREN L. CARR

It is so easy to get lost inside a sentence. It can happen so quickly; in just the amount of time it takes to dip a teabag up and down in a cup or tangle a strand of hair. Words move in a sweeping horizon, rolling here and there with ascent and descent. Later, when they have begun to build their landscape, the vertical plane appears, as if filled in from a feathery sketch. These days, of course, many of us write without writing. The fingers that wrap the pen, the side of the hand that rests, inky, by the paper, are remnants of another practice from another time. The tapping of keys, the flat bounce, the view of blinking cursor and bright screen, so distanced from the hand, crystallizes our sense of modern remove. It has been this way, too, for photography, long seen as an interrupting apparatus, a technological demon, pulling into the space between sight and seen, a mechanical bully, displacing the symbiosis between hand and eye.

The photograph asks that we see and see right now. Its insistence makes it challenging to force the kind of pause or reckoning that the written word compels. Its questions are often hidden behind or inside its ability to produce awe in the viewer. A photograph on a page, mingling with words, is often read as explanation, in the same way that certain fashion decisions have to do with things matching. If I write about a memory of a long-ago bubble-bath bottle, lost down a copper stream, one might expect a photograph of a brown stream, or a bubble-bath bottle, or even an abstracted slice of clouds, which could stand in for the ephemerality of objects, of life itself, the sorrow that gathers in bouquets with our losses. Because photography has been so yoked to the literal, it is often pinned to the representational field. If, instead, I imagine something in the visual realm that can offer a connection to the lost bottle, a way to pull the writing further into something like recollection rather than illustration, then the photograph becomes part of the text, part of a dialogue that works on two different but related registers, like left hand and right hand on the piano.

How does one bend a sentence towards a particular shadow, or fill the viewfinder with the emptiness of loss? What can be conveyed if we begin to think of photographs as equal presences in a written text, or text as more than caption in a photograph? What can be made from the threshold, where discipline and genre are, for a time, ignored? In the melding of photography and writing, we are engaged in lively and implicitly creative acts, of writing, of seeing, of harbouring the constitutive pieces of history, memory and moment. The photograph on a page must find a way to contain itself, humble itself. It is used to being up and about, framed, witnessed, regarded as the object of art, or the evidence of something seen, or known. It has worked hard to climb to this perch. When photography and writing work together, they each offer something to the other, as well as asking the viewer/reader to make connections that they might not be used to making. When the photograph is brought into the writing arena, it needs to now regard itself as a part of the spatial relationship between page and text. Will the photograph stretch out and take up all the room it is used to having as art object, or will it offer itself up to the sacrifice of illustrative explanation? The writing on the page must now be mindful of the photograph that threatens to take up all the air in the room. How to manage the pull towards sight? If the writing competes, attempts to dazzle, distract, pull attention away from the photograph, then it is an uneasy relationship; if the writing recedes, and grants the space that the photograph is used to having, it is surrendering to the awe of light and shadow, pulling tongue closer to silence.

In *True Stories* (2017), Sophie Calle loosens the photograph from the realm of the illustrative. In her continuously revised and deliberately destabilized vignettes, there is movement between text and image, point to counterpoint. Her photographs complicate and unfold the stories with which they sit, working as both arbiters and disruptors of the slippery notion of truth that autobiography invites. W. G. Sebald (2001) walks and wanders, traverses time and land, moves against a linear pattern. His found photographs function as portals into the archive that they are, themselves, a part of, as he burrows in a Fibonacci shape. His history is refutation of the grand narratives that threaten the local and the personal. DeCarava and Hughes (1955) offer a carefully rendered daily, built with the tacit credulity of realism that pivots, so quietly that one might not notice, into fiction.

What tools of photography can writing make use of? How can we think, for instance, of lighting in writing practice? If I put one word on a page next to a photograph, I am using a spotlight for the language of the text. Does the text need a spotlight, or might it benefit from a different lighting setup that more emphasizes shadow and contour? If the writing is dense and layered, in the manner of impasto painting, then might the photograph offer a space to take a breath, or might it also evoke density as a way to keep the reader within the textual carapace? In the phototextual realm, both text and image must make concessions, compromises. Each must know of the other's presence.

The practitioner of the phototext finds ways to keep image and text in constant conversation. Sometimes, the conversation is convivial; other times, it may be contentious. The space that emerges on the page refuses strict divisions in favour of the liminal. It is not necessarily neat, as words may spill over and atop images, or might stall, just at the border of an image. Images might lose their borders and send themselves into corners of the page, ignoring all margins.

The space of *between* asks the writer/photographer – and the reader – to loosen the seams of genre, to allow the visual and the verbal to coexist. The fully realized phototext offers a challenge to the conventions of both reading and viewing, and, in so doing, refuses, in a sense, to be mastered, fully absorbed, settled and closed by reader/viewer. Writing and photography are pulled apart and pushed together, making an accordion of the page, whose indefinite music resists and compels closure.

References

Calle, S. (2017 [1994]), *True Stories*, Arles, France: Actes Sud.
DeCarava, R. and L. Hughes (1955), *The Sweet Flypaper of Life*, New York: Simon and Schuster.
Sebald, W. G. (2001), *Austerlitz*, London: Hamish Hamilton.

SEE ALSO

Drawing
Ekphrasis
Observation

Play

NICOLE WALKER

There is a saying that goes something like, 'I don't want to write. I want to have written'. There is something lovely about exhaling after finishing a project. Having stuck ink to paper or electrons to computer screen, you've added to the available reality. Accomplishment achieved. But achievement and joy are not necessarily the same thing. To write is a verb. To play is a verb. To have fun, you have to verb. And, if you're not having fun, I'm not sure why you're writing – I mean, I know it's terribly lucrative and rejection is so good for your ego, but why not have fun while you're raking in the dough?

Writing, because of literature classes, I presume, seems serious. We study every word. Plumb the etymologies. Diagram the sentences. Wonder whether Ahab's White Whale telegraphs white supremacy. But I can imagine, as Melville sat down to paint Queequeg's skin in tattoos, that the detailing of a code written upon a man was as fun to write, as it is to decipher. (1892: 29–30). I have laughed out loud while I'm writing when on page fifty-seven, I accidentally answer the question I'd written on page nine about the disappearance of penguins. The poles have flipped. Nothing to worry about here, at least on page fifty-seven of my imagination, the penguins have swum their bodies north.

One thing that has been hard about teaching on Zoom during the pandemic is that I can't act out the writing prompts I give my students. If you're going to play, you have to get your body involved. For a prompt about zooming in and zooming out, not with the technology, but with the lens of imagination, I ask my students to find something very small to focus on – a ladybug or a cracker. Zoom in, I say, tell me all there is to know. I take a cracker, or something more often available, like a pen, and hold it up to my eye. Look at the shine. Look at the invitation to click. Don't you want to click? Write about compulsion. Write about shining compulsion to click the pen.

And then I pop up on the table. Now zoom out. Look at the pencil in relation to the table, to the carpet, to the air in the room. The pen is part of an ecosystem of writing or education or boardrooms. Shall we emancipate the parts of a pen? Write for three minutes about the hardship pens suffer.

Then, zoom back in. Who knew there was such an ecosystem to a pen? Spring, tip, thrust device, thrust tube, end cap, clip! That damn spring. How did it escape?

The last in-person workshop I taught before Covid was at the University of Boulder. I asked the students, who were all fellow professors, to stick their hand in the envelope. I know that now it sounds very germirific but at the time, we didn't fear both paper and hands. Into the envelope I had placed pieces of paper with homonyms typed onto them. Or homophones. The brave hand-sticker-inners pulled out words like crimp and flee/flea and crest and frank. I began the writing prompt, asking them to write for two minutes using one definition of your word. I set a timer and stopped them at the two-minute mark. Then, I asked them to write another scene, another meditation, another word-jaunt using the second definition of their word. Two minutes later, I said, 'Go back to the first, or, if you're lucky enough that the word has a third or fourth definition, onward!' One of the writers read aloud a story about Frank, their brother, who is the kind of brother who ate his Recess Peanut Butter Cups really fast and then turned and looked sulkily at you until you gave them a bite of your candy bar, and to be frank, this assignment doesn't seem that important, and the best hot dog I ever ate was Nathan's Frank's in New York City. And it's true, this assignment may not make it as one of the tattoos on Queequeg's skin, but it might have prompted you to write a longer story about that brother who is now the one who expects you to arrange all the details for Mom's birthday party or a short essay about writers who swoop in from beyond and make you write essays about homonyms or homophones and you'd think they'd clear up which was what before they started jumping up on the table. Or maybe you write a poem about Kosher hot dogs and how Upton Sinclair, the American author who wrote in *The Jungle* (1985 [1906]) about the horrific conditions of slaughterhouses, would have never imagined such a pure hot dog – something made not of cow tails and pig ears but of the finest cuts of meat. Or at least the Kosherest ones.

Writing prompts may be the writerly version of a playground. Just like a playground, there is equipment provided. Nouns are the monkey bars – you swing from one definition to another until one propels you into significance. Verbs are slides that move you from memory to scene, from character to climax. Adverbs are one of those carousels that you turn yourself. You must run, holding onto the metal saddles, until you get it going fast enough to jump onto the hot, metal platform. Adverbs and self-driven carousels are not allowed in the playgrounds much anymore, but adjectives are everywhere. Adjectives are sand. You have to be careful. Too much grit ends up in someone's eye.

But say you're alone, without a writing professor jumping up on the table, telling you zoom in, zoom out? The writing prompts work because the writers don't know what to expect from the workshop leader. The workshoppees come in with an open mind. They're willing to go anywhere on the page. How do you surprise yourself? Turn to page 532 in the OED (Oxford English Dictionary). Or lie down on the floor and look at the underside of the table. Have you smelled a ponderosa pine lately? Butterscotch or vanilla. If you want to have fun in your writing, you might have to have some fun in your life. When is the last time you've been to the playground? Can you find an illicit carousel? If you run as fast as you've ever run, kick up your feet until the centrifugal force is almost too much. Then jump on. Try writing a couple of sentences while the world and the carousel spin around.

References

Melville, H. (1892), *Moby Dick, or The White Whale*, Boston: St Botolph Society.
Sinclair, U. (1985 [1906]), *The Jungle*, New York: Penguin Books.

SEE ALSO

Imagination
Aswang
Procrastination

Preposition

MARTIN VILLANUEVA

1

When I googled 'preposition', I got 'a word governing, and usually preceding, a noun or pronoun and expressing a relation to another word or element in the clause, as in "the man *on* the platform", "she arrived *after* dinner", "what did you do it *for*?"' Its roots are Latin: *prae* or before, *ponere* or to place. So when I chose 'prepositional thinking' as my contribution to this volume, it turns out I mistook 'preposition' for 'conjunction'. Privilege is happenstance left un-remarked – to say, for example, that where I'm from and my writing in English were not constitutive of this opportunity.

2

When I got around to the second word ('thinking'), I was glad it was a gerund, which both activates action and suspends it as a state through nouning. What's pinned down is flux, modified by an adverb ('prepositional') that posits concurrently, against 'thinking', some-thing else. I trust only motion – knowledge as occupying time and space, as procedural and propositional, as hypothesis at best and at its best, to be proven false by as early as the next clause. What is there to believe in as writers but that: perpetual drafting, form as both evidence and enactment of enunciating-through the variables.

3

A Filipino word I've seen used to denote prose is *tuluyan*, from the root *tuloy* – continue; prose then as continuum. I first encountered this word (and not *prosa*) in a journal published by the university from where I attained my MFA, where a professor scarred me with their definition of poetry: the language of discontinuity. What is art but that: forms of opacity, complication to the received or inherited, purposive miscommunication that proceeds from a distrust in language, not a mastery of it – the vigilance towards *breaking* continuums. Pro-position: A de-contextualized writing practice is at ease with the status quo.

4

I chose 'prepositional thinking' thinking I saw an *o* and not an *e*, and I've always been drawn to staking claim to space in the world, but stance as merely a suggestion to question, body in the square the other kids try to push you off from. How one's posture is an assumption. A hypothesis. A theory. The space it occupies an improvised public square of an encounter – another opportunity to step beside or aside, or to occupy another stance, re-posture an attempt at understanding. Prepositionality is thus relational and is a practice – to be carried out, and with care.

5

Because there is no writing practice worth cultivating that does not reckon with power. Mine is a practice wrought with guilt over privilege – what I am able to do, for example, with craft choices and matters beyond that, like venues offered because of the contacts I can make with my degrees and my CV, from where I live and from my writing in English. Prepositional thinking in a glossary for creative writing suggests that the practice is positional and provisional. Writing and its vis-à-vis's. Consider all that can link nouns and verbs to complete a clause. Consider all the propositions.

6

Notes Above a Native Son. Notes Against a Native Son. Notes Around a Native Son. Notes Before a Native Son. Notes Behind a Native Son. Notes Beneath a Native Son. Notes Beside a Native Son. Notes Between a Native Son. Notes by a Native Son. Notes Despite a Native Son. Notes in a Native Son. Notes into a Native Son. Notes Near a Native Son. Notes Off a Native Son. Notes Through a Native Son. Notes to a Native Son. Notes Toward a Native Son. Notes Upon a Native Son. Notes with a Native Son. Notes Within a Native Son.

7

Philippine Literature from English. Philippine Literature in English. Philippine Literature into English. Philippine Literature Near English. Philippine Literature Off English. Philippine Literature Past English. Philippine Literature to English. Philippine Literature Toward English. Philippine Literature Under English. Philippine Literature Upon English. Philippine Literature with English. Philippine Literature Within English. Philippine Literature Without English. Philippine Literature Above English. Philippine Literature Across English. Philippine Literature Against English. Philippine Literature Among English. Philippine Literature Around English. Philippine Literature Before English. Philippine Literature Behind English. Philippine Literature Below English. Philippine Literature Beneath English. Philippine Literature Beside English. Philippine Literature Besides English. Philippine Literature Despite English.

8

Prepositional thinking *above* creative writing, the former's precedence within the practice over output or outcome, not a method but a way of being. Prepositional thinking *across* creative writing, or where we've seen it: the open texts and not the closed ones, how in my head I divide my loves – texts and people alike – between the two. Prepositional thinking *before* creative writing, not just precedence but in process, like when I drafted these ninety words at a time off-and-on for three weeks, and again months later, 100 words exactly per section without fail after two weeks of prepositioning with other propositions.

9

Prepositional thinking *beside* creative writing, as in always, hand in hand or one in the same. Prepositional thinking *behind* creative writing, sadly what it felt like when I was in school, technique then above all and a requisite set, poetry as status bestowed upon a reading by checklist and thus complete on/within its own, 'well crafted' at its best, 'prose' at its worst. Prepositional thinking *by* creative writing, as when the process does not document but shape the author's thinking while in flux – a gerunding of proximities and of relations, of orientations and of convictions, of acceptance and of resistance.

10

Prepositional thinking *from* creative writing, which is to say we have allies from other arts, fields and disciplines. Prepositional thinking *in* creative writing: poetry with/that traces, essays that essay, notes on notes and the infinity of lists, prose that poetries, poetry that proses. Prepositional thinking *of* creative writing (see behind, by, or in). Prepositional thinking *on* creative writing – like a glossary, with differences within and vis-à-vis others (un-)like it. Prepositional thinking *toward* creative writing: a manner of approach, things turned askew, Picasso or a convex mirror. Prepositional thinking *within* creative writing: a movement. Prepositional thinking *upon* creative writing: a manifesto.

Further reading

Those this (the above) prepositioned with/through/from/within (among others):

Abad, G. (2013), 'Filipino Poetry from English', *Prairie Schooner*. Available online: https://prairieschooner.unl.edu/fusion/trees/filipino-poetry-english (accessed 6 April 2021).

Cappello, M. (2020), 'Notes on Notes', *The Paris Review*, 1 October. Available online: https://www.theparisreview.org/blog/2020/10/01/notes-on-notes/ (accessed 3 April 2021).

Cruz, C. (2016), 'Authoring Autonomy: The Politics of Art for Art's Sake in Filipino Poetry in English', (Publication No. 10240433), Doctoral Dissertation, University at Albany, State University of New York.

Cruz, C. (2017), 'The (Mis)Education of the Filipino Writer: The Tiempo Age and Institutionalized Creative Writing in the Philippines', *Kritika Kultura*, 28. Available online: https://journals.ateneo.edu/ojs/index.php/kk/article/view/KK2017.02802 (accessed 17 April 2021).

Lexico.com (2021), 'Preposition', *Lexico*. Available online: https://www.lexico.com/definition/preposition (accessed 26 April 2021).

Rendle-Short, F. (2020), '"Tissue of Making" in Practice-Led Research: Practi-care, Prepositional Thinking and a Grammar of Creativity', *TEXT: Journal of Writing and Writing Courses*, October, 24 (2): 1–17. Available online: http://www.textjournal.com.au/oct20/rendleshort.pdf (accessed 16 April 2021).

SEE ALSO

Experimentation
Vocabulary
Taxonomy

Procrastination

ARITHA VAN HERK

Procrastination is mocked as a writer's ultimate moral failing, a damnable offence. Innumerable manuals offer emotional and psychic analyses along with solutions to the 'problem', and ways to combat its insidious creep. Whatever the cause – self-deception or insecurity, arrogance or narcissism – procrastination serves as productivity's special demon.

Cures for procrastination slap with triage: it must be resisted, or cured, or quashed, or subdued; it epitomizes avoidance, vacillation, laziness and delay. Creative ideas flee the procrastinator, postponement judged the thief of talent. But avoidance does not measure procrastination, and procrastination is not equivalent to entropy. Does constructive dilatoriness not slyly underline the dullness of expectation, and how slavish adherence to unity, coherence and persuasion will blunt a wayward air? I confess, in my creative practice, that blithe procrastination and productive procrastination both proclaim writing's exuberance.

Romantic depictions of writers and writing seem perfectly willing to validate loneliness but unwilling to acknowledge the necessity of procrastination. Many arguments declare (with Virginia Woolf) that loneliness and creativity work together, but in that room, I would insert procrastination as the wayward ghost, the shiver that keeps company with the creative mind and the elasticity of time.

Persuasive excuses for procrastination? I have many. I need to reach a deeper understanding of the subject. Evasion will spark a better word. Digression and distraction serve as helpful accomplices to impatient patience. The wait is worth the end result, waiting not passive but anticipatory. Creativity needs to dream and wool-gather, to muse and wonder, to re-order and speculate. It is procrastination that suggests, in Michael Ondaatje's *In the Skin of a Lion*, 'Trust me, this will take time but there is order here, very faint, very human' (1987: 146). A trace.

If avoidance is one way that I survive the imperatives of writing or the dull appendages of requirement, procrastination is my ally. I resort to rage-baking or soup-making. I revel in laundry, the orderly sorting of colours from whites, the snap and fold of clean linens. Julian Barnes makes marmalade; I make rhubarb chutney. Menial usefulness.

Creative procrastination offers fertile ground for insight or discovery, the possibility of leaps from a windowsill to a balcony, an opening door rather than a lid-snugged casket. But writers are obliged to resort to subterfuge in order to enjoy the temptations of detour, escape from the despotism of directional maps. One of procrastination's requisite diversions is research, the chance to unearth the archaeology of a subject, test its etymology and probe its provenance. But extended investigation is too often castigated as temptation, potential for pollution, the worry that the writing will stink of research. Or be damned for the generative digressions of travel, that magnet pulling a writer away from the tyranny of rote. Wandering defamiliarizes ideas: we think while we move, we invent when we notice new details. Dickens's daily twelve-mile walk was more than exercise, certainly procrastination: 'my walking is of two kinds: one, straight on end to a definite goal at a round pace; one, objectless, loitering, and purely vagabond' (1895: 546). Truly, nothing is more stifling than the atelier's rarified isolation. The orchid tendency, to stay hot-housed in one situation, has contributed to many a crisis of imagination.

Procrastination is treated as the stepsister of boredom, and the biggest lie fed to writers is that boredom is boring. Boredom incites invention, childhood boredom prerequisite for the unorthodox idea, the as-yet untried experiment. Although often attributed to Dorothy Parker, who understood the vagaries of curiosity and doubt, it was Ellen Parr who declared: 'The cure for boredom is curiosity. There is no cure for curiosity' (1980: 172). Only boredom could prompt such an astute observation, more penetrating than the *bon mot* it has been relegated to, even misattributed to a writer who 'herself had practically elevated procrastination to an art form' (Meade 1988: 315). I am of the firm belief that no writer need apologize if procrastination aligns their praxis with insatiable curiosity.

It is strange to me that 'effective' writers avoid curiosity, as if it will lead them astray. Digression's encirclement dodges a charted outcome to reach the core of an expressive undertaking. Curiosity is inconvenient, arriving as it does at inappropriate times, feeding unexpected desires, and serving as condiment for novelty. Tasks at hand do not countenance curiosity's slipshod ways, its invitations to the dance, its deliberate elopement. And so, the writer accuses herself of procrastination, and returns to the page with a set face and a joyless determination not to digress. Digressions are dissolute, the stuff of promiscuity. Those who measure every journey (How far did you go? How long did it take?) are irritated by temptations and turnarounds. Rambles and brambles gravitate to traipses and jaunts, perambulations, *flaneuring*. Sean Silver declares, in his born-digital museum of eighteenth-century thought, *The Mind is a Collection:* 'Digressions are, in other words, little side journeys, but not the main thrust of the argument, and we feel that we need to apologize to everyone for not getting to the destination as fast as possible' (2015). Ah, the lure of detours.

I have learned – the hard way – that digression and procrastination give me leave to explore, and while on traverse, to discover the crux of the writing I commit to. Writers have much to learn from Muriel Spark's *Loitering with Intent* and the main character's observation that, 'I was finding it extraordinary how [...] characters and situations, images and phrases that I absolutely needed for the book simply appeared as if from nowhere into my range of perception. I was a magnet for experiences I needed' (1981: 15). Spark may seem dated to contemporary writers but her summary, of how a writer open to her own inquisitiveness will be given what is needed, is one worth cherishing. It is certainly a condition of my own practice.

Swift, Salinger and Bradbury expressed firm opinions about digression on the page, declaring it a pollution of style. But others revel in its possibilities, digressions capturing how thought moves between a mind and the objects and ideas that the mind lays bare. And it can, invaluably, remind us of where we have been, as with Alberto Manguel's *Packing My Library: An Elegy and Ten Digressions* (2018).

Procrastination 139

In truth, my writing life seeks to enable the restlessness that is my cherished companion. In searching for a better word, a cleaner sentence, I perform a wanderlust of language, flavoured by creative dissonance, with a soupçon of postponement and a pinch of dissatisfaction. And I am always ready for that excursion to another writer's country, not as a tourist but a fellow wordsmith. Some writers read with deadly design, as if to target an archive of ideas relevant to their purpose. How much better to read wantonly, entering a book as prevarication, in search of both memory and respiration. Such temporizing resists the modem of focus and end-product. If over-preparation is procrastination in disguise, perhaps writers must stop thinking of time as a sculpture and instead merely inhabit what time offers.

References

Dickens, C. (1895), *The Uncommercial Traveller*, Chapman and Hill: University of California.

Manguel, A. (2018), *Packing My Library: An Elegy and Ten Digressions*, New Haven: Yale University Press.

Meade, M. (1988), *Dorothy Parker: What Fresh Hell Is This?* New York: Villard Books.

Ondaatje, M. (1987), *In the Skin of a Lion*, Toronto: McClelland and Stewart.

Parr, E. (1980), 'Quotable Quotes', *Reader's Digest*, 117 (December). Available online: https://quoteinvestigator.com/2015/11/01/cure/ (accessed 20 September 2021).

Silver, S. (2015), *The Mind Is a Collection: Case Studies in Eighteenth-Century Thought*. Available online: http://www.mindisacollection.org/digression (accessed 2 May 2021).

Spark, M. (1981), *Loitering with Intent*, London: Bodley Head.

SEE ALSO

Permission
Not-knowing
Uncertainty

Queering

MARION MAY CAMPBELL, LAWRENCE LACAMBRA YPIL, FRANCESCA
RENDLE-SHORT, DEBORAH WARDLE, AMES HAWKINS, QUINN EADES,
STAYCI TAYLOR, PETA MURRAY, NATALIE HARKIN, ANTONIA PONT
AND ANONYMOUS

To queer: 2subvert 2disrupt 2defy but is it enough to show up in my queerness? To throw my words down and split my infinitives?

For me, striving as a writer to *queer* form, there's been huge inspiration from Ross Chambers's seductive exploration of literary digression, *Loiterature* (1999); from Jean Genet's fabulous autofictional essays, especially *Fragments of the Artwork* (2003 [1982]); from Roland Barthes's beautiful autobiographically inflected *A Lover's Discourse: Fragments* (2002 [1978]); from the Belgian-born, Paris-based philosopher Luce Irigaray's *This Sex Which Is Not One* (1979), and especially her 'When Our Lips Together Speak'. I remain in awe of French writer Monique Wittig's radical lesbian poetic experimentation across her work, especially *The Lesbian Body* (1986 [1973]) and *The Opoponax* (1976). In Australia, the effect of the stunning intervention of Kathleen Mary Fallon in *Working Hot* (1989) is immeasurable.

I looked at history, once, and then it looked back, but in the way history does which meant it did not look but knew it knew, and did not know my name, in this way was I known queerly.

Method-ing queer-ing ||| I find my method in my hands these hands that write these hands that fist taking hold of and doing and playing | and trans-egressing |it's a misnomer saying fist it's more like let your hand compress let it be drawn in let it change shape what/how you like | as erotic moment | tunneling __ desire uneasiness | uncertains | cross-transgenres | un-spokens | queer out-of-reaches and difficults and | slip-slides ||| when I squirt all over you your look of delight in the 3.00 am light blinds down pink lamp lick the salt the thick residue how you taste out in the open settle (unsettle) towards looseness preposition-gender non-binary-eees |disturb discomfort off-bounds obliques | seek pleasure in the body in rise in expand in expunge in expel insist persist *sistere* 'stand' on (*in-contact-with*) resistance

step/tread/stoop/advance/go out of line | no supposed-tos | play in the muck tarps and towels underfeet play in write in the ruins eschew necessities for-always shouldswould-scoulds | #rudeandmessy | find flow *because of* | un-genred un-gendered un-nameable spaces ||| make a root book

queering from queer from Middle Irish 'cúar' from *quer* from *twerh* from the root *terkw* | 'to turn, twist, wind' (Online Etymology Dictionary).

Q for queer in LGBTQICAPGNGFNBAZ+++

I love collaborative queering: improvisation, skewed perspectives, prismatic lenses come readily because that's how we move through the world & next thing you know you're assembling sonic samples or heckling each other in the cloud.

Queering puts me in the mind of phosphorescent illuminations. I shift my writer's palette away from heteronormativity. I ask questions of the world to explore slanted ways to challenge dominant paradigms. Timescales might warp, plots are inconclusive and characters are rule breakers. I return time and again to Monique Wittig's *Lesbian Body* (1986 [1973]), to Mama Alto's queering of divas' songs. It's beside and more than feminism. It is the fierce voice of challenge and change. It's the lightning bolt of knowing, loving and embracing human and more-than-human diversity in writing research and practice.

Halberstam said of queer spaces we 'do not "outgrow" certain forms of cultural activity' (2012: 2) so let's write punk, write mortifying adolescence, write beyond conventional temporality.

QUEER-ing in this moment I am feeling – desiring – as quirk, quest and quark. As a quail moves. Or rather, my translation of how the quail moves, all zippy-like. Speed as camp, as bobbing-joy, until a force unseen bursts, most seriously, as explosive flight. Another way: Queering is as the letter Q itself. A circle interrupted. A cycle that calls attention to new directions; to the lean, the list, the veer. Both a feather and a tail.

There's no pre-re-queer-site for queering, you're here, you're queer, get youse to it.

Also: Don't forget the ampersand. Queer-ING (as the) BIG REVEAL: it is the Q &! Q with me & you & we! Queer-ing LOVE: &!

Phoraging in quare wordage I lullabide in husk(i)ness. Trackskirting the ronageist to qubble in cunninglinguality for the lasagnification of our liddlelives. Lockdowner daze and sundrowning nights. Waitloss. Vacillinations. Dutyfreed and taking leaf of our censors. Audicles of juvenescence. Etymolomania meets fomophobia. Pistachiology meets legumebriousness. Euphorealia meets lachrymimosa. The youthage and the pellage; the queenagers and the bruized, the wideberthdays and the anachronaversaries. Deersmantling for kondominimumism. The enswampments and vicisscheweds, the pinktures and the blazetrailers, the tartanic drolling and the verbotomy and the odonatic pilot of we drag'n'plaighs!

Do you reed me? Did you seed me? Do I make myself queer?

QUEERING | to commit, wholly, to the intersectional possibilities of a spoken or material word as echo, tremor and motion in shades of shadow to light and composed on a temporal-breeze, fleeting in touch and impossible to fully comprehend or receive | to project love while dismantling harm in all its best literary guises | to feast on revolutions of *Eat the Rich* and *Always Was Always Will Be* and spit bitter-marrow from bones that give shape to borders and margins-within-margins | to commit, wholly, to decolonizing space where raced-gendered-classed-based violence still creeps, nestles and so comfortably resides.

To commit to queering (in writing, living, relating and *as* time) involves not deciding one's desire in advance and not shutting off (disavowing) avenues that it might take (note: wanting is not behaving, and ethics is, of course, to insist on, and be capable of, a pause between). To queer (or to fail at straightening) oneself involves not pre-empting the thread, vein, gush, roil and swell of nimble life that animates you, nor the direction it may take, nor the shapes that may wake it up, repurpose it or blink into its irises. It is to be alarmed, tickled, humbled, astonished and graced by what want can want, and to be relieved of our dullest, certain trajectories, our death-trajectories that always know everything. They purport to know what we like, and they also claim to be certain of what others (are) like. Queering does away with this double disrespect; its practice is unsettling (thus sometimes joy-ridden) and makes futures that are generous, roomy, fearless, unresentful, intergalactic.

References

A kind of stream of consciousness from influential pieces to the individuals who create a queer constellation from/with these ideas in/to/for your own writing.

Barthes, R. (2002 [1978]), *A Lover's Discourse: Fragments*, New York: Vintage Classic.

[Yes,] Barthes. But also, Ms. Snyder, my grade school gym teacher. And Phranc, and Martina, and Emily and Amy, and then, of course, there are the first kisses and first fxs, and all of that.

Chambers, R. (1999), *Loiterature*, Lincoln: University of Nebraska Press.

Fallon, K. M. (1989), *Working Hot*, Fitzroy, Melbourne: Sybylla Co-operative Press and Publications.

Genet, J. (2003 [1982]), *Fragments of the Artwork*, trans. C. Mandell, Palo Alto, California: Stanford University Press.

Halberstam, J. J. (2012), *Gaga Feminism: Sex, Gender, and the End of Normal*, Boston: Beacon Press.

Irigaray, L. (1979), *This Sex Which Is Not One*, Ithaca, New York: Cornell University Press.

Online Etymology Dictionary. Available online: https://www.etymonline.com/search?q=queer&ref=searchbar_searchhint (accessed 4 October 2021).

Wittig, M. (1976), *The Opoponax*, trans. H. Weaver, Vermont: Daughters Inc.

Wittig, M. (1986 [1973]), *The Lesbian Body*, trans. D. LeVay, Boston: Beacon Press.

Xtra piece (n.d) that we think folx really would benefit from reading and then connect that to a cosmology of influences that are not of the literary sort.

SEE ALSO

Hybrid
Communitas
Vocabulary

Radical effrontery

JEANINE LEANE

I belong to the Wiradjuri people from the Murrumbidya (Murrumbidgee) river in southwestern New South Wales, Australia. I was born in the 1960s into a large extended family of Wiradjuri women, descending from my Gunhinarrung/Grandmother's people who have always lived in this area. The lands and waters between Gundagai in the southwest to Wagga Wagga, further south have always been my peoples' Country. These lands and waterways were first invaded by white settlers from the 1820s onwards. Foreign encroachment began after the crossing of the Blue Mountains to the west of the original site of occupation at Sydney. Settler invaders lobbied the colonial governor, Lachlan Macquarie and later Thomas Brisbane to go beyond the crown, to annex the fertile freshwater cradles further west of what is now known today as the town of Bathurst. Few settlers are aware of the implications of these three words: *Beyond the crown.* In being granted this permission settlers could occupy these lands on the understanding that they were no longer protected as British citizens *by* the crown and the radius its powers extended to in the Sydney basin. The advantages of encroaching beyond the protection of the crown far outweighed any disadvantages, because being *beyond the crown* also meant that the early invaders were no longer subjected to the laws and the punishments *of the crown.* Beyond the crown meant beyond the limits of retribution. The lands could be 'secured' for settlement by any means.

As I write this the euphemisms of the introduced language of English are already invading the story of lands stolen through and by the killings of the Country's first peoples. Terms such as 'the lands were secured', 'taken up', 'settled', 'farmed' and 'the Aborigines (sic) were displaced', 'dispersed' are all colonial euphemisms for the brutal truth: *the Wiradjuri clans were killed or captured and sent elsewhere, and the lands were stolen and occupied.* The violent-politeness of retrospective colonial tellings, spread thick and murky lies over the story of my people. They also fail to speak to the resilience and survivance of my people, along the Murrumbdiya and across the mythscape of the constructed nation.

Australia is a settler colony. Land was invaded not ceded. If you are not a First Nations Australian you are a settler, or a visitor (long or short term). Settlerism in Australia is layered and not all settlers identify as part of the British diaspora. Settlers make up the largest demographic in the country. Initially Australian settlers were Anglo and up until 1972 settlers had to be white under the White Australia Policy. Post 1972 Australian settlers become more diverse, but the majority are still Anglo/white and identify as such (ABS 2016). Too few settlers are familiar with the systematic violence that continues to impact on the speaking/writing positions of First Nations people.

In 1884, the Minister for Education favoured separate schools in areas with large Aboriginal populations. Where there were few Aboriginal students, they were to attend the nearest public school if they were 'habitually clean, decently clad and they conduct themselves with propriety' (Minister for Public Instruction George Reid [1883–4] cited in Fletcher 1989b: 74–5). In 1902, the policy of Exclusion on Demand was formalized and circulated to all New South Wales Public Schools (Fletcher 1989a: 88). Under this policy government schools in NSW were told to exclude Aboriginal children if other parents made a complaint about Indigenous children being in their child's classroom. Until 1972, the policy of Exclusion on Demand justified the expulsion of Aboriginal children in NSW by 'the will of the people with the Minister's sanction' (Minister John Perry [1899–1904] cited in Fletcher 1989b: 89). I was born in the colonial calendar to be the first generation after the invasion to have access to the settler-invader culture of power – the Western education system. The 1960s was a time when it became possible to attend a Western school (although still conditionally), and to learn to read and write. I am the first generation of my family and community to be in a position to mount a radical affront against and towards settler language and behaviours that continue to perpetuate the untruths of the violence that is not only confined to Australia's past, but which continues in the epistemic violence of the present, in conversations, in classrooms and the media.

Silencing by the 'politeness' of settlerism is a deep-seated ongoing practice continuing unchecked until the late twentieth and early twenty-first century into the present. Euphemism obscures truths of invasion, occupation and continued settler profit and skin privilege built on and nourished by dispossession and continued silencing of First Nations people who speak out against this. Silencing is well served by Western notions of 'politeness', 'restraint', 'courtesy' and 'not wishing to cause offence'. Radical effrontery is pushing away from accepted forms of settler language. It requires breaking a pattern of behaviour that is expected from First Nations peoples, that which was expressed in the Exclusion on Demand Policy, to a behaviour that confronts the language of invasion and settlement directly. It requires the risk of being described as 'rude', 'aggressive', 'offensive' and/or 'blunt'. Martin Heidegger (1971) noted that a border or boundary is signified not by where something ends, but where something else begins its presencing. The role of the limit and the limitations of what *is* and *isn't* allowed to be or supposed to be said is at the heart of radical effrontery in writing and speaking. As Munanjahli and South Sea Islander academic and writer Chelsea Watego observed in her new collection of essays, *Another Day in the Colony,* 'The "problem of the Aborigine" in the colony is our very presence; always was, always will be' (2021: 46). Watego's whole collection is a radical affront to settler representations of us and sensibilities towards us. She describes in detail the reactions towards, and the consequences for First Nations people who challenge the euphemisms of settler language when our questions come too close to the truth. Too close to offending settler sensibilities of living on and benefitting from stolen land.

Radical Effrontery works in speech and on the page as a style and practice of communication that is direct and one where the speaker/writer is prepared to run the risk of being described as abrupt, 'presenting biased information' (meaning too much content from a First Nations perspective) or 'reverse racism'. As Watego says: 'the Black critic is framed as a threat, not just to the white author, but to creativity and freedom, it would seem' (2021). Radical effrontery is about asking difficult questions like who has the authority to tell someone

Radical effrontery   145

else's story; and what is the legacy of literary representation. And challenging 'Eurocentric-constructed universalisms' such as 'freedom of the imagination' that normalize the settler state. Because what Black writing and speaking does is claim back space in classrooms and on pages that was not previously been afforded to us, and it interrupts the previously unquestioned privilege of white settlers to represent us.

References

ABS (Australian Bureau of Statistics) (2016), Cat No. 2071.0, Census of Population and Housing: Reflecting Australia – Stories from the Census, Canberra, Australia.

Fletcher, J. J. (1989a), *Clean, Clad and Courteous: A History of Aboriginal Education in New South Wales*, Marrickville, Sydney: Southwood Press.

Fletcher, J. J. (1989b), *Documents in the History of Aboriginal Education in New South Wales*, Marrickville, Sydney: Southwood Press.

Heidegger, M. (1971), *Poetry Language and Thought*, trans. A. Hofstadter, New York: Harper Colophon Books.

Watego, C. (2021), *Another Day in the Colony*, St Lucia, Brisbane: University of Queensland Press.

SEE ALSO

Archival-poetics
Permission
Resistance

Reading

BELINDA CASTLES

The difficult thing about the writing life is the uncertainty. Creative practice requires that we produce work over sustained periods in the face of ongoing doubt. What helps writers is often reading, and a particular kind of reading may be of value and comfort to us over the long haul. That is the reading of unfinished writing, approached with an ear for the fragments of tune singing fitfully from the messy page.

Reading unfinished work with an open mind takes practice. For many, this training begins or develops in a collaborative form, by reading the work of others, in a creative writing class or group. In such groups we are not reading according to personal taste. We may reject nothing as beneath our attention. The participants have agreed, merely by signing up, to read each other's work, and intentions, and help one another to carry them out. In the first class I attended, I recall vividly a classmate's poem: the rounded word 'tomato' in a graceful fat font, the white space around the words, a revelation, as you turned the page, about slicing – and a violence to do with a world beyond tomatoes. I wrote on her work; I tentatively spoke up in class. Students gave me notes on my poems and stories, about what worked, what was missing or unrealized. It was a galvanizing instance of exchange and possibility.

Later, I worked in publishing, and happened to open a package containing a typewritten manuscript of a new novel by one of my favourite authors, covered in edit marks, notes and queries made by the author and an editor. At the time, I would have said that what reading that particular manuscript gave me was a compulsion I wanted to create in my own writing: a kind of tension – you must read on, you can't read on. But it was the form in which this novel came to me that was important in the end. In the mistakes and corrections, or resolutions, the evidence of a process, I saw a mind at work, in conversation with another and with the text, dissatisfied, pushing itself on. I saw that no piece of writing, no matter how brilliant, arrives fully formed.

In the Australian novella *Snake* by Kate Jennings (1997), the wayward country wife Irene plays Mahler on her new record player, listening intently for a particular kind of evidence. 'In certain sections, if you concentrated, you could hear the conductor stamp his foot and grunt. Irene could barely contain her excitement as she waited for these moments. She did not view the extraneous noises as flaws. Instead, she was reassured by them. The music had not been handed down from Olympus; humans like herself had created it' (Jennings 1997: 92). To read the draft of a published writer is to catch a glimpse of one's own imperfect self in the work of those we admire. It was one thing, in class, to know that my own writing and that of my peers were smudged by our own clumsy thumbprints. But to read a messy manuscript by a celebrated author revealed an enabling connection between the writers I admired, and humans like myself.

These days I teach writing. In workshops, I guide students to articulate their reading of each other's work in a way that is helpful. A certain kind of generosity is required. We glean intentions. We sense heat, energy and the coolness when it dissipates. By reading others' works in progress, we learn the trick of distance needed to read our own. Practising this helps me identify the weaknesses in my own writing: the time-passing, the breath-clearing, the falling back on old tricks. My manuscripts are filled with blunt notes to self, *waffle, no tension, who cares?* I do not take offence – it is a kind of joke, a form of ribbing with purpose. Give this another try, the notes say. What can be done?

Toni Morrison said, 'As a writer, a failure is just information [...] I recognize failure [...] and fix it, because it is data, it is information, knowledge of what does not work' (qtd in Sutton 2014). I read with my feelings and knowledge of language, people and story, and it is data that I am collecting and acting upon. Like a scientist, a writer can read the meanings in data: in patterns, errors and gaps. What we are developing is a method of calibration. George Saunders writes of the iterative, repetitive work of continually testing and adjusting one's work. He says that 'the artist [...] is like the optometrist, always asking: Is it better like this? Or like this?' (2017). Our reading requires the steadiness of a technician focused on the data that will help us to see better.

This kind of reading requires a patient, enquiring disposition – scientists cannot prejudge the results of a true experiment. Novelist and writing teacher, Stephanie Bishop, writes of the way in which we must learn to read our drafts with acceptance, rather than judgement of their distance from the work we first imagined. 'Half the challenge, or maybe all of it, is just trying to understand what is there, to see it for what it is' (Bishop 2021: 275–6). What is needed is a 'kind of attention that can tolerate a maximum of uncertainty and instability. An attention that is both loose and sharp, curious, probing, exploratory, alert to uneasy sensations and contradictions' (275–6). We need to learn the kind of reading that will serve the work best: clear-eyed, open, purposeful, the kind of reading that will allow the work to be what it can be. By the time we have drafted our work several times, we know more about it than the people we were when we first imagined it.

Such reading can be practised collectively. Other writers need what we need: careful readers, deadlines and encouragement. By committing to read without prejudice in writing groups, workshops and informal partnerships we can develop both our ear and our patience for uncertainty. Our generosity to others and their work can be honed and turned towards ourselves. We might learn to read our own writing, alert to its failures and the information they provide: an attuned reading, keeping us alive to possibilities, and where they will take us next.

References

Bishop, S. (2021), 'Lines of Sight: The Short Fiction of Gerald Murnane', in B. Castles (ed.), *Reading Like an Australian Writer*, 272–85, Sydney: NewSouth Publishing.

Jennings, K. (1997), *Snake*, New Jersey: Ecco Press.

Saunders, G. (2017), 'What Writers Really Do when They Write', *The Guardian*, 4 March. Available online: https://www.theguardian.com/books/2017/mar/04/what-writers-really-do-when-they-write (accessed 15 December 2020).

Sutton, R. (2014), 'The Art of Failure: The Importance of Risk and Experimentation: Interview with Toni Morrison: Write Erase, Do It Over', *American Artscape Magazine*, 4, National Endowment for the Arts. Available online: www.arts.gov/stories/magazine/2014/4/art-failure-importance-risk-and-experimentation/toni-morrison (accessed 15 December 2020).

SEE ALSO

Zim
Notebooking
Listening

Resistance

JAMES BYRNE

> For me, poetry has no point unless it's a prompt or aid to political and ethical change. This is not to say that a poem should be political or ethical instruction, but rather that it might engender a dialogue between itself and the reader or listener, between itself and other poems and texts, and between all of these and a broader public (whatever that might be). I see myself as a poet activist – every time I write a poem, it is an act of resistance to the State, the myriad hierarchies of control, and the human urge to conquer our surroundings (Kinsella 2013: 16).

Language is active (the echo: is activism). Language as flux.

Language is a privilege. The examination of wounds. A speaking out against injustice.

All this echolalia of silence before we even begin to tune up a line.

Years ago, at a poetry festival in England, I enjoyed a lunch with Sarah Maguire, Fadhil Al-Azzawi and Margaret Atwood. Twirling her spaghetti, Atwood said that for every year of peace in the world there have been over 400 years of war. Al-Azzawi coughed on his soup: 'I'm surprised it's not *higher* than 400'.

Maguire's opening statement at the launch of the Poetry Translation Centre in London: 'Translation is an alternative to war' (2004) (the echo: writing is an alternative to war).

Creative resistance to all that looting and pillaging.

Yes, poetry vs. war. War wins. But writing keeps a record and can hold crookedness to account. Enough for politicians to enact the censoring scythe.

When working with Myanmar poets a decade ago, I learnt that the dictator General Ne Win once banned the world 'sunset'. His own name roughly translates as sunrise. Ne Win presumed poets of the time might be trying to assassinate him. Other censored words included 'mother' and 'red'. Imagine not being able to write the word 'mother'?

Why resist? Why rebel? The world is on fire.

David Marriott: 'the wound is language' (2008: 79). Echo: Allen Ginsberg and Amiri Baraka's owl-wise 'who who'.

'Poetry makes nothing happen', W. H. Auden miserably declared (1979: 80). I remember talking about this with Somali poet Maxamed Xaashi Dhamac (or 'Gaarriye' as he was better known). Gaarriye devised a metrical form for Somali poetry (there were no dictionaries, the language was first written down in 1972). Gaarriye made Somali poetry *happen*. Poetry itself *is* a happening.

It was common in Somalia for Gaarriye to read in front of thousands, many people travelled from nearby villages. There were no book signings. Readers were also listeners who had collected his poems on audio tapes, often bootleg copies, which he then signed at the readings.

Writing is both solitary and social. Even the act of writing might change something within ourselves and how we perceive the world.

'Poetics is born of a crisis – the need to change' (Sheppard 2002: 3).

'Poethics' as poetics. An ethical consideration of my place in the world. Who am I to be writing anything? And yet, the dare or nerve to do it.

Writing as forming(s). Not necessarily incoherent but often decoherent. Fragmentation is an organic use of form because we ourselves are fragmented, subdivided, plural. Anything else is artifice, is a performance of the self (which writing also is).

What did you *do*? Ilya Kaminsky: 'we protested/but not enough' (2019: 3).

What are you resisting? Why are you speaking to unspeak?

It would have been easier if I had been an astronaut. I could have explained to my family that I simply go up into space and come back down again. How else to explain the chanting out of a poem at 2.00 am?

Vertigoes within hierarchical space. To write against being *up there*.

Resisting state conformity because the state – unlike how it was presented in ancient Greece – has not been able to protect either myself or my fellow citizens.

Writing outside of 'the good life'. Of institutions. Writing from inside.

I-spy. Something beginning with 'P' … Power? Politricks? Yes, to both, but keep guessing.

To resist corporate-imposed docility. If I write about popular culture, it is to examine its essential *use*. But it is enough to ventriloquize Daffy Duck?

Unless dreaming myself awake, I don't have time to sleep during the day.

To resist all forms of literary corporatism (prizes, competitions, all that jostling for position when writing should be more communal). And yet, I still like the look of my own name on the book covers. Narcissus. Echo.

To know a little of who you are and what you're up against. 'Before you kick against the pricks, be sure you're not a prick yourself' (Lumsden 2003: 22).

A poetics of listening. Because everyone talks-talks-talks so much. Listening as ethical responsibility, as rebellion, as resistance.

A poetics of listening in … I am 'torn awake' (Gander 2000: 45).

Inhale-exhale, the world breathes like a lung.

'Who am I? Who are you? To understand the question is on repeat without magicking up the idea of a definitive answer.

Nuar Alsadir: 'I am never merely writing, but always writing to *you*' (2017: 11).

Know your place, offer support and a voice to those who have been silenced. Franz Fanon: 'The constantly affirmed concern with "respecting the culture of the native popula-tions" accordingly does not signify taking into consideration the values borne by the culture […] Rather, this behaviour betrays a determination to objectify, to confine, to imprison, to harden. Phrases such as "I know them", "that's the way they are" show this maximum objectification successfully achieved' (1970: 34–5).

So much writing about the colonies from inside the British Library.

Unwriting, unknowing. Knowing to be humble. All writing is merely a lifelong apprenticeship.

Resistance 151

Language is artificial, we had to make it up. But its 'consciousness implies a presence, an exposure to grasp, to taking: comprehension, appropriation' (Levinas 1998: 143).

Writing towards the idea of you, not speaking for you.

Extinction Rebellion kettled at the protest gates. Who was it for, if not you?

It seems to come around each year, the warning *against* being political. But what about dangers within shunning the political, of turning away? 'In our age there is no such thing as "keeping out of politics". All issues are political issues' (Orwell 2001 [1946]): 7).

A few weeks before he was murdered by the military regime in Myanmar on 3 March 2021, the poet K. Za Win posted on his Facebook account: 'Though I have different views than you, I'll lay down my life for you all.'

Writing is our essential gesture towards humanity.

References

Alsadir, N. (2017), *Fourth Person Singular*, Liverpool: Pavilion.

Auden, W. H. (1979), 'In Memory of W. B. Yeats', in *Selected Poems*, 80–3, New York: Vintage Books.

Fanon, F. (1970 [1964]), 'Racism and Culture', in *Towards the African Revolution*, 29–44, London: Pelican Books.

Gander, F. (2000), *A Faithful Existence: Reading, Memory and Transcendence*, New York: Counterpoint.

Kaminsky, I. (2019), *Deaf Republic*, London: Faber and Faber.

Kinsella, J. (2013), *Activist Poetics: Anarchy in the Avon Valley*, Liverpool: Liverpool University Press.

Levinas, E. (1998), *Entre Nous: Thinking of the other*, trans. M. B. Smith and B. Harshav, New York: Columbia University Press.

Lumsden, R. (2003), *The Wolf*, London, 4, issue 4.

Marriott, D. S. (2008), *Hoodoo Voodoo*, Devon: Shearsman.

Orwell, G. (2001 [1946]), *Politics and the English Language*, London: Penguin.

'Poets are the Martyrs in Myanmar Coup Protests'. Available online: www.vice.com/en/article/xgzj94/poets-are-among-the-martyrs-in-myanmar-coup-protests (accessed 18 March 2021).

Rettalack, J. (2004), *The Poethical Wager*, Berkley: University of California Press.

Sheppard, R. (2002), *The Necessity of Poetics*, Liverpool: Ship of Fools Press.

SEE ALSO

Aswang

Code

Radical effrontery

Rites

MANOLA-GAYATRI KUMARSWAMY

Entering

Fellow poet, Busisiwe Mahlangu, tells me about her new fiction writing, 'Yeoh! When I sit down to write, the story just takes me somewhere else. I never know where I'm going to go. I'm just going' (pers. comm.). Where does she go? How does she get on that trip? Some writers may be able to snap their fingers and get there. I often can't. My way of getting on board that journey Busi talks about is ritual. Maybe you already have one? The ritual acts as a passage of entry and a portal. Ritual happens over a demarcated space, compressed or longitudinal time, a commitment of intention and action, a noticing, a sense that in this time and space while doing this intended action – you are in a concentrated space or durational time. Your being, your attention and energy are focused on what is emerging and being directed through you here. In this space and for this time – you are present only to this.

First wRite: clearing air

You may need to speak before you can write. If there is no one to speak to, orgasm a free write.
Two drafts. Confession. Confronting. Second, I've showed no one. Buzzing. Eyes sting. Foggy. Who are the editors again? Why am I writing this? What's Bloomsbury's copyright tracks like? Where is the money going? This tongue. These words. This language. The Canadian Nuns on my Insta feed. The lost children. Silent. The silenced tongues. Catholic matriarchs in my line. Lips whispering confessions. Fingers slipping over rosary beads. The convent I studied in. Sacred Heart. The English classes. My favourite hours. The exams excelled. The Church refuses to apologize for the mass murders. Beginning knowing that our hands all have blood. Stigmata. The page too. The ink as well. Schooling. Even to be literate feels like a betrayal. To know, to read and write in this tongue. For this to be the language I think in. Dream in. Love in. Love. That I also love this language. And a whole bunch of dead and living white, black, coloured mxn and womxn writing in this tongue. I speak to someone. The 'other'/ my 'self'. What are we doing? I have doubts. This is what I feel. She says this. Listens. Clueless. Knowing. Holding. Letting go. I write a letter to my lover before I can look at the draft again.

Second Rite: body opens space

A ritual is an embodied practice. So is writing. Prepare your body. A somatics practitioner I've worked with says that we must prepare for material that emerges from the unconscious (Dunlea 2019).

The Second Rite is physical. A breath taken in, a walk, an ocean dip, coffee, a bath, yoga or breath-impulsed movement. The second rite is mental. I have been thinking about what I might want to write as I walk, eat, drink, swim. I notice what is moving into words. I play a current mood favourite song on loop. In some phases, I've decided on certain times that I write. As soon as I wake up, before I sleep. In the morning till about lunch. I try to keep meetings for certain times in the day and days in the week as far as possible and have uninterrupted hours for the writing. But sometimes I just have to do small slots. Ten mins. Twenty mins. Thirty mins. When struggling, I free write with a sand-glass timer. I light a candle when I'm starting something new. It helps me feel contained when what is coming through feels overwhelming. When writing through personal or collective trauma, we need to contain and hold as we heal and work.

Third wRite: working projections, waiting, wRiting

Clear my table. Relight a lamp. Sit at the table. Stare out of the window, At the sky, the sea. Ready. Turn the hourglass.

Though many writers will speak of the discipline of daily writing, I find myself holding a sensing or seeds of a thought for weeks and even months in silence, needing much touch by wind, light, sea, movement and conversation before flowing on the page. I learn to be less afraid of these silences and seeming non-activity. I do not see it as 'not doing work' anymore. And when I am ready, I freewrite or can bear to look at earlier drafts. I work on my own blocks. I rethink what was projected, assess continuing differences. Everything that continues to make this difficult. I notice the suffering of yet another unfolding injustice somewhere in the world or in my own body or life. Books I have still not read. I choose again to write, in spite of everything else happening. This choice marks a decisive movement. I have often not made this choice, or been able to, and the wRites ended before they moved into Writing.

Fourth wRite: community wRites

In December 2016, following the loss of a fellow poet from Johannesburg, who had abruptly ended his life, two South African poets (Xaviso Vili and Lebogang Lebese) and I co-founded Scribe Rites. After several months of hazy grief, over the course of a highly inebriated night, we decided to create a writing group that would be healing, creative and rigorous. We ran a series of writing workshops, divided across four quarters over the year with four three-hour Sunday sessions and an invited external facilitator for each quarter. The final quarter had each of us and then the participants facilitate the workshops. By the end of two years, a formula had emerged. We'd meet and greet. Do a short warm-up or playful writing exercise or listen and talk about a theme or poem. Next, we would have between 10 and 15 minutes to free write. We then paired up and read our freewrites to our partners, or to the group, and received feedback on them. We then re-wrote our pieces with an edit exercise. We'd read aloud our edited versions, be applauded and loved, ending each Sunday session remarkably happy with ourselves, the little piece in our notebooks and feeling close to this little community of writers. This Sunday mix had experienced writers, old slam kings, a visiting new queen, deadly upstarts, shy novices, philosophical ruminators, hobbyists and self-healers but across the table in our room, everyone's voice and words became golden, tender, shy, surprising, sad, powerful, victorious, tragic, hopeful, funny – making us scream with laughter or go silent or click or whistle or jump up and do a little jig for some completely unusual turn of phrase or powerful revelation on the meaning of it ALL or for a heartbreakingly poignant self-confession. Scribe Rites was a joyful riot of a community. But over the years, there have also been smaller, quieter ones made of a friend or two, who listens, gives feedback and helps me shape and share my words. I have sent them work as voice notes or word documents or in-lined emails and a couple for very special times in post. Writing is a tender mix of solitude and community.

Fifth Rite: rest, repetition, writing, reading, rewriting

Before I can come back to the page on my own, I must go away for the weekend. A Saturday night with mycelium intelligences awakening over the Western Cape coast, a girl-friend's exuberant loving and my lover's listening in another hemisphere as close as my heartbeat. Now I come back to the page with different feedback from my community of writers and non-writers. Anyone who has listened or read the drafts written. I even read my draft aloud to my plant. I come back to the editor's much invited strikethroughs and edit on my own again. This last rite is the most attentive and concentrated, requiring close reading and rewriting and time alone, in silence and with few distractions.

Sixth Rite: offering

Sending it out. This is less difficult, finally. I am waiting for it to find new places of connection.

Seventh Rite: return

Take a walk, have a drink, have another orgasm, call a friend, meet a lover, take your plant into the sun, find things that make you chuckle and repost them on your Insta feed.

When we write, we really do transition between worlds and while you need to ritual this entry, the exit needs to be rited with care too. You can feel an emptiness when you return from your draft. The room around you may feel weird. You wonder where your friends are and if you went away too long. You may feel relief that the work is done but also a little sad to stop. Breathe. Allow the journey you went on to synthesize. Journal about the poem, the article, the essay you just sent out into the world. Each time you write may change a little or a lot of who you are, how you live, love and think. You may have opened new neural pathways. wRiteing is a kind of photosynthesis for your being. It can be exhilarating and tiring. Rest. Talk to a plant.

Exit

This is my path for the riot of trauma violence – personal, epistemic, historical, linguistic – to be rited into writing. Why do I do it? Healing. Legibility. Because there are things to be said. Because wRiteing surprises me. Because it is not only about the trauma but joy and a way to return to life, *find* life. It changes me and the world around me. As Mahlangu would say,

'This is how you return to yourself' (2018: 51). When the different workshops ended and I came back to writing on my own again, I had a heightened sense of awareness of how useful rituals are not just for times of great joy or grief but for the act of writing itself. I write now, not as much as an act of mourning but of living. I have simply wRIoTED myself here.

References

Dunlea, M. (2019), *Bodydreaming in the Treatment of Developmental Trauma: An Embodied Therapeutic Approach*, Oxon: Routledge.

Mahlangu, B. (2018), 'This Is Yours', in *Surviving Loss, 51*, Tshwane South Africa: Impepho Press.

SEE ALSO

Ghost Weaving

Communitas

Camping

Sensing

CM BURROUGHS

The bulk of my work is bound to the body. My writing method is one of sensing the body through the poem, and I always wish my reader to sense that most essential figure, as well. This process requires a great amount of empathy, because the speakers of my poems are various: imperfect, half-made, unwell, desirous, loving, powerful and vulnerable. Making a poem that speaks through the senses necessitates an awareness of how the body is made and thusly moves within the poem.

My book *The Vital System* (2012) begins with the poem 'Dear Incubator', which distils three months I spent in an incubator after being born prematurely. The poem is the foundation of the book, and writing it was a practice in patience. It would have been a simple (read: easy) task to write the poem in third-person perspective, simply observing and imagining speakers and setting, but that would have created a gulf between the reader and the primary bodies of the poem. I chose to compose the poem using the first-person perspective, which would close the distance between reader and (my body). However, beyond this choice, my difficulty was figuring out how to write a poem that communicated from the perspective of a premature self – an incomplete body and half-formed mind. What could be experienced in that state? How could I bridge the premature body with the reader's body? Here is an excerpt from the completed poem:

Dear Incubator,
At six months gestation, I am a fabrication born far too soon. My body, a stone in a steaming basket.
I remember you.
– [Figureless]
– A black kaleidoscope. Turn. Turn. The dangerous loom of the loom of you. Patterns pressing upon – me inside. Nothing luminous as my mother's womb. This second attempt at formation; a turn.
The nurse slides her wedding band past my hand, beyond my elbow and over my shoulder. I am 1lb. 12oz. and already feminine. Knowing nothing of it. I am trying to be clear –

I was first fascinated then afraid of the shapes' rise from your darkness. And their growth toward me. I wailed under their weight. My eyes were shuttered by lids. My skin was translucent; anyone could see me working.
How can I ask you from inside the poem – what senses did I have so early … So unformed. I was tangled in tubes (that kept my heart pumping; that kept my lungs from collapsing; food to the body; oxygen to the brain) (2012: 3).

Early in the writing process, I chose direct address as my entryway into the poem in an effort to set up the most intimate and immediate confrontation between the speaker and incubator. It was a way to give agency to the incubator and to the body within it, and the first-person perspective, a frequent agent of the epistolary form, facilitated a confessional and revelatory experience for the reader. As if to say: *Hear me. Here is a body begging for empathy.*

After choosing to compose an epistolary poem through first-person perspective, I researched incubators from the time I was born, and, while rooting around in family archives, found a photograph my parents had taken of me *in* the incubator; a large sign on the outside of the incubator reads *Do Not Overstimulate!* These resources brought me closer to understanding the poem's site. To understand the smallness of my body, I used web searches to find images of premature babies – 1lb 12oz babies as I had been – and this gave me a way to imagine my body more fully, to conceive how it measured against an adult hand for instance and against the incubator, as well. After understanding the primary figures of the poem, I spent time considering the emotional tone. Vulnerability was vital to the poem; luckily, I had a story to tell; a nurse had pushed her wedding band up my arm, and this way an easy way to communicate the exact smallness of my body to a reader.

I had all the components for a rich piece, but how could I create the empathetic sensory experience I wanted for my reader? My writing 'dear incubator, premature body, wedding ring, my vulnerability' means nothing at all – to me or to you. I had to put the parts in concert and grant them a narrative, and the poem that results uses sensory imagery as its primary tool. There's a Billy Collins essay (2020) that reviews seven kinds of imagery; I use the essay to teach my beginning poetry students about the complexity of imagery as a poetic device. Collins lists imagery as: visual, auditory, gustatory, tactile, olfactory, kinaesthetic (sense of motion) and organic (internal sensations). This list of kinds of imagery helps to demystify what elements can combine to form a whole image. This list also presents the building blocks for what a writer may heed when trying to build imagery for a reader. To impress a reader's senses – to give your reader an experience – it is crucial to use sensory imagery.

In creating Dear Incubator and its sensory environment, I focused first on the container rather than the contained and chose the experience of claustrophobia to address the state of being inside the incubator. I use 'steaming basket' and 'kaleidoscope' – visual and tactile images – to convey a sense of instability, and there are references to figureless, darkness and a dangerous loom – kinaesthetic and organic images – used to convey a sense of fear, foreignness and anxiety. I address the incubator throughout the poem as a reference to stability and fixed form and use it as a viewing platform for the speaker's body, that is not fully formed, that can be touched but cannot touch, and whose biological needs are all that's legible. I play between the poem's two bodies – and between kinds of imagery – to craft a site of intimate vulnerability where my readers can reside. Only readership would gauge my success or failure in this effort.

In 2013, I read this poem to an audience at the Virginia Festival of the Book. Following the reading, a Neonatal Intensive Care Unit nurse found me; she was weeping when she told me that she'd always wondered what the premature babies were feeling in their incubators and said that my poem helped her to understand their experience. Her admission was one of the most insightful and rewarding experiences I've had as a poet. She taught me that my desire to communicate with my reader had resulted in a truth that mattered mightily to her life's work.

References

Burroughs, CM (2012), *The Vital System*, Massachusetts: Tupelo Press.
Collins, B. (2020), 'Poetry 101: What Is Imagery? 7 Types of Imagery in Poetry', *Masterclass*, 8 November. Available online: https://www.masterclass.com/articles/poetry-101-what-is-imagery-learn-about-the-7-types-of-imagery-in-poetry-with-examples#what-is-imagery-in-poetry (accessed 30 April 2021).

Further reading

Burroughs, CM (2021), *Master Suffering*, Massachusetts: Tupelo Press.
Cixous, H. (1994), *Three Steps on the Ladder of Writing*, New York: Columbia University Press.
Sellers, H. (2007), *The Practice of Creative Writing: A Guide for Students*, New York: Bedford, St Martin's.

SEE ALSO

Experience
Feelings
Bung wantaim

Speculation

ROBIN HEMLEY

Without speculation, there would be no creation. No gods creating people. No people creating gods. Every day, unceasing entertainment and stimulation carve roads into the great Speculative Range, where our ancestors were known to wander lost for months, feared missing, only to emerge transformed into geniuses. When my daughter says she is bored on a long car ride, I am hopeful. 'Good,' I tell her. 'Dwell there for a while.' From boredom, springs speculation.

The essay, steeped in a long tradition of praising uncertainty and ambiguity, has never confined itself to fact. My go-to example of this has long been Virginia Woolf's 'Death of a Moth' (1942), in which the author watches a moth flutter and die against a window. The moth is simply a vehicle for her to speculate on mortality and it matters not at all (to me at least) whether in fact she ever saw a moth beat its last against the windowpane. No one reads Woolf's essay to learn anything factual about the lifespan of a moth, but to speculate with her on the brief intensity of the universal life force.

In *Holy the Firm*, Annie Dillard (1977) likewise finds a moth which flares into metaphor and speculation. She writes of a camping trip on which a large moth that flew into a candle became affixed to the wick. For two hours, the moth melded with the wick while retaining its form until Dillard blew her out and went to bed. Certainly, this is an image begging to be transformed into metaphor and a vehicle for transformation, 'like a hollow saint, like a flame-faced virgin gone to God' (Dillard 1977: 16). Dillard takes the flame consuming the moth as a metaphor for life, as a cause for speculation on commitment and passion, exhorting a class of less-than-committed writing students to 'go at your life with a broadax' (18). Again, we don't know whether Dillard's moth really flew into her candle. Perhaps this all happened in her mind or happened to someone else, as in the case of the big tom cat that opens her book, *Pilgrim at Tinker Creek* (Dillard 1974). She writes that the cat would leap through her open window at night, 'stinking of urine and blood' (3), and would knead her chest with its paws, sometimes leaving bloody prints that looked like roses when she awoke in the morning. It's a visceral but beautiful image that Dillard returns to at the end of the book, but the cat is purely a speculative cat, a vehicle for connections made through metaphor. The cat actually belonged to someone else, as it turned out. Dillard subsequently took ownership of the metaphorical cat.

Other practical sorts, thinking the cat real, have pointed out that Dillard might have put a stop to her cat's antics by closing her window at night. Dillard didn't want to close her window – she wanted to keep it open and invite it in. The fact that it didn't exist, at least physically for her, made no difference to the pain and pleasure of which she was writing. She invited the cat in, which is my number one rule for writing speculatively. Always invite the cat in, whether real or imagined, but know that once you invite the cat in, it's real *and* imagined at once. Its origins don't matter if your goal is speculative and not one of chronicling events.

In the same section of *Holy the Firm* in which Dillard writes of her candle moth, she also writes of a spider in her bathroom. My daughter who is deathly afraid of boredom is likewise deathly afraid of spiders, and on more than one occasion she has called me to her room to dispatch a poor spider. I tell her that, for the most part, spiders are better roommates than some and that most of those found in our part of North America do more good than harm. Of course, my defence of these creatures does not move my daughter in the least.

You might be wondering at this point whether I indeed have a daughter or if I'm just using the idea of a daughter as a speculative tool. To me, such a move would be rubbish and not a device in the spirit of speculation. If I told you, I had no daughter (I have four, actually), this would not constitute speculation but manipulation. But what's the difference between an invented daughter and an invented cat? Am I stating that under no circumstance are you allowed to write an essay with an invented daughter? I would love to have that power to make whimsical essay edicts with the expectation that I must be obeyed, or you will suffer some speculative punishment (and it would be serious because it would be terrifyingly imaginary), but I don't have that authority. Poets, who are on a much longer speculative leash (no leash) than essayists, it seems, have no trouble inventing daughters. Weldon Kees does it famously in his poem, 'For My Daughter' (1940), in which he begins by looking into his daughter's innocent eyes and speculating with horror on all the awful fates that might possibly await her. But he ends his poem with, 'I have no daughter. I desire none' (Kees 1940). Do I feel cheated? Not at all, as I see that Kees's purpose is not to play a trick on me but to speculate on the terrors of attachment.

But those poor spiders. I killed two of them last week, when Naomi had her best friend Sadie over for a sleepover, and I heard them both screaming. Naomi insisted I stand on her bed (which I feared might not support me) and crush the spider. I did so, with great sadness, and the dead spider landed on her bed. Ten minutes later, the screaming resumed. Another spider had appeared in the same spot as the first. I dispatched that one, too. Is there anything speculative about these spiders? I might wonder about the coincidence of two spiders marching out to meet their deaths in the same spot within minutes of one another, but to what end? I'm not really in a speculative mood right now. Spiders to me are just spiders.

Not true for Naomi and not true for William Hazlitt in his 1826 essay, 'On the Pleasure of Hating' (1903), in which he takes the occasion of a spider crawling across his floor as an opportunity to speculate on all manner of hatreds. Hazlitt insists that his spider is real, unlike an allegorical spider in a poem published three years earlier by Leigh Hunt, 'To a Spider Running Across a Room' (1823). I believe him but I don't care. What I care about is how his essay triggered my own speculation. After reading Hazlitt, I wrote my own speculative essay on the pleasures of hating.

Speculative essayists are intrigued and even obsessed with possibility. Consciousness is itself a kind of speculation, and our musings are our bold footfalls as we make our way, presumptively across deserts of stasis, of boredom, of doing nothing. The speculative is the mirage turned real.

References

Dillard, A. (1974), *Pilgrim at Tinker Creek*, New York: Harper's Magazine Press.

Dillard, A. (1977), *Holy the Firm*, New York: Harper and Row.

Hazlitt, W. (1903), *The Collected Works of William Hazlitt*, 7, London: J. M. Dent and Company.

Hunt, L. (1823), 'To a Spider Running across a Room'. Available online: https://www.poetrynook.com/poem/spider-running-across-room (accessed 7 September 2021).

Kees, W. (1940), 'For My Daughter', from *The Collected Poems of Weldon Kees*, D. Justice (ed.), Lincoln: University of Nebraska Press. Available online: https://www.poetryfoundation.org/poems/47574/for-my-daughter (accessed 7 September 2021).

Woolf, V. (1974), *Death of a Moth, and Other Essays*, New York: Houghton Mifflin Harcourt.

SEE ALSO

Metaphor-me

Play

Non-human imaginaries

Taxonomy

LAVANYA SHANBHOGUE ARVIND

A writer must first observe. She must then be able to – with the intention of a surgeon and the skill of a sculptor – excerpt the grief of inappropriately named things and people. With what she has so excerpted, she must classify, un-name and rename them while chiselling their grief on to books, with only her words.

Migrant. Alien. Refugee. Squatter. Stateless. Homeless.

Human, she classifies.

The writer is a taxonomist. And, if she gets it wrong, because the names have a longer history than her own existence, she must console herself.

In the course of her taxonomical journeys, the writer will encounter strange phenomena.

A flower named after sorrow, for instance. How will she catalogue them?

The night-flowering jasmine, the parijat, is native to South and South-East Asia. The flower is known as the tree of sorrow for it blossoms at night and dries up at the first touch of daylight, almost as if it is afraid of light. The parijat has an orange-red centre, broad, seven-eight lobed corollas, white flowers that bloom at dusk and fade at dawn. The botanical name for the parijat is nyctanthes arbor-tristis.

Arbor. Tree

Tristis. Sad. Mournful.

Sad tree.

People name things to understand them better. But what if the names are wrong?

Why call a tree sorrowful?

For all you know, the writer writes, the parijat is really, really happy.

The parijat was incorrectly named, and so it grieves. And so, grieves the writer-taxonomist.

Now, naming the unnamed is one thing, but sifting through antiquity, sorting through the taxonomies of emotion, probing for meaning, followed by self-dialogue, a critical gaze inward as she labels and classifies … the ailments of the writer-taxonomist.

The kingdom of sentiment. Phylum? Sentient. Class? Being. Order? Feeling. Genus? Precarity. Family? Ephemeral.

Species? Fragile humans misnaming a flower.

The taxonomist must retreat until she finds a better name.

The taxonomist must examine facsimiles and deceits.

Two summers ago, the writer's husband travelled to China for work. When he returned, they sat together on the sofa looking at pictures of a beautiful Chinese countryside.

Looks like a painting, the writer said.

He had also brought home a painting of another landscape.

Looks so real, the writer said.

We want art to imitate life and life to imitate art. We love the imitations and the duplicities; their names might have been interchanged; you see.

The writer-taxonomist must tell you if that is the case.

Pausing in English.

(Note: I send out the previous version of these ruminations to my beta-reader-friend for his comments. He says that I am not to use the word 'post-colonial' [hereafter referred to as the Fancy Word] in ruminations such as this. It's pretentious and jargon-y, he writes. I thank him for his time and tell him that the Fancy Word has some connection to my relationship with English. He does not respond to that email. He must be exhausted, no doubt. Relationship advice does that to people.)

The taxonomist must classify space and time. She must name them correctly. What block of time is 'pre' and what is 'post'? She must also classify people in connection to their language. What do you call a person whose language is different when they count, different when they think and different when they speak? Look at the exemplar below, the audacity of linguistic identity.

The writer counts in English unlike her father who counts in Kannada. Her late mother would pray in Tamil but would count in English. Her maternal grandmother who was born in 1913 and educated in a convent school was taught by British nuns. When she counted, the accent was English. Growing up, they watched the news in English. Not BBC or CNN but their own homegrown channels where the news anchors spoke like them, only better. Now, the writer's sister lives in America. Sometimes she rolls her Rs when she speaks.

'It's so that they understand me better,' she explains, 'It's for them, not me.'

'It's all right,' she says, 'We all speak hoping to be understood better.'

The writer knows that it's tough for her sister to carry the burdens of her language, her colour and culture around at a time when the world is growing smaller hearts. It's not so difficult for the writer, here in this part of the Fancy Word world where people love English speakers whether they are good or not. The writer thinks in English. She argues with internet trolls in English. She emotes in English when she writes long, whiny text messages to her husband, who responds in English. When she applies for a visa to another country, she pauses at the field 'Mother Tongue'. She even pauses in English. But only long enough to enter 'Tamil' in the visa form. What do you name a person whose silence is in English?

She knows that English does not belong to her, and her mother tongue is tough on her tongue. She lives in a constant state of dissonance, a discord with the self. What is hers she cannot use and what she uses is not hers. What do you name her?

The 'post' in the Fancy Word does not simply mean 'after', but also what's been left behind, what continues, what stays back like a stubborn but familiar and comforting habit that you do not have the luxury of letting go of. Because then, you'd be somewhat languageless.

How will the taxonomist categorize such audaciousness in all its diversity?

What does the taxonomist do when she notices new names appear under 'Network and Connections?' *Wi-fi*. She thinks of new neighbours, for old names have disappeared. People have come, lived their lives nearby, separated only by walls and left.

Proximate Strangers, she labels.

What do you call life in a megacity? This estrangement of human from human, a life where one no longer goes to the neighbourhood kirana store to buy groceries. A life far away from the time one would stay a minute after the grocer bundles cardamom and gram flour into small newspaper cones held intact by a deft twine. Now, we use the grocery app on our phones. Two taps and Big Basket delivers home.

Like a genie trapped in a phone, she writes.

When the pandemic comes, the taxonomist doesn't know what name to give it. That which destroys homes and people, breaks hearts and builds walls?

Everyone she knows seems to be angry with China. She thinks of the doctor from Wuhan who wanted to speak to the world, to tell them the truth. She thinks of how he died.

This generation seems to have a strange relationship with truth. People are so afraid of it, they choose *dare* and invent new names for our times. It's the new normal, they say about grievous reality. The taxonomist has to sift through stories, the ones where fierce truth is dressed up in colourful corsages just so that the world is less afraid of it, a giant act of self-consolation.

SEE ALSO

Atmosperhics
Note-booking
Iterative thinking

Translation

RÚNAR HELGI VIGNISSON

Jæja!

Here is a famous Icelandic word that has often been considered untranslatable because it has so many different meanings, one of them being something like: Let's start! Untranslatability is as good a starting point as any for a writer looking for fresh associations and original juxtapositions. What does a non-native speaker of Icelandic, as you most likely are, make of a word like this? How would you pronounce it? It includes a letter that is rarely seen in an English text any longer, a combination of a and e, but does not tell you much about its pronunciation. I have added an exclamation mark that might send you in a certain direction. I could also have left the exclamation mark out which would have reversed the meaning, suggesting instead of a cheerful call to arms that I was about to start a rather boring project.

Which is not the case.

The verb 'translate' means etymologically 'to bring over' or 'to remove from one place to another' (Online Etymology Dictionary 2021). The equivalent Icelandic word, 'þýða', derived from the word 'þjóð' (nation), denotes translation as the act of nationalizing foreign words, so to speak, which is more or less the same thing. What if there is a will but not really a way to bring the freight across because there is no vehicle for the ferryman? Interestingly enough, you still have a lot of transfer modes at your disposal.

Let's look at a few of them.

Even though you don't understand the source text, you can always try to reproduce the formation of the text by writing words, sentences, and paragraphs of similar length. That would create a kind of metre with which to work; you would be emulating the form which would require innovation. As for the content, you could try to activate your acutest senses to get at the meaning. Maybe you're a linguistic psychic. Most people would be taking a wild guess.

The wild zone can engender a lot of things, even without drugs.

If you like to work with visual poetry, you could delete all but the letter combinations that seem to signify something in your own language. This may leave the translator with odd words and acronyms, even dislocated prepositions, scattered throughout the text being translated, depending on the affinity of the two languages; the more closely related they are, the longer list you are likely to end up with. In and of itself that could be meaningful as a translation of sorts, indicating, for example, that most of what writers around the world have to say is inaccessible to readers because of language barriers. You could also try to conjoin these scattered words and prepositions, rearranging them so that they make up a meaningful (or not so meaningful) sentence, or fill in the gaps between them. Minding the gap would then take on a new meaning and produce unexpected juxtapositions. You can find countless ways to mind the gap, inventing formulas and systems. Using Google Translate might as well be one of them for it often yields the most absurd results.

Should you be fluent in the language of the original, you have found a vehicle for the ferryman and can load it with all the words of the source text. The hitch is that when you unload them you must repackage them and to do that decently you need many skills, most of which are also relevant for the writer. An American author whose work I have translated, Jhumpa Lahiri, has taken up translating from the Italian and claims that translation has shown her 'how to work with new words, how to experiment with new styles and forms, how to take greater risks, how to structure and layer [her] sentences in different ways' (2021).

Translating, no matter the supposed difficulty of the source text, requires you to find an equivalent in the target language that works on several levels at the same time. First, you must get the meaning across. But meaning can be a beast with many legs. Part of the meaning is mediated through stylistic features such as rhythm, alliteration, rhyme or register. A devoted translator tries to find a way to embody all these features in the translation, sometimes bringing in a creative solution from a different semantic field to generate a comparable effect in the target text. This makes one acutely aware of the complexities of language and meaning making. For one thing, translating sends you to the dictionary more often than to the fridge, so that you are constantly looking closely at words, weighing their meaning, resonance and connotations. The outcome is sometimes translationese, where one inadvertently imitates the syntax of the original, creating a text that, in my case, is a far cry from regular Icelandic. This again highlights one's shortcomings in the mother tongue but may also produce imaginative wording. In the process, you learn a lot about both languages, but probably more about the target language (usually the translator's native tongue), which is likely to increase your vocabulary and make you more agile stylistically. You create special effects that you would never have thought of otherwise. If you try to translate *As I Lay Dying* by William Faulkner you need to change register and style in almost every chapter for the narrators all have their distinct voices.

Don't start there! You might as well start with Chaucer or the Icelandic Sagas

Writing in a second language may also prove to be a creative experience, even though you have limited command of it. Your limitations combined with the thought patterns inherent in the other language will force you to express yourself in unexpected and novel ways, both in content and style. Lahiri believes her writing in Italian, with which she has experimented recently, belongs to another part of her and has no doubt she wouldn't have written certain things if she had stuck to English (Leyshorn 2021). Writing in a second language may take on yet another dimension when you translate the text back into your native language. Then the translated text can function as a copy editor since translation requires extremely close reading. Milan Kundera, who wrote most of his works in the Czech language, discovered that he found flaws in his own texts when mirrored in the translations of his work. Consequently, he rewrote the original to make it more precise (Rafnsson 1985).

Jæja, there you have some tools should you be interested in experimenting with a second language to generate new ideas and presentation options. For me it's time to translate back into Icelandic to see if something needs clarifying.

References

Lahiri, J. (2021), 'Jhumpa Lahiri on the Joy of Translation as Discovery', *Literary Hub*, 23 April. Available online: https://lithub.com/jhumpa-lahiri-on-the-joy-of-translation-as-discovery/ (accessed 30 April 2021).

Leyshorn, C. (2021), 'Jhumpa Lahiri on Missing Rome', *The New Yorker*, 8 February. Available online: https://www.newyorker.com/books/this-week-in-fiction/jhumpa-lahiri-02-15-21?fbclid=IwAR3_IQqRz1bAdkmYyOJbXub-TYyG3fvWxiEZWNtBLBoL9FdM9StmXEvmA0o (accessed 27 April 2021).

Online Etymology Dictionary. Available online: https://www.etymonline.com/word/translate (accessed 30 April 2021).

Rafnsson, F. (1985), 'Öll erum við börn skáldsögunnar – Viðtal við Milan Kundera' [We Are All Children of the Novel – An Interview with Milan Kundera], *Tímarit Máls og menningar*, 3: 355–9. Available online: https://timarit.is/page/6293374?iabr=on#page/n91/mode/2up/search/Vi%C3%B0%20erum%20%C3%B6ll%20b%C3%B6rn%20sk%C3%A1lds%C3%B6gunnar (accessed 29 April 2021).

SEE ALSO

Writing-foreign-language
Listening
Resistance

Uncertainty

LAWRENCE LACAMBRA YPIL

When I think about the role of uncertainty in writing, I think of a poem that I wrote more than twenty years ago on a very hot summer afternoon on one of my trips back home to Cebu for vacation. It's a poem about doubt, about Thomas, Doubting Thomas as he is usually called, remembered notoriously for being the apostle who insisted on seeing proof, before believing that the Christ he had seen crucified on the cross had now been resurrected. He was usually taught us in Catholic school as the prime example of what not to do: not to question, not to ask for proof, not to dare to say in the face of the wound of the lord in a painting, *can I touch? I will be restless until I see. I want to touch, you see. If you will show me.*

I kind of liked Thomas for expressing such brazen audacity. I suspect I must have written this poem after a homily given by one of the priests in the neighbourhood who liked Thomas as much as I did – for believing that the Lord was a kind of god that did not shy away from this questioning of faith and in fact welcomed it. This story felt like a wonderful testament to the power of the senses. I was a biology major as an undergrad, and like any obedient son to a doctor father, I was on the way to studying medicine. In the past semester, I had dissected a cat. I was about to dive deep into the complicated structures of organic chemistry, and I did not know it then but would eventually fail terribly at higher physics. I was beginning to be sure I was falling in love with poetry. I was beginning to realize that words were more than the meanings they were designated, and that there was a way of approaching them, of gathering them on the page of the mind, that would unravel a new way of speaking and of seeing the world. I was beginning to ask of language something that might have been too much, but which I believed it was perfectly capable of acceding to, if only we learned *how* to ask: politely, audaciously, in doubt as in belief: *will you show us the wound, can we touch.*

Touch

The first sense to ignite, touch is often the last to burn out: long after our eyes betray us, our hands remain faithful to the world. – Frederick Sachs, The Sciences

Thomas knew this of course,
when he asked to touch the Lord,
feel where the nails dug deep,
where the spear's tip bit.

He knew that light,
this sight of hair, mouth, eyes,
would be the first to go,
followed by the memory of His words

till all that would be left
would be the faint sensation
of his finger on the lacerated
resurrected flesh.

His friends, thought him foolish
for demanding such sacrilegious proof,
and named him doubtful

when he was, in truth, the only one
who knew what believing meant
and did not mean.

There were wavelengths
his eyes could never perceive,
frequencies that would never reach
his inner ear.

And faith, he knew, did not lie
in thinking one could understand
what the eye and ear
could not hear or see.

The hands *they* knew
what faith was–
the held object
holding you.

And perhaps I am remembering 'Touch', after all these years, because it was the first time I wrote a poem – a real one! One borne not out of a mere need for the reckless expression of emotion, or even the whim of play, but made of the careful deliberation and appreciation of everything that we had so far known: religion and science, knowledge wrested out of study and story, a way of making out of things we would not otherwise put together: the chemistry of light, a faith received from the heritage of one's culture, a dear, dear man who dared to ask what everyone was just a little bit afraid to do so. I wrote that poem in the afternoon, I know. A very hot one in Cebu. One of those summer days that one survives by sweating and lying on the bed in front of the electric fan holding a piece of paper, writing something out of the mind, unsure where it will go – and yet very sure too about what it can do – with music, and voice, and a story retold differently, so that we see things again, truly, and not some other person's version of the truth.

I think I understood form, for the first time, writing that poem: that it was not a set of rules to be followed blindly but a way of listening to the music of a first line and understanding that it forged a path of hearing and knowing. That if one allowed oneself to give one's ear, one would find a way of speaking and writing that would lead the poem to its rightful if tentative closure. Insight at the end. Or voila surprise. Or as in this poem, not knowledge, but mystery.

Not the certainty of the known, but that calm and wonderful space of being known. So this was what it meant to follow the lead of a word and see where it would go. So this was poetry!

And although I had meant to write about uncertainty and the role it plays in writing, maybe what I really wanted to talk about was the necessary place of faith in making any work of art – the belief that things will fall into place, the understanding that there is craft, yes, but also trust. And that perhaps craft is one way to stave off whatever uncertainty we may wish to dispel, or desire to fuel the pleasure of writing – whether in the form of a poem, the arc of a plot, the shape of a character's motivations, the sound of a line, the way it breaks in the mouth of the mind that tells us – it is fine, fine, fine.

SEE ALSO

Not-knowing

Speculation

Reading

Vocabulary

PETA MURRAY

Some people collect stamps, or Clarice Cliff ceramics or desiccated dragonflies. I collect words. *Obelisk. Doldrum. Balustrade. Contrabassoon.* Indeed, I had thought to call this *essaimblage* something less prosaic than Vocabulary. Nomenclature? Something bespoke if controversial, like *Vocabularium Colloquoloquium*? As a linguistics nerd I sound origins of 'our' English words, aware of etymology's utility to reveal shadow histories of invasion and colonization, assault, assimilation, acquisition and appropriation. Is my *assonance* showing?

And what of the sonics and phonics of polysyllabic assemblages as they fall on the ear in melodic morphemic mélanges of monophthongs and diphthongs, voiced or voiceless consonants whether plosive or fricative, labio-dental or alveolar, nasal, lateral or glottal?

Bathysphere. Quintessence. Umbridge. Tumble-turn. Concatenation.

Even words *about* words excite.

When we deploy vocabulary as method, multi-storied possibilities open before us. Scrivenings, spoken word, unsayings, glossolalia, language-as-choreography, diarology (Munro, Murray and Taylor 2020), over-writings and under-writings, utterings, stutterings, mutterings, Babel and babble and verbiage and ventriloquy. Punctuational practices, prepositional-thinking (Rendle-Short 2020), poly-linguality, polyphony and prosody, orality, typography and toponymy. These are some ways in which practitioner-researchers shake mechanisms and topple structures of meaning-making through language-based practices of enquiry.

Wheelbarrow. Jigsaw. Tartan. Kindred. Dragonfly. Yearning.

Words are ontological frames or vessels or _____ (INSERT METAPHOR OF CHOICE) for the carriage and dispersal of thought. At a forensic level, investigative wordage allows us to explore where, how or why meaning making resides, whether in a name (McMurray), a place (Maribyrnong) or a body (blak). Words may be sites of enigma containing multiplicities of meanings. They may foment fabulation, together and alone, or at our peril. A refusal to speak a certain tongue, even adopt a certain idiom may signify an act of resistance. A with-holding. *Use your words!*

We know the power of muteness, silence, refusal to speak.

Every writer's vocabulary is different, making for lexical fingerprints. Some have such distinctive cadence or lilt one can tell them by ear. Notwithstanding vocabulary's powers to include and exclude, to invite, connect, compare, label or reject. Then there is the other great paradox, to *wit*: the more extensive a vocabulary, the more targeted the quest for precision.

Besmirch. Timber. Gumboots. Avuncular. Venerable.

Compounding and *portman-towing* parts of speech into new configurations and playing with *-phones* for their *phunnery* never fails to delight. Fun fact. The Icelandic alphabet has thirty-six letters. Korean Hangul has twenty-four. The Scottish Gaelic alphabet uses a mere eighteen.

Sin agad e! Tha sin ceart!

According to authoritative sources, and staying with my forebears, wee canny (can-nae?) Scots have some 421 words for snow. These include *feefle* – to swirl, *flindrikin* – a slight snow shower, *snaw-pouther* – fine driving snow, *spitters* – small drops or flakes of wind-driven rain or snow and *unbrak* – the beginning of a thaw. Not to mention un-Scottish coinages such as *snaux* for the fake stuff used in fashion shoots. (No. Not *that* snuff-like stuff. The other s'nough!)

A word on the ear becomes two in the book. A stick in the hand becomes script, a system of marks holding meaning pinned to a specimen board like a preserved member of *phylum odonata*. Stylus becomes quill becomes pencil becomes fountain pen becomes keystroke. Meaning remains slippery. Words are crucibles for new ideas, even dangerous ones. Units of the text(ural) word-playthings – Malapropisms, Spoonerisms, syllepses – and other howlers. Not to mention homonyms, *lezzonyms* and *queeronyms* of all persuasions.

Forgive my excess. I am a Constant Neologiser. In solo and collective research projects I elaborate key concepts hence: *lasagnification, audicles, elder-flowering* and *essayesque dismemoir* (Murray 2017). This labour continues after hours at MMMMYCorona blogsite where I deliver a neologism a day through Covid's lockdowns. *Sundrowning. Fomophobia. Unschoolfulness. Jigsorcery.* New words for old! Among additions to the Oxford English Dictionary lately: verbs *body-shame* and *dox*, nouns *dog-fooding, virtue-signaller* and *Pasifika*, adjectives *gribble* and *toyetic*. Covid-19 took plenty, but gave us newbies: *corona-coaster, cluttercore, infodemic* and *super-spreader*.

Words are can openers. For this *paracademic* (Sempert et al. 2017) they are also a tool in the poetics of a queer praxis, the lexical equivalent of carrying an Opinel® or Leatherman® in one's pocket, and just as revealing about where you came from, your privilege or lack of it, and who the _____ (INSERT EXPLETIVE OF CHOICE) you think you are. Prising words apart, spilling their contents, welding bits and pieces of random vocab together can be a revelation. And not only a mother tongue, but in another tongue, say, Scottish Gaelic (Ghàidhlig) which I am learning as my way of understanding the urgency to recuperate threatened languages and what it might mean to 'decolonize and moisturize' a parched mind.

'Had we but world enough and time' this might have been a moment to Marvell (1621–78), too, at Murray's Theory of Cunninglinguality as a method of language-based practice. Queer, but with Lesbianese genealogy, cunninglinguality brings language back to the mouth and tongue where they may probe words for new meanings. It restores language from scripted to emergent orality, allowing for mistakes, errors of enunciation and an upending of other conventions of utterance. Cunninglinguality admits the unacceptable, the substandard and the unconventional, bringing sensory pleasures of orality to words, rather than the pleasure of words to orality. It draws elements of the devotional and the worshipful towards

Vocabulary 173

words and wordplay. It is an erotics of linguistics, repurposing vocabulary as a performative on the stage that is the page.

Tairbh nathrach.
Drag'n'phlaigh.
'S e do bheatha.
You're welcome.

Notes

1 McMurray signifies son of a Murray, *mac* being the Gaelic word for *son*. I am technically a *NicMurray,* from *nighean* which means *daughter.*

2 A significant river in Narrm (Melbourne), Maribyrnong is an anglicized version of the Aboriginal term 'Mirring-gnay-bir-nong' which translates as 'I can hear a ringtail possum'. See https://www.maribyrnong.vic.gov.au/Discover-Maribyrnong/Our-history-and-heritage/Aboriginal-Maribyrnong (accessed 30 May 2021).

3 'Blak' was first used in an Australian context in 1991 by artist the late Destiny Deacon to describe the lived experience of urban-dwelling Aboriginal and Torres Strait Islander peoples (Perkins 1994).

4 *Sin agad e! Tha sin ceart means Indeed! That's right.* In Scottish Gaelic.

5 Decolonize and moisturize is a catchphrase attributed to Australian ensemble, Hot Brown Honey, whose Performers of Colour combine cabaret, circus, hip-hop and burlesque, in shows that challenge audiences to confront racial bias and stereotypes. See https://www.abc.net.au/radio/programs/speakingout/hot-brown-honey/12012200 (accessed 15 June 2021).

6 Scottish Gaelic for *dragonfly* is *tairbh nathrach*, composed of separate Gaelic words for *snake* and *bull*. For *drag'n'phlaigh* and other neologisms that appear in this entry, see my blog MmmmyCorona.

References

Munro, K, P. Murray and S. Taylor (2020), 'Diarology for Beginners: Articulating Playful Practice through Artless Methodology', *New Writing: The International Journal for the Practice and Theory of Creative Writing*, 17 (1): 80–100.

Murray, P. (2017), 'Essayesque Dismemoir: W/rites of Elderflowering', PhD Thesis, School of Media and Communication, RMIT University. Available online: https://core.ac.uk/download/pdf/83608312.pdf (accessed 11 November 2020).

Murray, P. (2020–21), 'MmmmyCorona', Available online: https://mmmmycorona.wordpress.com (accessed 15 June 2021).

Perkins, H. (1994), 'Introduction', in C. Williamson and H. Perkins (eds), *Blakness: Black City Culture*, 4–7, Boomalli: Aboriginal Artists Collective.

Rendle-Short, F. (2020), 'Preposition as Method: Creative Writing Research and Prepositional Thinking, Methodologically-Speaking', *New Writing: The International Journal for the Practice and Theory of Creative Writing*, 18 (1), 17 March.

Sempert, M., L. Sawtell, P. Murray, S. Langley, and C. Batty (2017), 'Methodologically Speaking: Innovative Approaches to Knowledge and Text in Creative Writing Research', *New Writing: The International Journal for the Practice and Theory of Creative Writing*, 14 (2): 205–22.

SEE ALSO

Listing
Collecting
Paragraphing

Writing-foreign-language

FAN DAI

Writing in a foreign language is not the usual choice for a writer, though it has become more common in the last couple of centuries. Writers who have become known for foreign language writing include Joseph Conrad, Vladimir Nabokov, Samuel Beckett, Lin Yutang, Eileen Chang, Ha Jin and Yiyun Li. The phenomenon has caught enough attention for these writers to be called 'exophonic'. There has not been much research on why such writers wrote in a foreign language, though it is obvious that those writers lived in a country where the foreign language is spoken. For example, Ha Jin has said that he chose to write in English for survival purpose. Reaching a larger reader group is likely to be another reason for a language choice.

In 'Writing in Two Tongues', Wang Ping offers an insider's view of how it is to write in a foreign language. She points out that 'mother tongue soothes and nurtures like a cradle, but […] provides the ground for my imagination while setting the boundary' (2006: 13). She explains that when she writes in English, 'Chinese always runs as the undercurrents in the process. The two tongues gnash and tear, often at each other's throat, but they feed on each other, expand, intensify, and promote each other' (16).

Wang is one of those writers who lives overseas, and English is the mother tongue in her new country, while a few writers, in recent years, have chosen to write in a foreign language in their own country, myself being one. Having studied and lived in English-speaking countries for a total of close to six years and having taught English as a foreign language in China for close to thirty years, it is almost natural for me to want to write in English, to share what is interesting about China that would otherwise not be told, or mis-interpreted by non-Chinese writers. With the writing in English came the joy of having a new-found psychological distance to the story, and the sense of freedom of writing non-fiction without having to worry about how the subjects of my writing would feel or be affected by it, as they do not understand English, and neither do English-readers know who they are. Therefore, I can write as I wish while achieving anonymity.

Soon I realized that writing in English as a foreign language means that I write from a perspective that can only be provided by a native Chinese. I frequently experience frustration trying to find words for the cultural aspects of whatever I want to write about because there are no corresponding expressions for certain cultural norms. This coincides with the translators' plight in translating what is culturally specific in the original language. There was a cultural turn in the 1970s when translators saw that language was no longer understood as an isolated phenomenon suspended in a vacuum but as an integral part of culture. According to Hans Josef Vermeer, a translator needs to be not only bilingual but also bicultural (2000). The same applies to writing in a foreign language. This means that a writer of a foreign language should be culturally aware and alert. This is also where being a foreign language teacher helps.

The following is an example from one of my Chinese students' works:

They spent a lot of time pressing the road.

This line comes from a story about two people who have just fallen in love. To a non-Chinese reader, 'pressing the road' sounds like physical labour. To a Chinese reader, it is a metaphorical way of referring to new lovers who spend a lot of time together, which usually means taking long walks, resulting in 'pressing the road'. The writer, apparently, was not aware that this is a Chinese-specific expression which is rendered strange in a non-Chinese reader's mind.

The following line comes from a story in which another Chinese student wrote about how the main character's parents made money:

Her parents worked outside since she was a child.

Here, 'worked outside' would sound a bit strange to a non-Chinese reader, while a Chinese eye would not detect anything unusual, as this is a general expression used to refer to the rural-to-urban migration for better-paid jobs in the rapidly developing Chinese cities since the 1980s. Therefore, 'outside' means out of the village, or generally, out of the rural area.

The above examples demonstrate the need for and importance of writers of foreign languages to incorporate the explanation of cultural elements in the narrative. Such incorporation requires skills beyond translation in that the writer needs to strive to turn the explanation into an organic part of the narrative, so that the narrative voice does not become loud.

As a writer of English as a foreign language, I myself have been writing with awareness for cultural differences. The following is from my story 'Mother-son-hood':

'When are we going to see Grandma again?' Dai asked on our way home.
'Once a year during the Qingming Festival.'
'Qingming Festival?'
'It's April 5, the day in the lunar calendar for mourning the dead.'
'Can we go more often like once a week?'
  'We can, but we don't have to come here to remember grandma. We'll think of her every day, won't we?' (Dai and Zheng 2019: 666)

This is a dialogue between my seven-year-old son Dai and me on the way home from my mother's funeral. Qingming Festival would have been an unfamiliar expression to international readers. Therefore, I used a dialogue through which I explained to Dai who had never come across a death in the family before. The explanation is part of the dialogue in which Dai struggles to part with his grandma.

It is obvious that the cultural aspect of creative writing in a foreign language demands the smooth combination of crafting with storytelling.

Writing in a foreign language may become more common with the increasing scale of globalization. It requires writers to be mindful of the cultural context of the readership they are targeting. This is an aspect of writing that rarely poses a challenge when writing in one's mother tongue. As to how to employ the right method for a given context, this is a matter of creativity that the writer works on throughout the writing process, so as to draw cultural elements into the narrative in a manner that makes them consistent with the whole.

References

Dai, F. and W. Zheng (2019), 'Self-Translation and English-Language Creative Writing in China', *World Englishes*, 38 (4): 659–70.

Vermeer, H. J. (2000), 'Skopos and Commission in Translation Action', in L. Venuti (ed.), *The Translation Studies Reader*, 221–32, London: Routledge.

Wang, P. (2006), 'Writing in Two Tongues', *Beyond Words: Asian Writers on Their Work*, 18 (1): 12–16.

SEE ALSO

Translation
Experience
Taxonomy

Xenos

NIKE SULWAY

Xenos (from the Greek): *noun;* stranger, wanderer, refugee; *adj:* foreign, alien, strange.

When I first entered the forest, I went there to be alone. I thought I was seeking solitude. Instead, I entered into a great community of alien beings. I feel lonely here, sometimes, but it is a false loneliness. Similar to the feeling that arises when travelling in a foreign land where nobody knows your language, your story, your kin.

Here, where I am the only one of my kind, everyone else – all of the other animals – are xenotic, are aliens. As Midgley writes, we often use the word 'animal' to refer only to nonhuman animals. Used this way, the word animal 'represents the forces that we fear in our own nature, forces that we are unwilling to regard as a true part of it [… it] dramatizes their power, but it also enables us to disown them. It implies that *they are alien to us* and are therefore incomprehensible' (1994: 136, emphasis added).

The nonhuman beings I encounter – bees and beetles, crows and snakes – seem alien to me. Even though they are deeply familiar, the differences between us seem monumental, irreducible. And yet, they are my kith and kin. My fellow travellers. And I want to find a method for writing about them that navigates ethically between two impossible and inauthentic extremes: to render the alien as completely alien to us, as incomprehensible, or (at the other extreme) to render the nonhuman as passive surfaces for human imaginings.

As Philo and Wilbert argue, 'If we concentrate solely on how animals are represented, the impression is that animals are merely passive surfaces on to which human groups inscribe imaginings and orderings of all kinds' (2000: 5). Going beyond this limit of representation seems necessary and urgent in the current context, where environmental changes are having a devastating impact on both human and nonhuman animals. And yet, writing about the nonhuman 'raises broader concerns about […] the extent to which we can say that animals destabilise, transgress or even resist our human orderings' (Philo and Wilbert 2000: 5).

When I consider a method for writing about those aliens – those nonhumans – in whose homelands I trespass, I experience the page as a site of crisis. The poet Borodale describes the page as 'a perishable object, the field of a ruin, or of crisis' (2016: xxii). A perfect way to express what it is to face the page both during and after the act of writing (when the page has become infected by a successful piece of writing). Writing – as both noun and verb – is indeed a perishable object, a field of ruin, a crisis.

And this particular crisis leads me to ask: how can we write well (with respect and compassion, with something approaching authenticity) about nonhumans? The first thing is to recognize that there is no single and right method, that constant questioning *is* the primary method of an ethical and sustainable life. As the poet Rilke writes: 'I beg you to have patience with everything unresolved in your heart and to try to love the questions themselves as if they were locked rooms or books written in a very foreign language' (2000: 35).

Loving the process is at the heart of a sustainable writing practice. To love the questions that writing constantly asks of us: how can we write this poem, this story? To have patience, and take deep and sustained pleasure, in loving the questions, loving the crisis. There is work to be done, and it is long and slow and steady work. Writing well, as you already know, requires more effort and time than writing poorly.

There are some risks, of course.

If we *imagine* our way into the hearts and heads, the culture and society, of nonhumans, we can fall into anthropomorphism, rendering them inaccurately as (like) ourselves. To write in this way, we draw on pre-existing human scaffolding for understanding things like identity, relationships and politics. At its most extreme, this kind of writing manifests as stories of badgers in boats, foxes in monocles. There is nothing wrong with these kinds of stories, but they are rarely about nonhumans; they are about human experiences and society.

Another possibility is to write about nonhumans as if they are objects, little more than animated cups and shelves, foils for and symbols of our own emotional landscapes. Birds that fly through the blue skies under which we kiss. Dogs that stand on porches, reflecting the mood of their human companions. Again, there is nothing wrong with writing in which animals are rendered roughly and imperfectly in the background (rather than in the foreground), but that is not what we are working towards here.

What can you do? I offer these methods to you in solidarity, in case you too are facing this particular crisis.

First, remember that there is very little in the practice of writing that is purely ethical or unethical, purely good. In writing about nonhumans, it is useful, however, to consider what is at stake for both yourself and for these enigmatic strangers. As soon as you begin, you will discover that even this is difficult, near impossible. You will get it wrong. You will misunderstand. There will be things you cannot begin to understand or imagine. The wider the gulf – the more tangled and mysterious the distance between you and the nonhumans you write about – the more difficult it will be to write authentically about them.

Second, consider that the only authenticity you can be confident of achieving is documenting your experience of the encounters and exchanges between you and them. Start there. Embrace, acknowledge and celebrate the limits of what you know. Think deeply, for example, about what is exchanged between you and the nonhumans you have encountered – a gesture, a touch, a look – and describe those exchanges in as pure and unadulterated a fashion as you can. Consider that when you write about these encounters, your work is an act of translation, and that translation is never precise, never literal. Avoid rendering the language of nonhumans in human terms; that is, avoid *interpreting* their gestures in terms of human abstractions like love, family, community and nations. Instead, describe the gesture itself, with precision and economy. The colour, the arc, the duration and heat of a beetle moving through leaf litter, the slow dart of a tadpole in the shallows.

Third, accept that writing about nonhumans with authenticity and compassion is intensely risky. With risk comes the possibility of failure. You cannot protect yourself against getting it wrong. No amount of consultation, learning, observation, attention, empathy or sensitivity will protect you. Getting it *wrong* is half of the beauty of a well-written poem. Telling stories, writing poems is dangerous partly because authenticity is at best an illusion, an aesthetic conceit. I urge you to risk writing with courage and honesty: it is, after all, the greatest and the most authentic offering you have to give.

References

Beston, H. (2019), *The Outermost House: A Year of Life on the Great Beach of Cape Cod*, London: Pushkin Press.

Borodale, S. (2016), *Bee Journal*, London: Vintage.

Midgley, M. (20013), *The Myths We Live By*, New York and London: Routledge.

Philo, C. and C. Wilbert (2000), 'Animal Spaces, Beastly Places', in C. Philo and C. Wilbert (eds), *Animal Spaces, Beastly Places: New Geographies of Human-Animal Relations*, 1–35, London and New York: Routledge.

Rilke, R. M. (2000), *Letters to a Young Poet*, trans. J. M. Burnham, Novato California: New World Library.

SEE ALSO

Non-human imaginaries
Speculation
Imagination

Yoga

ANTONIA PONT

Yoga has a foundational principle called *staying in the middle*. I learned this expression and its practice from my yoga teacher, Orit Sen-Gupta. At once a directive ('please try to stay in the middle'), as well as an experiential framework (what happens if you try to 'stay in the middle'?), it is a high-level technical requirement (without which difficult practices remain impossible/uneasy), as well as a *creative* constraint. As writers know, constraints are methodologies that we set going in order to invite unexpected, pleasing, even gracious spin-offs. 'Staying in the middle', as question, spawns other questions: *what/where is the middle? what would 'staying in it' be like? what would this staying enable or unleash*?

In this conception, the 'middle' is both soft and precise. We cannot reach it with rigidity or mechanical harshness. It might be a location *in* the body, but it could also involve a relation *to* our bodies. The middle, when we touch it, can feel like a portal onto vastness and silence. When we adhere to its suggestion over time, we may begin to relax. The 'middle' is a dignifying of *how* we are (structurally and on further levels). It strengthens our ability both to listen for what we long to contribute, offer, share (the *way* of our desire, our unique impulse), as well as to persevere with something seeming-illegible because wholly new.

Aligned with the middle, we find ourselves in less of a fight – we engage less in defiance and more in decision. I associate 'staying in the middle' with radical respect and a practice of *honouring*. It would therefore bear scant relation to what goes by the name 'hermeneutics of suspicion' (Sedgwick 2003: 124). This is a kind of approach where we are always reading for what is amiss; we suspect ourselves (and others) at every turn. We imagine that paranoia is the only accurate way. The 'middle' widens our understanding of accuracy, finally to reverse our received cultural ideologies of how change works. The 'middle', therefore, as it guides us away from a defensive suspicion, tends to curb our resentments (or at least let us know how often we are resentful!). Resentment broadly describes a mode where one conjures impoverished pseudo-positives from double negatives. It refers always to an outside, via competition and comparison. Comparison is imprecise; at a certain level, nothing, or only smudged generalizations, can be compared, and from this kind of generality neither art, nor expansiveness, ever comes.

Principles are animated, and tested too, by departing from, or forgetting, them. To 'stay in the middle' must take in the fallout of *leaving* this middle. Straying makes up the refrain of our usual lives. Its flavour is not uninteresting (but perhaps it is something we lose a taste for). At the beginning, we thus leave the middle constantly. The 'middle' can indicate a zone of approximation – *approaching the middle sometimes*. To become stable *there*, to paraphrase *Patanjali's Yoga Sutras* (Sen-Gupta 2013), is one of yoga's main preoccupations.

The 'middle' pertains to composure and steadiness in what one does, makes and wants (while knowing that one never really knows what one might do, make or want). Thus, the 'middle' involves a counter-intuitive constellation that includes its apparent opposite (this pair of straying/staying tumble and reinforce each other). Those who seem the most composed (as writers, makers, lovers, yogis, leaders) might be those who are at ease or relaxed in their *homelessness,* their constitutive oscillations, having trained seriously in the ontological accuracy of *not knowing* – from one second to the next, one creative moment to the next, one fresh question/impasse or sensation to the next. An unfaltering engagement with the middle (and with our near misses) might be the yogic equivalent of what Alain Badiou (2012) calls 'fidelity' or *obstinacy*.

Staying in the middle includes this strange paradox – pertaining at once to a composed stability (which can seem confident, assured, determined), as well as to a relationship to change and loss held seriously but not earnestly.

'Staying in the middle' reveals itself when one approaches the practice, not merely as a set of healthy exercises, or one mode of accomplishment among others, but rather as an inventive laboratory. When done 'intensively, properly and continuously over a long period' (Sen-Gupta 2013: 28 [chapter 1: sutra 14]), yoga (like writing) will begin to morph, and with it one's understanding of what one is even *up to*. You were trying to make a good story/touch your toes, or get published/heal your back, or change your life/enter a world that's cool and clever, but all of that was recast. Many begin writing to manage mental health and stay on because writing changes the very paradigm which would assess and label this. Many begin yoga to get a 'better' body and stay on to realize that they don't even know what a body is or what it can do.

The middle comes to be a principle in every practice because practising requires one to return to something, to meet it repeatedly (sitting down to write, returning to the cushion/mat), even if one doesn't fully understand the import or gravity of that direction, *yet*.

The 'middle' in yoga refers us straightforwardly to the physical body and its skeleton. The midline is the front face of the inside spine – a dark region (rarely or barely considered). When we abandon our middle, the front parts of our body lose their relationship with this darker core, and with it the silent, agile measure of aligned reference it offers. The front body can be a loud body, which comes to dominate our perceptions of ourselves to create meaty, energetic, psychic and subtler distortions. We see a version of it in the mirror; we meet others from behind its facade. When this emphasis *dominates* too much (it doesn't need to be disavowed), the yogi is more prone to 'injury' and things feel uneasy, meaner. We go too far. Trying to please the outside gaze, we sacrifice something precious. Without 'middle', there is strain, fatigue, costly compromise, shirking. We are likely to be activated too much by outside scenarios, ones that appear to require our urgent reaction, but which are skewed.

When trying to 'staying in the middle', we bump into what nudges us away from it, and what makes us malleable. We learn the conditions under which we consent to distortions in our expression. We may query why and at what point we abandoned our desire and what it had to say to us. With practising, this self-abandonment occurs less.

'Staying in the middle' has the further generative implication of opening us to *that which doesn't appear*. We begin to glimpse that which the status quo might prefer to render invisible or label obsolete. Via the apparently modest intention of 'staying in the middle', we might wake up to an altered relation to convention itself, to the habituated self, and therefore to what we thought was sayable, think-able, feel-able. We might forget to suffer in our usual ways; we may speak something plain and nourishing; or we might bump into uncharted intensities or unfathomable joy. We grow kinder, wider eyes, with which we can see more worlds and acknowledge more entities. We can breathe these worlds, observe them, adore, poem and champion them.

References

Badiou, A. (2012), 'On Being Happy', Keynote, Nexus Conference, Pt. II. Available online: https://www.youtube.com/watch?v=oEY14y4jThY (accessed 19 May 2021).

Sedgwick, E. K. (2003), *Touching Feeling: Affect, Pedagogy, Performativity*, Durham: Duke University Press.

Sen-Gupta, O. (2013), *Patanjali's Yoga Sutras*, Jerusalem: Vijnana Books.

SEE ALSO

Sensing

Fade out

Rites

Zim

ALVIN PANG

Zim is based on an idea of writing as immersion, exploration and experimentation. It contrasts with a view of writing as a kind of problem-solving, or as a task of recording thinking that has already been carried out towards a pre-determined end goal. Working with zims and zimming is a way of approaching creative writing not as the skilled production of fixed and complete outcomes awaiting editorial polish, but as a more fluid ongoing process of reflection, review, reconsideration, reuse, elaboration, extension and play:

> To struggle with the steep. To steep in the struggle; to zim in it, make room for, zimmering like a germane barge on the shoals of the senile, dubbed *Danceswithdifficulty*. Drenched, learning to swim the tidal collisions. Immersion, not sinking in nor jesusing the wavetop of muchness. *Zyme/Zymo* – indicating fermentation. Whatever the ithacas, the pretext, a void's usefully empty, no? But also itches: too appropriate appropriates. So a bit of sand in the sandal. A necessary document of frustrations. Stubs of stumblings past and to crumb. Sometimes juryrigging a salience, sometimes cloudy with a chance of raininess, some translucence, some tracer rounds. Knowing from time to time you hold the gun, worry your alloys. Not aloof, afoot. At least looking for fresh glasses. To hold place, sieve water, airlock the comingintoview. ~~To make safe space for dangerous interactions.~~ What mutters most when you can't sleep. What seams true. What you're sacred of (Pang 2020: 84).

The term *zim* echoes the Chinese Min/Hokkien word 浸 [*zìm*], meaning to *immerse, soak* or *steep*; it also recalls the German word *zimmer*, meaning a room or chamber, as well as the Latinate *zyme* (as in enzyme) suggesting fermentation and leavening. *Zim* also recalls the concept of the underground, proliferative 'rhizome', as put forward in Deleuze and Guattari's *A Thousand Plateaus* (1987). Zim is about allowing the material procedures of notetaking, drafting and writing to become translucent sites of innovation: where the nameless, formless and not yet expressed have time to brew, and to come into view. For a writer like myself, who works with several different forms of writing (fiction and non-fiction, literary and non-literary, poetry and prose), this is a liberating and open notion of what writing is and does.

I use the zim concept in my writing practice in several ways.

First, zim serves as a kind of genreless-genre: a container term for new writing that is still in the process of being fashioned. I refer to all my initial creative writing drafts as 'zims', regardless of text type. I keep a softcopy file for them with the title 'Zim', followed by the date the file is started (e.g. 'Zim 2020-11-20'). Each zim gives room for a particular writing idea to be played with: it makes space for the dynamic processes of experimenting, dreaming, scribbling, drafting, before the writing has settled into recognizable forms. Making zims helps shift attention: from what exactly is being made, to the making itself.

Second, I keep together in the zim any notes about ideas, fragments, sources, doodles, lingering questions, side musings and so on that might relate to my writing idea. These often accumulate after a zim has been active for a time, and serves, like leaf litter in a forest, to enrich the environment from which a zim emerges.

Third, I also keep together all the different versions and draft changes I make, as 'branches' of the zim. Each of a zim's branches could (and in my case, often does) have a separate life as different published texts! For instance, an initial writing idea might later become part of a social media post as well as a poem and a published essay: I keep these related 'branch' pieces together. I also record variant word choices and phrasing, knowing that these might lead me in different creative directions later.

Before organizing my writing practice around zims, I used to retain only final (published) versions of my written works, discarding most of the in-progress notes, drafts, initial questions and creative decisions that had led up to those 'finalized' versions. It may feel onerous to keep track of all these raw material bits and bobs. So instead of trying to exhaustively document every single little change or raw idea and its source, I include notes only of shifts or ideas that I want to remember or lingering questions I have. I also note down phrasings I am not fully happy with, alternative word choices or information I hope to research or include at a later time.

Sometimes, I make a zim by taking a 'finished' text that has already been written or published and reworking it. For instance, I might graft new sentences to existing ones, or give a technical document new imagery or syntax so it becomes legible as a poem. I call this approach of creatively repurposing or rewriting an existing text: *zimming*. A text that has been reworked by this method is said to be *zimmed*.

Through zims and zimming I allow myself the freedom not to presume a creative work's final form when I start writing. This sense of genrelessness can be freeing: I do not have to worry about what kind of writing I am supposed to be pursuing. One purpose of making zims is to expand the creative and critical possibilities of writing, allowing for textual outcomes that may not conform to recognizable literary conventions. By thinking of myself as writing zims (rather than 'a poem' or 'a short story' or 'an essay'), I can follow the flow of my creative ideas without being concerned with genre boundaries and expectations. The zim is a way of being kind to my creative process: of allowing embryonic ideas time and space to wander, to evolve and to settle by themselves into different shapes according to different practice contexts.

By retaining the rich background information surrounding a creative idea, I also afford myself a safety net: I have something to fall back on if I want to pursue a different angle later on. No idea need be 'lost' on the cutting room floor. More than once, when my writing lost momentum or hit a dead end, I have been able to return to my notes and fragments in a zim for renewed stimulus and a different direction to try. Fragments that go nowhere by themselves can spark something new when combined. The odd typo or omission might suggest new and unexpected associations from which to continue thinking and begin thinking again.

Zims and zimming relieve the pressure of that final draft: writing does not need to strive for finality or perfection but can continue to evolve and change and remain protean. With a zim, a piece of writing isn't closed off even when published: there is always the possibility of further transformation.

References

Deleuze, G. and F. Guattari (1987), *A Thousand Plateaus*: *Capitalism and Schizophrenia*, trans. B. Massumi, Minneapolis, Minnesota: University of Minnesota Press.
Pang, A. (2020), 'Writing the Multiple: From Chapalang to Confluence', PhD Dissertation, RMIT University, Melbourne.

SEE ALSO

Experimentation
Iterative thinking
Code

INDEX

Abramović, Marina 40
acrossness 47, 48
activism 4, 67, 80, 149
Adam, Barbara 95
affective dissonance 67
affective response 98
Agamben, Giorgio 34
Ahmed, Safdar 117–19
Alexievich, Svetlana 44
algorithm 37
Anthropocene 17, 102, 111, 124
Anzaldúa, Gloria 81, 84
appropriation 10, 81, 98, 152, 172
archival-poetics 7–9
archive 10, 105, 130, 140, 158
    colonial 7–8
    decolonizing 7
Aronson, Linda 18, 57
artwork 54–5
aside, the 35, 36, 48
association 21, 75, 93, 101–2, 166, 186
aswang 10–11
atmospherics 5, 13–14
authenticity 179, 180, 181
autobiography 37, 85, 117, 130
autobiographical 43, 44, 63, 64, 141

Bachmann, Ingeborg 83
Badiou, Alain 182
Balla, Paola 80
Bancroft, Corinne 16, 18
bardo 77, 78
Barry, Lynda 53
Barthes, Roland 14, 28, 34, 41, 84,
      102
    queering 141
    reader as creator 20
belonging 46, 70, 126
Benjamin, Walter 27, 104, 105, 118
betwixt and between 47
beyonding 47, 48
bilingual 176

Bishop, Stephanie 148
Blak 80–2, 172, 174
blood memory 7–8
boredom 139, 160, 161
Borges, Jorge Luis 24, 62, 101
Borodale, Sean 178
braiding 16–18
Braidotti, Rosi 111
breast cancer 78
bricolage 11, 20–2
Bunda, Tracey 80, 81
bung wantaim 2, 23–6
Burroughs, CM 157–9
Byrne, James 149–51

Calle, Sophie 130
camp 10, 142
Campbell, Marion May 83–5, 141–3
camping 4, 27–8, 160
Cappello, Mary 46, 77–9
Carleton, Stephen 120–2
Carlin, David 1–6, 28, 47, 101–3, 124
carousel 133
Carr, Karen L. 129–31
Carrière, Jean-Claude 71
Carson, Anne 33
Castles, Belinda 147–9
character/s 14, 30–2, 37, 57–9, 63, 87
    actor 13, 34
    braiding 16–18
    creating 53
    dialogue 49–51
    drawing 52
    flawed 127
    main 139, 177
    motivations 171
    nonhuman 112
    observation 120–2
    other cultures 126
    rulebreakers 142
    verbs 133
    writer as 47

characterization 64
Chekhov, Anton 86
chorality 4, 33–4
chorus 13
    Ancient Greek 34
    choral 33
    chorality 33–4
    noh (jiuti) 34
cis-heteronormative 40
climate 67, 81
    change 121
    fiction 111–12
Cobby Eckermann, Ali 47, 69–70
code 37–9
Coetzee, J. M. 63
collaboration 4, 40–2, 67, 71, 80, 93
    as love 48
collecting 43–5, 60, 148
colonial/ism 7–8, 80–1, 105, 112, 144–5
    Colonial Relic 2
comics 52–3
communitas 46–8
compression 93
computer 37, 43, 118, 132
    computer-generated 37
conceptual 66, 92, 93
conference 28
Copley, Martina 33–5
Covid-19 17, 40, 70, 120, 173
creative
    creative process 11, 89, 98, 118, 186
    creative process as research methodology
        89, 107
cultural exchange 46
culturescape of the Pacific 2, 24
curiosity 118, 139

Dai, Fan 176–8
dancing 81, 89
deafness 96
DeCarava, Roy 130
decolonial praxis 7
decolonize/ing 2, 142, 173, 174
deep listening 48
defamiliarization 120
Deleuze, Gilles 14, 28, 83, 185
Derain, Allan N. 10
Derrida, Jacques 20, 21
dialogue 3, 49–51, 71, 129, 150, 177
    bung wantaim 23, 24
    philosophical 83
    playful 1
    self-dialogue 163
    spoken 112

dialogic engagement 24
diarology 172
dictionary 37, 60, 62, 167
difference(s) 17, 21, 31, 102, 154
    cultural 177
    identities 107
    power and 2, 3
    prepositional thinking and 136
digital 102, 139
    Digital Age 72
    digital technology 40
digression 138, 139, 141
Dillard, Annie 160, 161
disbelief 92
discomfort 115, 127, 141
Doctorow, Edgar L. 114–15
double-line break 124
doubt 3, 115, 127, 139, 147, 169
drafts 50, 109, 127, 148, 153, 154
    as zims 185, 186
drag 89, 142, 174
Dragon magazine 43
drawing 52–3, 89, 118
Drucker, Johanna 34
Dunlea, Marian 153
Duras, Marguerite 41, 84

Eades, Quinn 40–2, 84, 141–3
ecocritical/ism 67, 102, 111
editing 44, 72, 90, 103
ekphrasis 7, 54–5
electronic literature 37
embodied 7, 84, 89, 90, 114, 153
English 134, 135, 164, 166, 172
    as foreign language 176–7
    introduced 144
    Old 101
Eno, Brian 72
ensemble 57–9
epistolary practice 83, 158
erasure 60–2, 72, 84
etymology 138, 172
Evasco, Marjorie 98–100
experience 63–5
experiment/s 1, 48, 115, 139, 148, 167
experimental 21, 37, 66, 67, 186
experimentation 66–8, 141, 185
exposition 50

Facebook 71, 152
facilitator 69–70
fade out 71–3
faith 58, 169–71
Falconer, Delia 123–5

Index 189

Faulkner, William 167
feelings 2, 35, 58, 74–6, 86
    and reading 148
    and ritual 46
feminism/s 8, 142
Feral Atlas 102
Ferreira Cabeza-Vanegas, Lina María 30–2
film practice 49, 71, 74
Firaaq 58
First Nations Peoples 144, 145
flow 27, 77–9, 98, 154, 186
    narrative 8, 124
forget 77, 78, 127, 142, 184
    erasure and 60–2
    forgetfulness 62
    forgetting 8, 72–3, 182
    unforgettable 84
Foster Wallace, David 44
Foucault, Michel 83, 101–2
fountain up 47, 48
fragment/s 21, 84, 102, 141, 147, 186
    cut up 40–1
    fragmentary 124
    fragmentation 83, 118, 151
    language 43
    memory 7, 96

Gayatri-Kumarswamy, Manola 153–6
gender 27, 58, 84, 141
    gender-aligned 83
    gender-based 8, 142
    gender-bending 21
    gendered 7
    violence 8
genre 4, 5, 11, 50–1, 55, 130
    cross / trans-genre 53, 83–4, 90, 141
    discipline and 129
    discourse 84
    genreless 185, 186
    literary 71
    screen play as literary 71
    subgenre 50
gesture/s 4, 35, 93, 124, 152, 180
ghost/s 8, 55, 62, 104, 138
Ghost Weaving 80–2
ghostliness 71
Gibson, Ross 115
gift 69–70, 75, 87, 90, 105, 122
    gifting 80
    from liminality 47
    of listening 4
Gíslason, Kári 63–6

Glissant, Edouard 67, 102
Global South 2
Grace, Patricia 86
grandmother stories 7, 69, 107

Halberstam, Jack 142
Harkin, Natalie 2, 7–9, 105, 140–2
haunt/ing 7–8, 101, 124
Hawkins, Ames 46, 89–91, 141–3
Hazlitt, William 161
Hecq, Dominique 20–3, 84
Heffernan, James A. W. 54
Heidegger, Martin 89–90, 145
Hemley, Robin 160–2
Holland-Batt, Sarah 54–6
homonym 132, 173
homophone 132, 133
Hughes, Langston 130
hybrid 21, 83–5

Icelandic 166–8, 173
identity 8, 31, 69, 83, 127, 180
    cultural 47
    identity-based poetics 66
    linguistic 164
    markers 50
Ihimaera, Witi 87
imagination 2–3, 69, 86–8, 98–9, 112, 176
    in classroom prompt 133
    crisis of 139
    freedom of 146
    metaphoric 99
    novel 114
    play 132
    readers' 92
    and reality 75
immersive 46, 114–15
imperative 2, 13–14, 50, 99, 124, 138
imperfections 127
Indigenous
    culture and intellectual property 7–9
    feminisms 8
    knowledge systems and cosmologies 2
    methods and methodologies 2
    New Zealand 126–7
    poetics 7–9
    resilience 144–6
    sovereignty 80–2
    standpoints and subjectivities 8
    worldviews and epistemologies 24–6
Ingelstrom, Ann 71
inspiration 28, 86–8, 141

190 Index

Instagram 72
instinct 86–8
integrated development environment (IDE) 38
intertextual 20–1, 54, 118
interview 50, 58, 114–15, 126
iterative thinking 4, 89–91

JavaScript 37–9
jigsaw 72, 172
journal 43, 89, 95, 155
    journaling 40
juxtaposition 17, 90, 92–3, 166, 167

Kantrowitz, Andrea 53
Kaplan, Caren 83
keepsake 95–7
Kees, Weldon 161
kineticism 38
knowing 78, 142, 151, 153, 183, 185–6
    in-action 114
    hearing and 170
    ways of 81
    the world 25, 27
knowledge 8, 20–2, 27–8, 83, 114–16, 170
    Blak knowledges 81
    body knowledge 89
    embodied 64, 89–9
    intergenerational transmission of 8
    of language 148
    in motion 134
    non-hierarchical 117
    non-knowledge 3
    perceptual 64
    and science 112
    social 2, 24–5
    of story 16
    taken-for-granted 107
    workers 28
Knudsen, Erik 2, 74–6
Koestenbaum, Wayne 124
Kothari, Shuchi 57–9
Kristeva, Julia 20
Kumarswamy, Manola-Gayatri 153–6
Kundera, Milan 168

Ladin, Joy 90
Lahiri, Jhumpa 167
Laird, Benjamin 37–9
language 20–1, 33–5, 150–2, 153, 169
    based thinking 66
    body 121
    and coding 37–9

Chinese 176–8, 185
as choreography 140, 172, 121
colonialist, settler 80–1, 145
and ekphrasis 54
everyday 120, 148
foreign 176–8, 180, 181
form 90, 130, 134
Icelandic 166–7
and listening 98, 99
memory 104
multiple 25
practices 3, 5, 43, 48, 49–51, 86
racist 51
restoration of 173
science 117
second language 167–8
symbolic 96
as taxonomy 164
Leane, Jeanine 2, 144–6
Leavitt, Sarah 52–3
lesbian 84, 141–2, 173
letter writing 89–90
Levertov, Denise 99–100
Lévi-Strauss, Claude 20–1
Lewis, Edwin Herbert 123–4
LGBTQI+ 83, 142
liminality 11, 47, 84
listening 98–100, 147, 155
    as *communitas* 46–8
    and facilitation 69–70
    as gift 4
    and imagination 87
    poetics of 170
    as radical practice 98
    as research method 80–1
    as resistance 151
    to speech patterns 49
listing 43, 101–3
literary 2, 5, 59, 102, 114
    art 44
    corporatism 151
    components and elements 92–3
    conventions, crafts, forms 43, 54, 92, 99, 186
    cultures 38, 47
    device 102
    ekphrasis 7
    experimentation 66–8
    genre 71, 185
    and material cultures 25
    queer 142
    representation 146

Index   191

theory 21, 84, 141
tropes and tools 8
work 98, 120
literature 2, 8, 62, 70, 132
    and coding 37–9
    and creative writing methods 64, 99
    and ecocriticism 112
    fields of 2, 11, 21, 84
    in-flux 71
    Philippine 135
    and science 113
Lorde, Audre 11, 90
love 7, 58, 155, 164
    of Ancestors 8
    of characters 31, 63
    collaboration-as 4, 40–1
    of collaborative queering 142
    of comics 52
    as *communitas* 46–8
    of language 153
    and letter-writing 90
    objects 96
    of poetry 169
    of questions 180
    and resistance 80, 82
    as verb 105
lyric
    and anti-lyric 66
    essay 16, 124
    form 17, 84, 92
    as music 77
    songwriting 118

Macdonald, Ian 71
Mahlangu, Busisiwe 153, 155
Makereti, Tina 126–8
Māori, te ao 126–7
Maras, Steven 71
Marsh, Selina Tusitala 107–10
Mayer-Schonberger, Viktor 72
McKinnon, Catherine 16–19
Melville, Herman 132
memoir 43, 63–4, 95–6, 98, 99
    dismemoir 173
memorabilia 43
memory 7, 43, 61–3, 86, 133
    gathering 118
    and imagination 33, 69
    and keepsakes 43, 95–6
    and notebooking 117
    and the photograph 129
    and remembering 53, 170
    and respiration 140

societal 72
spaces 80
traumatic 84
work 104–6
metaphor 11, 27, 111, 160, 172
    and memory 104–5
    and silences 21
metaphor me 107–9
metaphorical 7, 160, 177
methods 1–6, 63, 89, 113, 180
    and code sequences 37
    in creative writing 21–2, 46, 64, 114
    and the 'everywhen' 80
    as processes 114–16
middle 52, 114, 182–3
    Ages 123
    class 58, 74
    Dutch 101
    Irish 141
Midgley, Mary 179
milieu 14, 117
monologue 35, 72
Monson, Ander 43–5
Moore, Cath 49–51
more-than-human 102, 111, 142
Morris, Paula 86–8
Morrison, Toni 2, 148
motif/s 10, 17, 55
movement 32, 90, 99, 130, 136
    in character journeys 58
    and chorality 33–5
    and coding 38
    and *communitas* 47
    Graeco-Arabic translation 117
    and iterative thinking 89
    through multiple languages, worlds and
        histories 25
    in ritual 154
    of thought 33
multiple protagonists 57
murmuration 79
Murphy, Fiona 95–7
Murray, Peta 1–6, 46, 84, 101, 141–3, 172–5
mycelium 155
mythscape 14

Nabokov, Vladimir 86, 176
narrative 21, 30, 38, 49, 57, 115
    arc 30, 41
    braided 16–18
    cultural elements in 177–8
    dream 83
    drive 16, 49–51

historical 43, 130
Hollywood 57
instinct 87
juxtaposition in 92
key turning points in 95
medicine 64
tactics, techniques, tools 8, 64, 113, 158
thread 96
voice 64
neologism 173–4
Nhã Thuyên 60–2
Nogues, Collier 66–8
non-binary 4, 141
NonfictioNOW 146
nonhuman 111–13, 179–81
nonhuman imaginaries 111–13
not-knowing 114–16, 127
notebooking 117–19
notional ekphrasis 55

objects 7, 13–14, 54, 89, 95–6, 139
collecting 43–4
display of 46
ephemerality of 129
juxtaposition and 93
nonhumans as 180
observation 120–2, 180
Offill, Jenny 124
Oliver, Mary 99
Ondaatje, Michael 138
online 41
oppositional 54, 66–7
outlaw works 83–4

pact 72
Pamuk, Orhan 43–4, 86–8
panel 52, 70
unpanel 46
pandemic 40, 70, 81, 101, 120, 132, 165
Pang, Alvin 185–7
paragraph/ing 4, 123–5
collecting 102
writing 30, 52, 64, 90, 166
Parker, Dorothy 139
participatory 46
Patanjali 182
Perkins, Emily 114
performance 2, 34, 46, 89, 120, 151
writing about 4, 54
writing for 4, 72
permission 4, 44, 126–8, 144
Philippine literature 10, 135
phototextuality 129–31

play 27, 132–3, 141, 158, 170, 185
as collaboration 41
invitations to 109
not-knowing and 115
playful 1–5, 11, 46, 173–4
plays and playwriting 38, 120
plurality 46
poethic/al 67, 151
poetic/s 2–3, 34–5, 38, 71, 83–4, 120
archival 7–9
ekphrasis 54–5
experimentation 67, 141
imagery 157
of listening 151
metapoetic 54–5
mythopoetic 20
poetics, Global South 2
queer practice 173
in relation 102
trans poetic 90
poetry 40, 41, 69, 134, 169
ancient 33
conceptual 66
ecopoetry 67
form/s 4, 16, 37–8, 84, 108, 124, 185
practice of 84, 89, 107, 136, 158, 171
as resistance 150
visual 166
poet/s 10, 23–4, 47, 55, 77, 154
political 2, 74, 80, 83, 150–2
politics 2–5, 8, 83, 153, 180
polyphonic 4, 44
Pont, Antonia 141–3, 182–4
postcolonial 8, 84, 164
practising 81, 90, 148, 183
praxis 7, 8, 81, 139, 173
preposition/al 124, 134–7, 141, 166
prepositional space 47
prepositional thinking 48, 134–7, 172
Price, Steven 71
privilege 54, 134, 135, 145–6, 150, 173
creative writing 3, 114
method 35, 115
procrastination 4, 87, 138–40
prompts 47, 86, 132, 133
protagonist 57, 58, 112

queer 4, 8, 46, 90, 141, 173
queering 141–3

radical 84, 98, 118, 141, 145, 182
and memory 105
possibility 102

Index   193

radical effrontery 2, 144–6
radio 46, 92–3
reading/s 2, 18, 87, 136, 147–9, 161
    aloud 41, 158
    close 155, 167
    colonial 70, 80
    as a form of sharing 25, 69
    re-reading 20, 67
relationality 7
remembering 8, 60, 69, 80, 105, 170
remembrance 8, 62
Rendle-Short, Francesca 1–6, 46–8, 141–3,
    172
representation/al 120, 129, 146
    indigenous and settler 8, 145
    limits of 104, 179
    modes of 54, 83
research 10
    collaborative 173
    discomfort and 127
    experience and 64
    hybridity and 21
    methodology 89, 107, 172
    permission and 127
    procrastination and 138
    practice 1, 2, 5, 80, 114–16
    practice-led 81
    process 3, 114
    sovereign 80
resilience 112, 144
resistance 7–8, 80–2, 84, 136, 150–2, 172
    of nonhumans 112
    poetics 2
    queer 141
    radical 84
    and uncertainty 4
Retallack, Joan 66–8
rhyme 109, 167
Rilke, Rainer Maria 180
rites 82, 153–6
ritual 20, 46, 67, 72, 153–6
    disruptive 122
    idiosyncratic 117
    practice 121
rhythm 13, 34–5, 38, 64, 115, 125
    and drawing 52
    features of 120, 167
    and listening 35, 98
Rogers, Pattian 99

sand mandala 72
Saterstrom, Selah 44
Saunders, George 148

Scarry, Elaine 99
science 21, 28, 112–13, 115, 117, 170
    Social Science 46, 115
screenplay 50, 57–9, 71–3, 74
screenwriting 49–51, 71–3
screenwriting practice 49, 71–3
script 49, 53, 71, 83, 173
Sebald, W. G. 130
Sedgwick, Eve Kosofsky 77, 182
self-editing 72
Sen-Gupta, Orit 182–3
Sentilles, Sarah 3
sensation 14, 35, 96, 158, 170, 183
    and iterative thinking 89–90
sensing 157–9
settlers 80, 144–6
    settlerism 144, 146
Shanbhogue-Arvind, Lavanya 163–5
Sherry, Jamie 72
silence 2, 8, 24, 164
    as erasure 10–11, 62
    as a gap in the text 21, 54, 130
    profound 150–1, 182
    and the writing process 98, 121, 153–5,
    172
silencing 145
Silver, Sean 139
Sinclair, Upton 133
social knowledge 2, 24
software 37–9
Sousanis, Nick 53
space/s 25, 27–8, 34, 46, 92, 120
    blank, empty or unoccupied 13, 41, 60, 96
    geopolitical 80–1, 84
    imaginative 7, 90, 99, 114, 153–6, 171
    on the page 16, 52, 70, 123–4, 147
    paradoxical 127, 164, 184
    photographic 129–31
    physical 53, 118, 151
    prepositional 47–8, 134–5
    queer 4, 142
    resistance and 82, 102, 146, 185
spatial 37–8, 104, 130
spatialities 35
spark 43, 87, 138, 186
Spark, Muriel 139
Speculative/ion 14, 66, 112, 160–2
Spice Girls 43
Sternberg, Claudia 71
Stewart, Kathleen 13–15
story 1, 7, 44, 77, 96, 102
    and dialogue 49–51
    and erasure 60–1

form and structure 16–18, 52–3, 71–3, 92,
169–70, 180
of lands stolen 144, 146
and plot 16–18, 57–9
as relational 46–8, 80–2, 153, 176–8, 179
sources of 63–5, 69–70, 74–6, 86, 109, 112
storylines 57–9
storytelling 51, 63–4, 95, 111, 177
as colonial discourse 8, 74
through dialogue 23, 50
and economy 52
as facilitation 70
storyworld 16–19, 49
subtext 50–1, 121
Sulway, Nike 179–81

Taylor, Stayci 1–6, 71–3, 141–3, 172
taxonomy 163–5
teaching 69, 132
Thoreau, Henry David 77
tourist 27–8, 93, 140
translation 4, 117, 166–8, 177, 180
body 61
mistakes 62
and resistance 150
self- 66, 142
Tumarkin, Maria 104–6
Turner, Edith 46–7
Turner-Vasselago, Barbara 115
Tusitala Marsh, Selina 107–10
typography 172

uncertainty 4, 115, 127, 147–8, 160, 169–71
unfolding 7, 14, 24, 38, 46, 49–50
and rites 154
unknowing 151
unknown, the 16, 27, 87

van Herk, Aritha 138–40
van Loon, Julienne 1–6, 114–16
Veijola, Soile 27–9
vernacular 50, 77
Vietnamese language 62

Vignisson, Rúnar Helgi 166–8
Villanueva, Martin 134–6
violent-politeness 144
vocabulary 3, 62, 167, 172–5
vulnerability 114, 157–8

Walker, Nicole 18, 47, 132–3
walking 16, 89, 99, 118, 120, 139
Walters, Wendy S. 92–3
Wardle, Deborah 1–6, 111–13, 141–3
Watego, Chelsea 145
Webb, Jen 114
Webb, Ruth 54
Welty, Eudora 87
Winduo, Steven 2, 23–6
Wiradjuri 144
Wittig, Monique 141, 142
Wood, Charlotte 114
Woolf, Virginia 138, 160
Woolfe, Sue 121
workshops
bung waintaim 23, 25
culture and diversity in 2, 148, 154, 156
Wright, Alexis 8, 112
writer's block 43, 61, 87
writing
collaboratively, see collaboration
non-human others 111–13, 179–81
process 21, 71, 95, 98, 114–15, 118, 157
prompts, exercise and experiments 66–7,
72, 112, 115, 153
restorative 8, 81
in a second language 167–8, 176–8
wounds 8, 41, 150
writing-foreign-language 176–8

xenos 179–81

yoga 5, 89, 154, 182–4
Ypil, Lawrence Lacambra 141–3, 169–71

zim 5, 185–7
Zoom 95, 132–3